LUTHER'S WORKS

American Edition

VOLUME 53

*Published by Concordia Publishing House
and Fortress Press (formerly Muhlenberg Press)
in 55 volumes.
General Editors are Jaroslav Pelikan (for vols. 1-30)
and Helmut T. Lehmann (for vols. 31-55)*

LUTHER'S WORKS

VOLUME 53

Liturgy and Hymns

EDITED BY

ULRICH S. LEUPOLD

GENERAL EDITOR

HELMUT T. LEHMANN

FORTRESS PRESS / PHILADELPHIA

7982G79   *Printed in the United States of America*   *1-353*

GENERAL EDITORS' PREFACE

The first editions of Luther's collected works appeared in the sixteenth century, and so did the first efforts to make him "speak English." In America serious attempts in these directions were made for the first time in the nineteenth century. The Saint Louis edition of Luther was the first endeavor on American soil to publish a collected edition of his works, and the Henkel Press in Newmarket, Virginia, was the first to publish some of Luther's writings in an English translation. During the first decade of the twentieth century, J. N. Lenker produced translations of Luther's sermons and commentaries in thirteen volumes. A few years later the first of the six volumes in the Philadelphia (or Holman) edition of the *Works of Martin Luther* appeared. But a growing recognition of the need for more of Luther's works in English has resulted in this American edition of Luther's works.

The edition is intended primarily for the reader whose knowledge of late medieval Latin and sixteenth-century German is too small to permit him to work with Luther in the original languages. Those who can will continue to read Luther in his original words as these have been assembled in the monumental Weimar edition (*D. Martin Luthers Werke.* Kritische Gesamtausgabe, Weimar, 1883-   ). Its texts and helps have formed a basis for this edition, though in certain places we have felt constrained to depart from its readings and findings. We have tried throughout to translate Luther as he thought translating should be done. That is, we have striven for faithfulness on the basis of the best lexicographical materials available. But where literal accuracy and clarity have conflicted, it is clarity that we have preferred, so that sometimes paraphrase seemed more faithful than literal fidelity. We have proceeded in a similar way in the matter of Bible versions, translating Luther's translations. Where this could be done by the use of an existing English version—King James, Douay, or Revised Standard—we have done so. Where it could not, we have supplied our own. To indicate this in each specific instance would have been pedantic; to adopt a uniform procedure would have been artificial—especially in view of Luther's own inconsistency in this regard. In each volume the translator will be responsible primarily for matters of text and language, while the responsibility of the editor will extend principally to the historical and theological matters reflected in the introductions and notes.

Although the edition as planned will include fifty-five volumes, Luther's writings are not being translated in their entirety. Nor should they be. As he was the first to insist, much of what he wrote and said was not that important. Thus the edition is a selection of works that have proved their importance for the faith, life, and history of the Christian church. The first thirty volumes contain Luther's expositions of various biblical books, while the remaining volumes include what are usually called his "Reformation writings" and other occasional pieces. The final volume of the set will be an index volume; in addition to an index of quotations, proper names, and topics, and a list of corrections and changes, it will contain a glossary of many of the technical terms that recur in Luther's works and that cannot be defined each time they appear. Obviously Luther cannot be forced into any neat set of rubrics. He can provide his reader with bits of autobiography or with political observations as he expounds a psalm, and he can speak tenderly about the meaning of the faith in the midst of polemics against his opponents. It is the hope of publishers, editors, and translators that through this edition the message of Luther's faith will speak more clearly to the modern church.

J. P.
H. T. L.

CONTENTS

IX

CIC   — *Corpus Iuris Canonici,* edited by E. Friedberg
(Graz, 1955).

C. R.   — *Corpus Reformatorum,* edited by C. G. Bret-
schneider and H. E. Bindseil
(Halle/Saale, 1834-1860).

LW   — American Edition of *Luther's Works*
(Philadelphia and St. Louis, 1955-   ).

PE   — *Works of Martin Luther.* Philadelphia Edition
(Philadelphia, 1915-1943).

WA   — *D. Martin Luthers Werke.* Kritische Gesamtausgabe
(Weimar, 1883-   ).

WA, Br   — *D. Martin Luthers Werke.* Briefwechsel
(Weimar, 1930-   ).

WA, DB   — *D. Martin Luthers Werke.* Deutsche Bibel
(Weimar, 1906-1961).

WA, TR   — *D. Martin Luthers Werke.* Tischreden
(Weimar, 1912-1921).

INTRODUCTION TO VOLUME 53

Luther's liturgical writings occupy an uncertain and controversial place in his literary work. Compared with the bulk of his exegetical, homiletical, and polemical output, they form an insignificant fraction. All of them are very short. The longest, the *German Mass*,[1] contains forty-seven pages in the original. Most of the others run to no more than a couple of pages. And yet few of his writings became as influential and were reprinted as often as the liturgical orders published under his name. They passed into the church orders of the Reformation and became normative for Lutheran worship (with certain changes) up to the present time.

Luther's liturgical influence is more remarkable since he was not primarily interested in the forms of worship. His whole concern was with the preaching and teaching of the Word. And yet in the course of events the reform of the mass became the shibboleth of the Reformation, for the whole order and idea of the sacrifice of the mass ran counter to Luther's basic insights. The abolition or reformation of the mass became, therefore, the signal heralding the accession of priests and people here and there into the camp of the Reformation.

These and other developments forced Luther to provide alternate forms for the ones that were being discarded. He was by no means anxious to do so. Many of his friends and followers were far less hesitant than he was to try their hand at liturgical reconstruction. Kantz,[2] Karlstadt,[3] and others had new orders in use while Luther was still celebrating mass according to the traditional order. There was nothing in him of the faddist with an itch for the novel

---

[1] See pp. 51-90.
[2] Kaspar Kantz (d. 1544), the reformer of Nördlingen, was the first to prepare and use a German order of service for the Lord's Supper according to evangelical principles: *Von der Evangelischen Mesz. Mit Christlichen Gebetten vor und nach der empfahung des Sacraments* (1522).
[3] Andrew Bodenstein Karlstadt (1480-1551). During the first years of the Reformation Karlstadt was a supporter of Luther (*LW* 31, 309-311), but growing tension between him and Luther resulted in an open break on the reformation of the liturgy in Wittenberg (*LW* 36, 129-132; *LW* 51, 69-100).

and untried. On the contrary, he shrank from innovations and avoided liturgical sensationalism because he had a pastor's concern for the faith and piety of the common people.

But when he realized that practical reforms could no longer be postponed and that his people were getting ready for them, he acted with vigor and verve. The forms he designed were at once more conservative and more creative than those of any of his contemporaries. That is not to claim perfection for every part. Luther had no time or inclination to work out every pedantic detail and could not be bothered with fussing over liturgical minutiae. Many of the ideas he proposed, such as a revision of the *de tempore* Epistles,[4] the placing of the sermon at the beginning of the service, or the position of the officiant behind the altar, he failed to work out in practice. But regardless of particulars, his liturgical reforms show such a firm grasp of the essentials and such a bold and sure expression of them that his reforms became a pattern for centuries to come and set forth principles that are as valid today as they were in Luther's time.

Nevertheless, it is difficult for the modern observer to understand the mind of Luther in the reorganization of worship. He seems both too tradition-bound and too subjective: so much so that many modern liturgical scholars refer to him, somewhat disdainfully, as an "amateur" in matters of worship. As a matter of fact—and this must be the point of departure in understanding Luther—he was much more of a traditionalist than either low or high church liturgiologists in the present, for today liturgical reformers agree that existing liturgical practices in their respective churches are unsatisfactory. They may not agree on the ideal form of worship, but even the most conservative do not want to preserve the existing liturgical traditions. Frequently they are the ones most critical of the status quo, because they advocate a return to earlier, more ancient forms. Historical research is the basis of their proposals and their watchword, restoration. But this whole idea of restoring the sunken glory of ancient ritual is a product of nineteenth-century Romanticism and was as foreign to Luther as to the

---

[4] *De tempore* refers to the propers for the Sundays and festival days of the church year. It is distinguished from *de sanctis*, a term that refers to the propers for the calendar of saints.

Romanist theologians of his day.[5] He and the defenders of the Roman mass knew no other liturgical forms from which to start than the ones in actual practice in the sixteenth century. Neither party thought seriously of going back to the orders of early medieval, patristic, or apostolic times. All of Luther's reforms were simply revisions of the service then in use. He never engaged in liturgical research or reconstruction. That is one of the reasons modern scholars are apt to view with scorn his liturgical competence. But in the sixteenth century only the enthusiasts attempted to devise a completely new service.

Luther would have been somewhat nonplused by the plaudits of those who pay tribute to his conservatism, as though the preservation of ancient forms was a liturgical mark of merit. Neither Old nor New were ultimate values to him. He approached the tangled problem of tradition versus innovation with the freedom of the Christian man.

On the one hand, he asserted over and over again that the Christian—as far as he is righteous through faith—needs no forms or orders. He is a possessor of all things. "Externals" are unimportant and unnecessary for him. But this frequent reference to externals has sometimes been misunderstood. Rationalists have tried to stamp Luther as the advocate of a purely spiritual, intellectual religion. Romanists and others have defended externals as helps and aids to worship. But both parties fail to see that Luther was not against externals as such. It is well known how much he stressed the external Word and sacrament in his controversies with the enthusiasts. His opposition to externals was directed against the current legalism of his church, which insisted on the necessity of these outward forms and so invested them with a spurious sanctity of their own. In other words, he did not denounce externals as such, but he did denounce the place they held in the ecclesiastical system and in the faith, or rather superstition, of the people. Externals had become a fetish which the believer in Christ did not need and which would prevent the unbeliever from finding God. That is why Luther constantly stressed the freedom of the Christian man

---

[5] The more radical reformers of the sixteenth century, such as Zwingli and the Anabaptists, did seek to restore apostolic orders of worship, but much less from a desire to introduce new liturgical forms than with the intent of abolishing them altogether.

from externals and *in* externals, i.e., the freedom to use or not to use them and to change them as the need arose.

On the other hand, Luther recognized that the Christian is not only a righteous man, but also a sinner. His faith is not a static, but a growing, struggling thing. Therefore, he needs the daily nurture and exercise in the Word as provided in the church's liturgy, and even though he might not need it for himself, he must provide it for others.

In this spirit of liberty and with this concern for the man in the pew, Luther planned the reformation of the cultus. Like a good doctor who is as careful in protecting and building up the healthy organs in his patient as he is ruthless in removing the diseased, Luther preserved and strengthened every vital feature in the traditional liturgy and deleted all corrupt intrusions. He did not invent preaching; but he made the sermon a regular part of every service. He did not invent congregational hymns in the vernacular. A number of them were known long before the Reformation and tolerated by the church on great festivals or at processions and pilgrimages. But Luther accorded them legitimate status and a regular place in the church service. In the proper sense of the word, his hymns are therefore "liturgical," i.e., they are firmly imbedded in the service and in the church year. Long before Luther different dioceses preserved regional differences in their forms of worship. Luther refused to sanction a Lutheran common order and encouraged each principality to strive for uniformity within its own borders without imposing these orders on others.

There had also been considerable differences between the elaborate services in cathedral and convent churches compared to the ordinary village or country church. This distinction continued and was made sharper when Luther and others introduced the German language. For ecumenical, academic, and musical reasons, Luther wanted the Latin services retained wherever the Latin language was still taught and used (and that meant everywhere except in villages and very small towns). Therefore, he arranged the German service in such a way that it could be used in even the smallest church. This fact has been overlooked by many critics of the *German Mass*.[6] It would have been easy for Luther to trans-

---

[6] Such as, e.g., Paul Zeller Strodach in *PE* 6, 26-27.

late *An Order of Mass*, 1523,[7] into German with very minor changes. But he realized that the physical conditions for the German service were altogether different from those for the Latin, e.g., the presence of a choir could not be depended on. Faced with the necessity of devising a service that could be used in the country and (for less important occasions) in the city, he went all the way and created a service along functional lines which, omitting all the "extras," provided the essential elements of the mass. After all, the man in the pew would benefit more from a German hymn in which he could join than from a Latin gradual mumbled by the celebrant which he could neither hear nor understand. In this connection it must also be remembered that the practice of adding German hymns to corresponding Latin chants, e.g., the Creed or the sequences, existed long before Luther. The Reformation only extended this principle by introducing more hymn paraphrases and by allowing these to take the place of a liturgical chant·in the church service.

In this and many other practices Luther simply built on existing traditions. At the same time, he did not hesitate to discard traditional forms and usages that obscured rather than expressed the gospel. Much offense has been taken at his complete excision of the canon of the mass, but this ruthless operation freed the Words of Institution from the rank growth around them and placed the gospel squarely in the center of the eucharistic rite.

Luther's liturgical writings span a wide compass. Besides the basic works in which he developed the general premises for liturgical reform, with practical suggestions for their realization, they include orders for the occasional services, such as baptism, private confession, and marriage, collects and other prayers, hymns and liturgical chants, prefaces to hymnals and other musical collections, and even a brief motet of his own composition. Luther's liturgical writings include not only the text, but also the music, for Luther gave serious attention to the melodies for chants and hymns whether they came from his own pen or from his musician friends and advisers.

This volume is the first attempt to collect all these materials

---

[7] See pp. 15-40.

with their music and to present them in an English version.[8] The sixth volume of the Philadelphia Edition of Luther's works covers the same sector of Luther's literary activity, but it disregards the music entirely and offers for the hymns not the texts proper, but merely an annotated index. Admittedly, the texts of Luther's hymns are available in several English translations. John Hunt,[9] Richard Massie,[10] John Anderson,[11] and others translated the entire body of Luther's hymns, but these works do not contain the music. Indeed, some of them change the original meters so freely that it would be impossible to sing them to the original melodies. Two collections have appeared which give Luther's hymns translated by various authors and with their music, but neither one of them affords a correct and dependable picture of the hymns in their original musical garb. James F. Lambert's[12] transcription of the melodies shows that he was ignorant of the rules of mensural notation. It is full of mistakes. L. W. Bacon and N. H. Allen[13] are more dependable, but they follow later sources, rather than the original prints from Luther's lifetime.

Concerning the editing of words and music and the editorial comments in this volume, the following should be noted:

1. Luther's literary style in his liturgical orders is as direct, earthy, and realistic as it is in his other writings. He did not need to affect an unctuous dignity to make a religious impact; for in his lifelong occupation with the Bible he had made the Hebraic mode of expressing divine truths in vivid, dynamic terms his own. No English translation can hope to preserve this feeling. Scripture passages in the liturgical orders have been given according to the King James Version of the Bible; elsewhere they have been given according to the Revised Standard Version, with necessary changes when Luther's German translation differs significantly from these English ones. Prayers and other liturgical forms are given in the idiom of the Book of Common Prayer, however without slavish de-

---

[8] Not included are Luther's occasional poems that have no relation to public worship (WA 35, 568-608) and his prayers for private devotion.
[9] The Spiritual Songs of Martin Luther (London, 1853).
[10] Martin Luther's Spiritual Songs (London: Hatchard and Son, 1854).
[11] Hymns from the German by Dr. Martin Luther (2nd ed.; Edinburgh, 1897).
[12] Luther's Hymns (Philadelphia: General Council Publication House, 1917).
[13] The Hymns of Martin Luther Set to Their Original Melodies. With an English Version (New York: Scribner's, 1883).

pendence on the style of Archbishop Cranmer. The modern reader will do well to remember that Luther's German did not have the archaic quality for his readers that sixteenth-century English conveys to the modern reader.

2. In Luther's day two kinds of musical notation were in use: chorale and mensural notation. Chorale notation, which was used for plain-chant melodies, did not indicate the exact value of the notes, though a distinction between long and short notes was possible. The Lutheran sources used this notation mostly for chants, e.g., the chants in the *German Mass*, but not for hymns unless they were written in a chant-like style, e.g., "Isaiah 'Twas the Prophet." All other hymns were printed in mensural notation.

Mensural notation, as the name implies, allowed an exact measurement of note values. In this respect it agreed with and was indeed a forerunner of our modern notation. Because it lacked one distinctive feature of modern notation, the bar, it failed to indicate stress. This is important for Luther's hymns. In both his texts and tunes, accents are not as regular (on every third or fourth beat) as in modern hymns. Accordingly, our edition omits bar lines and time signatures. It will be seen that duple or quadruple time underlies most of the hymn melodies (as indicated by ¢ in the original print). Yet they cannot always be pressed into 4/4 or 2/2 measures. In keeping with modern practice, in chants we use the eighth note as the basic unit to represent the punctum (♦), and small eighth notes to indicate optional notes. In hymns and other musical forms we reduce the note values to one fourth of their original value and substitute quarter notes for the semibreves (◇) that mark the beat in the original prints.[14] A bracket above the music indicates a ligature. The eight under the treble clef shows that it should be read an octave lower. For purposes of comparison, we always precede the modern transcription with the original key, key signature, time signature, and first note.

3. Finally, the editor wishes to acknowledge his indebtedness to all those who have plowed the same ground before him; the fruits of their labors have been distilled in the footnotes and other editorial comments. Our edition would have been impossible without the basic research contained in the respective volumes of *WA*.

---

[14] See p. 205.

Especially the careful studies on Luther's hymns by Walter Lucke and Hans Joachim Moser in WA 35 proved invaluable, as did the monographs on several of Luther's hymns and hymnals in *Jahrbuch für Liturgik und Hymnologie*.[15] Our edition of the chants depends largely on the studies by Konrad Ameln and others in the first volume of *Handbuch der deutschen evangelischen Kirchenmusik*.[16] Our edition of the liturgical writings and of the collects has greatly profited from the translations, comments, and commentaries by Paul Zeller Strodach and others in *PE* 6.

However, we have been on guard against letting the editorial comment overshadow the text proper. The footnotes are intended to clarify the meaning of various terms (where obscure) and to indicate the principal sources for the various orders. But this volume did not seem to be the place for explaining such common liturgical terms and forms as the Gloria in Excelsis or *Te Deum*, or for giving a history of these or other basic liturgical forms.[17]

The editor would also like to express his gratitude to all those who assisted him with advice and counsel, especially to Dr. Robert Schultz, who read the manuscript and offered many valuable suggestions.

U. S. L.

---

[15] Konrad Ameln *et al.* (eds.), *Jahrbuch für Liturgik und Hymnologie* (Kassel: Johannes Stauda Verlag, 1955-1963). Helpful for the study of Luther's hymns were also the following: Hans Joachim Moser, *Die Melodien der Lutherlieder* (Leipzig: Gustav Schlössmann, 1935); Otto Schlisske, *Handbuch der Lutherlieder* (Göttingen: Vandenhoeck und Ruprecht, 1948); and Wilhelm Stapel, *Luthers Lieder und Gedichte* (Stuttgart: Ev. Verlagswerk, 1950). On Luther's musicianship, see Paul Nettl, *Luther and Music* (Philadelphia: Muhlenberg Press, 1948); Ulrich S. Leupold, "Luther's Musical Education and Activities," *Lutheran Church Quarterly*, XII (1939), 423-428; Ulrich S. Leupold, "Luther's Conception of Music in Worship," *Lutheran Church Quarterly*, XIII (1940), 66-69; Theodore Hoelty-Nickel, *Luther and Music* ("Martin Luther Lectures," Vol. IV [Decorah, Iowa: Luther College Press, 1960]); Walter E. Buszin, *Luther on Music* (St. Paul: North Central Publishing Co., 1958).

[16] Published in Göttingen: Vandenhoeck und Ruprecht, 1933 ff.

[17] Much fuller and more detailed historical and liturgiological references will be found in *PE* 6. In fact, Paul Zeller Strodach was so anxious to demonstrate Luther's loyalty to the Roman rite that he not only gave the text and complete bibliography for every traditional prayer and collect that Luther used, but he even extracted from Luther's *Abomination of the Secret Mass* (*LW* 36, 307-328) the text of the Roman canon, while omitting Luther's caustic criticism of the same (*PE* 6, 125-132).

LUTHER'S WORKS

VOLUME 53

THE BASIC
LITURGICAL WRITINGS

INTRODUCTION

Luther never published a blueprint of the ideal Lutheran rite. His liturgical writings are concerned more with the purpose and meaning of worship than with its forms. For example, *A Christian Exhortation to the Livonians Concerning Public Worship and Concord,* 1525, simply explains the basic principles of liturgical reform without offering any actual orders or forms. And even those writings that go into practical detail lay greater stress on the theology of worship than on rubrics. Three of the four writings here deal with the reform of the mass and of the Canonical Hours. The earliest and shortest is the pamphlet *Concerning the Order of Public Worship,* 1523, in which Luther outlined the most urgent reforms in the service. The other two are more detailed and come closest to what may be called a "Lutheran liturgy." *An Order of Mass and Communion for the Church at Wittenberg,* 1523, details the changes that Luther wished to effect in the Latin services. *The German Mass and Order of Service,* 1526, as the title indicates, does the same for the services in the German tongue. These two orders contain Luther's liturgical legacy and became, either singly or in combination, determinative for the whole subsequent history and development of Lutheran worship.

CONCERNING THE
ORDER OF PUBLIC WORSHIP

1523

Translated by Paul Zeller Strodach

Revised by Ulrich S. Leupold

INTRODUCTION

On January 29, 1523, Luther promised to provide the congregation at Leisnig (Saxony) with an "order for singing, praying, and reading." The situation in Wittenberg lent impetus to the fulfilment of this promise. Having rejected Karlstadt's violent reformation of the cultus, Luther could not simply return to the traditional order. He had to point the way which led between the Scylla of reaction and the Charybdis of revolution. In other words, he had to spell out the basic principles of an evangelical reform of the liturgy and their practical application. This he did in *Concerning the Order of Public Worship*.

A case in point is Karlstadt's discontinuance of the daily private masses in Wittenberg. Nothing had been put in their place, and church doors were no longer open on weekdays. Luther established the Word of God as the principal element in the service and provided for daily Matins and Vespers with Scripture reading and explanation.

In Wittenberg these weekday services began on March 23, 1523. Whether the publication of Luther's *Concerning the Order of Public Worship* preceded or followed this date is uncertain. A Zwickau reprint of this order appeared as early as May 19, 1523. The work itself, however, does not refer directly to Wittenberg or to Leisnig; it may have been written as a guide for all those who felt the need for liturgical reform, but did not know how and where to begin.

The German text of the original Wittenberg print, *Von ordenung gottis diensts ynn der gemeyne*, is given in WA 12, 35-37; the following translation is a revision of P. Z. Strodach's translation in *PE* 6, 60-64.

9

CONCERNING THE
ORDER OF PUBLIC WORSHIP

The service now in common use everywhere goes back to genuine Christian beginnings, as does the office of preaching. But as the latter has been perverted by the spiritual tyrants, so the former has been corrupted by the hypocrites. As we do not on that account abolish the office of preaching, but aim to restore it again to its right and proper place, so it is not our intention to do away with the service, but to restore it again to its rightful use.

Three serious abuses have crept into the service. First, God's Word has been silenced, and only reading and singing remain in the churches. This is the worst abuse. Second, when God's Word had been silenced such a host of un-Christian fables and lies, in legends, hymns, and sermons were introduced that it is horrible to see. Third, such divine service was performed as a work whereby God's grace and salvation might be won. As a result, faith disappeared and everyone pressed to enter the priesthood, convents, and monasteries, and to build churches and endow them.

Now in order to correct these abuses, know first of all that a Christian congregation should never gather together without the preaching of God's Word and prayer, no matter how briefly, as Psalm 102[1] says, "When the kings and the people assemble to serve the Lord, they shall declare the name and the praise of God." And Paul in I Corinthians 14 [:26-31] says that when they come together, there should be prophesying, teaching, and admonition.[2] Therefore, when God's Word is not preached, one had better neither sing nor read, or even come together.

---

[1] A conflation and free rendering of Ps. 102:21-22.
[2] When Luther refers to I Corinthians 14, he assumes that the Scriptures are read in Latin, a practice he associates with speaking in tongues. Hence teaching and admonition, i.e., explanation of the lesson, should follow for the benefit of those who do not understand the Latin. WA 18, 124-125; WA 12, 31.

11

This was the custom among Christians at the time of the apostles and should also be the custom now. We should assemble daily at four or five in the morning and have [God's Word] read, either by pupils or priests, or whoever it may be, in the same manner as the lesson is still read at Matins; this should be done by one or two, or by one individual or choir after responding to the other,[3] as may seem most suitable.

Thereupon the preacher, or whoever has been appointed, shall come forward and interpret a part of the same lesson, so that all others may understand and learn it, and be admonished. The former[4] is called by Paul in I Corinthians 14 [:27] "speaking in tongues." The other he calls "interpreting" or "prophesying," or "speaking with sense or understanding." If this is not done, the congregation is not benefited by the lesson, as has been the case in cloisters and in convents, where they only bawled against the walls.

The lesson should be taken from the Old Testament; one of the books should be selected and one or two chapters, or half a chapter, be read, until the book is finished. After that another book should be selected, and so on, until the entire Bible has been read through; and where one does not understand it, pass on, and give glory to God. Thus Christian people will by daily training become proficient, skilful, and well versed in the Bible. For this is how genuine Christians were made in former times—both virgins and martyrs—and could also be made today.

Now when the lesson and its interpretation have lasted half an hour or so, the congregation shall unite in giving thanks to God, in praising him, and in praying for the fruits of the Word, etc. For this, the Psalms should be used and some good responsories and antiphons. In brief, let everything be completed in one hour or whatever time seems desirable; for one must not overload souls or weary them, as was the case until now in monasteries and convents, where they burdened themselves like mules.

---

[3] This is a reference to the two parts of a chancel choir which face each other in the stalls.
[4] I.e., the reading of the lesson just mentioned.

In like manner, come together at five or six in the evening. At this time one should really read again the Old Testament, book by book, namely the Prophets, even as Moses and the historical books are taken up in the morning. But since the New Testament is also a book, I read the Old Testament in the morning and the New Testament in the evening, or vice versa, and have reading, interpreting, praising, singing, and praying just as in the morning, also for an hour. For all that matters is that the Word of God be given free reign to uplift and quicken souls so that they do not become weary.

Should one desire to hold another such service during the day after lunch, that is a matter of choice.

And although these daily services might not be attended by the whole congregation, the priests and pupils, and especially those who, one hopes, will become good preachers and pastors,[5] should be present. And one should admonish them to do this willingly, not reluctantly or by constraint, or for the sake of reward, temporal or eternal, but alone to the glory of God and the neighbor's good.

Besides these daily services for a smaller group, the whole congregation should come together on Sundays, and mass and Vespers be sung, as has been customary. In both services there should be preaching for the whole congregation, in the morning on the Gospel for the day, in the evening on the Epistle; or the preacher may use his own judgment whether he would want to preach on a certain book or two.

If anyone desires to receive the sacrament at this time, let it be administered at a time convenient to all concerned.

The daily masses should be completely discontinued; for the Word is important and not the mass. But if any should desire the sacrament during the week, let mass be held as inclination and time dictate; for in this matter one cannot make hard and fast rules.

Let the chants in the Sunday masses and Vespers be retained; they are quite good and are taken from Scripture. However, one may lessen or increase their number. But to select the chants and

---

[5] *Seelsorger.*

13

Psalms for the daily morning and evening service shall be the duty of the pastor[6] and preacher. For every morning he shall appoint a fitting responsory or antiphon with a collect, likewise for the evening; this is to be read and chanted publicly after the lesson and exposition. But for the time being we can shelve the antiphons, responsories, and collects, as well as the legends of the saints and the cross, until they have been purged, for there is a horrible lot of filth in them.

All the festivals of saints are to be discontinued. Where there is a good Christian legend, it may be inserted as an example after the Gospel on Sunday. The festivals of the Purification and Annunciation of Mary may be continued, and for the time being also her Assumption and Nativity, although the songs in them are not pure. The festival of John the Baptist is also pure. Not one of the legends of the apostles is pure, except St. Paul's. They may either be transferred to the [closest] Sunday or be celebrated separately, if one so desires.

Other matters will adjust themselves as the need arises. And this is the sum of the matter: Let everything be done so that the Word may have free course instead of the prattling and rattling that has been the rule up to now. We can spare everything except the Word. Again, we profit by nothing as much as by the Word. For the whole Scripture shows that the Word should have free course among Christians. And in Luke 10 [:42], Christ himself says, "One thing is needful," i.e., that Mary sit at the feet of Christ and hear his word daily. This is the best part to choose and it shall not be taken away forever. It is an eternal Word. Everything else must pass away, no matter how much care and trouble it may give Martha. God help us achieve this. Amen.

---

[6] *Pfarrer.*

AN ORDER OF MASS
AND COMMUNION FOR THE
CHURCH AT WITTENBERG

1523

Translated by Paul Zeller Strodach

Revised by Ulrich S. Leupold

INTRODUCTION

In his pamphlet *Concerning the Order of Public Worship*, 1523,[1] Luther had indicated the basic principles of liturgical reform and also given a few hints for their implementation. But the detailed outline of an evangelical mass was still wanting, and Luther's friends outside Wittenberg were anxious to know the order Luther had adopted. It was due to the repeated urging of his friend Nicholas Hausmann[2] in Zwickau that Luther in December, 1523, published a step-by-step account of the evangelical mass (in Latin) and of its rationale, entitled *Formula Missae et Communionis pro Ecclesia Vuittembergensi.*

The Latin text of the original Wittenberg print is given in *WA* 12, 205-220; the following translation is a revision of P. Z. Strodach's translation in *PE* 6, 83-101. A German translation by Paul Speratus, which appeared the following year in Wittenberg, is reproduced in *St. L.* 10, 2230 ff., and in *MA*³ 3, 111-127.

---

[1] See pp. 7-14.
[2] Hausmann (1478/79-1538) was a close friend of Luther and lead the Reformation in Zwickau (1521) and Dessau (1532). Practical advice was urgently needed in Zwickau, where the enthusiasts were particularly strong. The Wittenberg riots of 1521/22 were largely due to the influence of three "prophets" from Zwickau; see *LW* 51, 69; *LW* 48, 364, n. 28.

AN ORDER OF MASS
AND COMMUNION FOR THE
CHURCH AT WITTENBERG

Grace and peace in Christ to the venerable Doctor Nicholas Hausmann, bishop of the church in Zwickau, saint in Christ, from Martin Luther.

Until now I have only used books and sermons to wean the hearts of people from their godless regard for ceremonial; for I believed it would be a Christian and helpful thing if I could prompt a peaceful removal of the abomination which Satan set up in the holy place through the man of sin [Matt. 24:15; II Thess. 2:3-4]. Therefore, I have used neither authority nor pressure. Nor did I make any innovations. For I have been hesitant and fearful, partly because of the weak in faith, who cannot suddenly exchange an old and accustomed order of worship for a new and unusual one, and more so because of the fickle and fastidious spirits who rush in like unclean swine without faith or reason, and who delight only in novelty and tire of it as quickly, when it has worn off. Such people are a nuisance even in other affairs, but in spiritual matters, they are absolutely unbearable. Nonetheless, at the risk of bursting with anger, I must bear with them, unless I want to let the gospel itself be denied to the people.

But since there is hope now that the hearts of many have been enlightened and strengthened by the grace of God, and since the cause of the kingdom of Christ demands that at long last offenses should be removed from it, we must dare something in the name of Christ. For it is right that we should provide at least for a few, lest by our desire to detach ourselves from the frivolous faddism of some people,[1] we provide for nobody, or by our fear

---

[1] I.e., the enthusiasts.

of ultimately offending others,[2] we endorse their universally held abominations.

Therefore, most excellent Nicholas, since you have requested it so often, we will deal with an evangelical[3] form of saying mass (as it is called) and of administering communion. And we will so deal with it that we shall no longer rule hearts by teaching alone, but we will put our hand to it and put the revision into practice in the public administration of communion, not wishing, however, to prejudice others against adopting and following a different order. Indeed, we heartily beg in the name of Christ that if in time something better should be revealed to them, they would tell us to be silent, so that by a common effort we may aid the common cause.

We therefore first assert: It is not now nor ever has been our intention to abolish the liturgical service of God[4] completely, but rather to purify the one that is now in use from the wretched accretions which corrupt it and to point out an evangelical use. We cannot deny that the mass, i.e., the communion of bread and wine, is a rite divinely instituted by Christ himself and that it was observed first by Christ and then by the apostles, quite simply and evangelically without any additions. But in the course of time so many human inventions were added to it that nothing except the names of the mass and communion has come down to us.

Now the additions of the early fathers who, it is reported, softly prayed one or two Psalms before blessing the bread and wine are commendable. Athanasius[5] and Cyprian[6] are supposed to be some of these. Those who added the Kyrie eleison also did

---

[2] I.e., the Romanists.
[3] Latin: pia. In Luther's usage in this context, the word pius means "in accord with the gospel." Speratus translates: "Christian." Similarly, impius denotes everything connected with work righteousness, in spite of the "piety" seemingly attached to it.
[4] Cultus dei.
[5] Cf. Athanasius, De Fuga. MPG 25, 676: "When I sat on the throne, I told the deacon to read the Psalm and the people to respond with 'for his mercy endureth forever'" [Ps. 136:1]; see also the reference to Athanasius' practice of Psalmody in Augustine, Confessions, X, 33, 50. MPL 32, 800.
[6] Cyprian (d. 258), bishop of Carthage. Perhaps Luther was thinking of Cyprian's advice to Donatus (Epistle I. ANF 5, 280), "Let the temperate meal resound with Psalms."

well. We read that under Basil the Great,[7] the Kyrie eleison was in common use by all the people. The reading of the Epistles and Gospels is necessary, too. Only it is wrong to read them in a language the common people do not understand. Later, when chanting began, the Psalms were changed into the introit; the Angelic Hymn *Gloria in Excelsis: et in terra pax*,[8] the graduals, the alleluias, the Nicene Creed, the Sanctus, the Agnus Dei, and the *communio*[9] were added. All of these are unobjectionable, especially the ones that are sung *de tempore*[10] or on Sundays. For these days by themselves testify to ancient purity, the canon excepted.

But when everyone felt free to add or change at will and when the tyranny of priestly greed and pride entered in, then our wicked kings, i.e., the bishops and pastors, began to erect those altars to the images of Baal and all gods in the Lord's temple. Then it was that wicked King Ahaz removed the brazen altar and erected another copied from one in Damascus.[11] What I am speaking of is the canon, that abominable concoction drawn from everyone's sewer and cesspool. The mass became a sacrifice. Offertories[12] and mercenary[13] collects were added. Sequences and proses[14] were inserted in the Sanctus and the Gloria in Excelsis. Whereupon the mass began to be a priestly monopoly devouring

---

[7] Luther seems to refer to the note in Guillaume Durand, *Rationale divinorum officiorum* (Argentine, 1484), lib. iv, fol. 12, 4, that before Pope Gregory the Great (*ca.* 540-604) and among the Greeks, the Kyrie was sung by both clergy and people. This note is contained in the paragraph which begins with a reference to the intonation of the Kyrie by Basil the Great, bishop of Caesarea (*ca.* 330-379).

[8] The Gloria in Excelsis was commonly called the Angelic Hymn because of its derivation from Luke 2:14.

[9] The chant sung during the distribution of the Lord's Supper.

[10] Cf. p. xiv, n. 4.

[11] Cf. II Kings 16:10-14.

[12] Of the propers of the mass, the offertory was the most offensive to Luther, because it stressed the sacrificial concept of the Lord's Supper.

[13] Luther calls the prayers (for the departed, for special favors, etc.) in the canon "mercenary" because they were based on the assumption that the sacrifice of the mass would evoke a readier response from God.

[14] As commonly understood, a sequence or prose is a kind of Latin hymn that was sung after the Alleluia. Luther thought highly of some of these (cf. pp. 25 and 255). Here he seems to refer rather to tropes, which in a manner similar to the sequences and proses added new words to an existing melody in the Gloria or Sanctus.

the wealth of the whole world and engulfing it—as with an apocalyptic plague—with a host of rich, lazy, powerful, lascivious, and
corrupt celibates. Thus came the masses for the departed, for
journeys, for prosperity—but who can even name the causes for
which the mass was made a sacrifice?

Nor do they cease to enlarge the canon even today: now it is
for these feasts, then for others; now these *actiones* then other
communicantes[15] are adopted—not to mention the commemoration
of the living and the dead.[16] And there is no end of it yet. And
what shall I say of the external additions of vestments, vessels,
candles, and palls, of organs and all the music, and of images?
There was scarcely a craft in all the world that did not depend
on the mass for a large part of its business.

All these have been tolerated and—with the gospel revealing
so many abominations—they can be tolerated until they can be
completely removed. In the meanwhile we shall prove all things
and hold fast what is good [I Thess. 5:21]. But in this book we
are not going to prove again that the mass is neither a sacrifice
nor a good work—we have amply demonstrated that elsewhere.[17]
We do accept it as a sacrament, a testament, the blessing (as in
Latin), the eucharist (as in Greek), the Table of the Lord, the
Lord's Supper, the Lord's Memorial, communion, or by whatever
evangelical name you please, so long as it is not polluted by the
name of sacrifice or work. And we will set forth the rite according to which we think that it should be used.

First, we approve and retain the introits for the Lord's days
and the festivals of Christ, such as Easter, Pentecost, and the Nativity, although we prefer the Psalms from which they were taken
as of old.[18] But for the time being we permit the accepted use.

---

15 The passage of canon called *intra actionem* and beginning with the word
communicantes is altered on certain days.

16 The canon contains prayers for the living (*Memento, Domine*) and for the
dead (*Memento etiam*) that provide for the insertion of the names of certain
beneficiaries.

17 *A Treatise on the New Testament, that is, the Holy Mass,* 1520. LW 35,
79-111; *The Babylonian Captivity of the Church,* 1520. LW 36, 47-56, *passim;*
The Misuse of the Mass, 1521. LW 36, 162-198.

18 Cf. pp. 38-39.

And if any desire to approve the introits (inasmuch as they have been taken from Psalms or other passages of Scripture) for apostles' days, for feasts of the Virgin and of other saints, we do not condemn them. But we in Wittenberg intend to observe[19] only the Lord's days and the festivals of the Lord. We think that all the feasts of the saints should be abrogated, or if anything in them deserves it, it should be brought into the Sunday sermon. We regard the feasts of Purification[20] and Annunciation[21] as feasts of Christ, even as Epiphany[22] and Circumcision.[23] Instead of the feasts of St. Stephen[24] and of St. John the Evangelist,[25] we are pleased to use the office of the Nativity. The feasts of the Holy Cross[26] shall be anathema. Let others act according to their own conscience or in consideration of the weakness of some—whatever the Spirit may suggest.

Second, we accept the Kyrie eleison in the form in which it has been used until now, with the various melodies for different seasons, together with the Angelic Hymn, Gloria in Excelsis, which follows it. However, the bishop[27] may decide to omit the latter as often as he wishes.

Third, the prayer or collect which follows, if it is evangelical (and those for Sunday usually are), should be retained in its accepted form; but there should be only one. After this the Epistle is read. Certainly the time has not yet come to attempt revision here, as nothing unevangelical is read, except that those parts from the Epistles of Paul in which faith is taught are read only rarely, while the exhortations to morality are most frequently read. The Epistles seem to have been chosen by a singularly unlearned and

---

[19] Literally, to keep the Sabbath.
[20] February 2.
[21] March 25.
[22] January 6.
[23] January 1.
[24] December 26.
[25] December 27.
[26] The Invention of the Holy Cross, May 3; the Exaltation of the Cross, September 14. On Luther's marked opposition to these festivals, cf. WA 10ᴵᴵᴵ, 113-119; 332-341; 361-371.
[27] *Episcopus,* "bishop." Luther sometimes refers to the parish pastor as "bishop." Speratus translates *Pfarrherr.*

superstitious advocate of works. But for the service those sections in which faith in Christ is taught should have been given preference. The latter were certainly considered more often in the Gospels by whoever it was who chose these lessons. In the meantime, the sermon in the vernacular will have to supply what is lacking. If in the future the vernacular be used in the mass (which Christ may grant), one must see to it that Epistles and Gospels chosen from the best and most weighty parts of these writings be read in the mass.

Fourth, the gradual of two verses[28] shall be sung, either together with the Alleluia, or one of the two, as the bishop may decide. But the Quadragesima graduals and others like them that exceed two verses[29] may be sung at home by whoever wants them. In church we do not want to quench the spirit of the faithful with tedium. Nor is it proper to distinguish Lent, Holy Week, or Good Friday from other days, lest we seem to mock and ridicule Christ with half of a mass and the one part of the sacrament.[30] For the Alleluia is the perpetual voice of the church, just as the memorial of His passion and victory is perpetual.

Fifth, we allow no sequences or proses unless the bishop wishes to use the short one for the Nativity of Christ: "*Grates nunc*

---

[28] Most of the graduals consist of two verses, of which the first is repeated after the second. The Alleluias are usually short and consist of only one verse with its Alleluias.

[29] Quadragesima, the first Sunday in Lent, here refers to the whole Lenten season. In Lent the "tracts," consisting of up to thirteen verses, took the place of the gradual.

[30] The Mass of the Presanctified. This is a celebration without the consecration of the host or wine. Two hosts are consecrated on Maundy Thursday and one is reserved in a specially prepared place for use on Good Friday. On Good Friday the wine is not consecrated by the usual prayers, but rather by placing a third part of the preconsecrated host into it. The prayers in connection with the wine are omitted in this Good Friday use, but the unconsecrated wine together with the portion of the host placed in it is consumed by the priest. Though not forbidden to commune, the people at that time were directed to commune in silence (*sub silentio*). WA 12, 210, n. 2; PE 6, 104, n. 54. In his *Defense and Explanation of All the Articles*, 1521, Luther speaks of a "half-sacrament" (*halb sacrament*), though in a different context. LW 32, 56; WA 7, 389. Cf. also WA 7, 123, when he speaks of "the one part of the sacrament," *altera pars sacramenti*.

omnes."[31] There are hardly any which smack of the Spirit, save those of the Holy Spirit: *"Sancti Spiritus"*[32] and *"Veni sancte spiritus,"*[33] which may be sung after breakfast,[34] at Vespers, or at mass (if the bishop pleases).

Sixth, the Gospel lesson follows, for which we neither prohibit nor prescribe candles or incense. Let these things be free.

Seventh, the custom of singing the Nicene Creed does not displease us; yet this matter should also be left in the hands of the bishop. Likewise, we do not think that it matters whether the sermon in the vernacular comes after the Creed or before the introit of the mass; although it might be argued that since the Gospel is the voice crying in the wilderness[35] and calling unbelievers to faith, it seems particularly fitting to preach before mass. For properly speaking, the mass consists in using[36] the Gospel and communing at the table of the Lord. Inasmuch as it belongs to believers, it should be observed apart [from unbelievers].[37] Yet since we are free, this argument does not bind us, especially since everything in the mass up to the Creed is ours, free and not prescribed by God; therefore it does not necessarily have anything to do with the mass.

Eighth, that utter abomination follows which forces all that

---

[31] *"Grates nunc omnes reddamus Domino Deo, qui sua nativitate nos liberavit de diabolica potestate";* attributed to Notker Balbulus of St. Gall (d. 912). *MPL* 131, 1005. Translated into German as *"Danksagen wir alle,"* it is found in many early Lutheran hymnals. Cf. Johannes Zahn, *Die Melodien der deutschen evangelischen Kirchenlieder* (Gütersloh: Bertelsmann), V (1892), No. 8619. Following John Julian's *Dictionary of Hymnology* (London, 1892), Strodach erroneously states that Luther's *"Gelobet seist du, Jesu Christ,"* was based on this sequence. *PE* 6, 105, n. 58.

[32] Attributed to Notker, *"Sancti Spiritus adsit nobis gratia, quaecorda nostra sibi faciat habitaculum"* was an eleventh-century sequence appointed for use following the reading of the Epistle for Pentecost. *MPL* 131, 1012.

[33] *"Veni sancte spiritus et emitte coelitus,"* a thirteenth-century sequence formerly used on Whitmonday (cf. Julian, *Dictionary of Hymnology,* pp. 1212-1215), which Luther prized highly; cf. *WA,* TR 4, No. 4627, p. 409. Strodach in *PE* 6, 105, confuses this sentence with the antiphon *"Veni sancte spiritus, reple tuorum corda fidelium,"* on which Luther's hymn "Come, Holy Spirit Lord and God" is based. Cf. p. 265.

[34] Does Luther mean during Matins?

[35] Cf. Matt. 3:3.

[36] Luther distinguishes the "use" from the "preaching" of the gospel. It is heard by all, but "used" only by the believers.

[37] Cf. p. 64.

precedes in the mass into its service and is, therefore, called the offertory. From here on almost everything smacks and savors of sacrifice. And the words of life and salvation [the Words of Institution] are imbedded in the midst of it all, just as the ark of the Lord once stood in the idol's temple next to Dagon.[38] And there was no Israelite who could approach or bring back the ark until it "smote his enemies in the hinder parts, putting them to a perpetual reproach,"[39] and forced them to return it—which is a parable of the present time. Let us, therefore, repudiate everything that smacks of sacrifice, together with the entire canon and retain only that which is pure and holy, and so order our mass.[40]

I. After the Creed or after the sermon[41] let bread and wine be made ready for blessing[42] in the customary manner. I have not yet decided whether or not water should be mixed with the wine. I rather incline, however, to favor pure wine without water; for the passage, "Thy wine is mixed with water," in Isaiah 1 [:22] gives the mixture a bad connotation.

Pure wine beautifully portrays the purity of gospel teaching. Further, the blood of Christ, whom we here commemorate, has been poured out unmixed with ours. Nor can the fancies of those be upheld who say that this is a sign of our union with Christ; for that is not what we commemorate. In fact, we are not united with Christ until he sheds his blood; or else we would be celebrating the shedding of our own blood together with the blood of Christ shed for us. Nonetheless, I have no intention of cramping anyone's freedom or of introducing a law that might again lead to superstition. Christ will not care very much about these matters, nor are they worth arguing about. Enough foolish controversies have been fought on these and many other matters by the Roman and Greek

---

[38] I Sam. 5:2.
[39] Ps. 78:66; cf. I Sam. 5:12.
[40] I.e., the mass in the narrower sense of the word, namely, the celebration of the Lord's Supper.
[41] Original: *post canonem*, an obvious misprint for *post concionem*.
[42] *Benedictio* is regularly translated as "blessing" or "benediction," except for *verba benedictionis*, which is translated "Words of Institution."

churches.[43] And though some[44] direct attention to the water and blood which flowed from the side of Jesus,[45] they prove nothing. For that water signified something entirely different from what they wish that mixed water to signify. Nor was it mixed with blood. The symbolism does not fit, and the reference is inapplicable. As a human invention, this mixing [of water and wine] cannot, therefore, be considered binding.

II. The bread and wine having been prepared, one may proceed as follows:

The Lord be with you.

Response: And with thy spirit.

Lift up your hearts.

Response: Let us lift them to the Lord.

Let us give thanks unto the Lord our God.

Response: It is meet and right.

It is truly meet and right, just and salutary for us to give thanks to Thee always and everywhere, Holy Lord, Father Almighty, Eternal God, through Christ our Lord . . .

III. Then:

. . . Who the day before he suffered, took bread, and when he had given thanks, brake it, and gave it to his disciples, saying, Take, eat; this is my body, which is given for you.

After the same manner also the cup, when he had

---

[43] Jerome Emser attacked Luther's restructuring of the mass on many points. On this point, he asserts: "Not only in Rome, but in Egypt, Asia, Africa, Europe, and throughout the whole Christian world, the rite of mixing water with wine is observed; and the Greek author, Theophilus, also approves." *Missa Christianorum contra Lutheranam missandi formulam assertio,* 1524. *Corpus Catholicorum,* 28, 30-31; cf. *WA* 12, 212, note.

In his argument Luther followed Guillaume Durand, a thirteenth-century French canonist and liturgical writer. Durand states: "It is said that the Greek church did not add water to the sacrament." *Rationale divinorum officiorum,* lib. iv, fol. 70. Similar statements were made by Peter Lombard, *Sententiarum* (Venice, 1563), lib. iv, dist. XI, ques. 8 (cf. *MPL* 192, 864), and by others (cf. *MPL* 58, 1044).

[44] Pseudo-Ambrose in *De sacramentis,* lib. v, cap. 1. *MPL* 16, 447; Gennadii, *De ecclesiasticis dogmatibus,* cap. 75. *MPL* 58, 998.

[45] John 19:34.

supped, saying, This cup is the New Testament in my blood, which is shed for you and for many, for the remission of sins; this do, as often as ye do it, in remembrance of me.

I wish these words of Christ—with a brief pause after the preface—to be recited in the same tone in which the Lord's Prayer is chanted elsewhere in the canon so that those who are present may be able to hear them, although the evangelically minded should be free about all these things and may recite these words either silently or audibly.

IV. The blessing ended, let the choir sing the Sanctus. And while the Benedictus is being sung, let the bread and cup be elevated according to the customary rite for the benefit of the weak in faith who might be offended if such an obvious change in this rite of the mass were suddenly made. This concession can be made especially where through sermons in the vernacular they have been taught what the elevation means.

V. After this, the Lord's Prayer shall be read. Thus, let us pray: "Taught by thy saving precepts. . . ."[46] The prayer which follows, "Deliver us, we beseech thee . . . ,"[47] is to be omitted together with all the signs[48] they were accustomed to make over the host and with the host over the chalice. Nor shall the host be broken or mixed into the chalice. But immediately after the Lord's Prayer shall be said, "The peace of the Lord," etc., which is, so to speak, a public absolution of the sins of the communicants, the true voice of the gospel announcing remission of sins, and there-

---

[46] The introduction to the Lord's Prayer in the Roman canon: "Taught by thy saving precepts and guided by the divine institution, we make bold to say: Our Father," etc.

[47] In the translation by Luther D. Reed (*The Lutheran Liturgy* [2nd ed.; Philadelphia: Muhlenberg Press, 1960], pp. 727-728), this prayer reads: "Deliver us, we beseech thee, O Lord, from all evils, past, present and to come, and by the intercession of the blessed and glorious ever Virgin Mary, Mother of God, together with thy blessed apostles Peter and Paul, and Andrew, and all the saints, mercifully grant peace in our days: that through the bounteous help of thy mercy we may be always free from sin and secure from all disturbance. Through the same Jesus Christ, thy Son our Lord, who liveth and reigneth with thee and the Holy Ghost, one God, world without end."

[48] The signs of the cross.

fore the one and most worthy preparation for the Lord's Table, if faith holds to these words as coming from the mouth of Christ himself. On this account I would like to have it pronounced facing the people, as the bishops are accustomed to do, which is the only custom of the ancient bishops that is left among our bishops.

VI. Then, while the Agnus Dei is sung, let him [the liturgist] communicate, first himself and then the people. But if he should wish to pray the prayer, "O Lord Jesus Christ, Son of the living God, who according to the will of the Father," etc.,[49] before communing, he does not pray wrongly, provided he changes the singular "mine" and "me" to the plural "ours" and "us." The same thing holds for the prayer, "The body of our Lord Jesus Christ preserve my (or thy) soul unto life eternal," and, "The blood of our Lord preserve thy soul unto life eternal."

VII. If he desires to have the communion sung,[50] let it be sung. But instead of the *complenda* or final collect,[51] because it sounds almost like a sacrifice, let the following prayer be read in the same tone: "What we have taken with our lips, O Lord . . . ."[52] The following one may also be read: "May thy body which we have received . . . (changing to the plural number) . . . who livest and reignest world without end."[53] "The Lord be with you," etc.

---

[49] In the Roman canon the prayer continues as follows: ". . . and the co-operation of the Holy Ghost, didst through thy death give life to the world: deliver me by this thy most sacred body and blood from all mine iniquities, and from all evils: and make me ever to cleave to thy commandments; nor ever suffer me to be separated from thee: who with the Father and the Holy Ghost livest and reignest with God, world without end. Amen."

[50] Literally, "If he desires to sing the communion." But the communion was one of the propers to be sung by the choir, not by the priest. Speratus also translates, "If one desires to have," etc.

[51] This is evidently a reference to the final collect in the canon of the Roman mass: "May the homage of my bounden duty be pleasing to thee, O holy Trinity; and grant that the sacrifice which I, though unworthy, have offered in the sight of thy majesty may be acceptable to thee, and through thy mercy be a propitiation for me and for all those for whom I have offered it. Through Christ our Lord. Amen." Reed, *op. cit.*, p. 734.

[52] In the Roman canon this prayer continues: ". . . may we with pure minds receive; and from a temporal gift, may it become to us an everlasting remedy."

[53] In the Roman canon, this prayer continues: ". . . cleave to mine [our] inmost parts: and grant that no stain of sin may remain in me [us] whom this pure and holy sacrament hath refreshed, O thou. . . ."

29

In place of the *Ite missa*[54] let the *Benedicamus domino*[55] be said, adding Alleluia according to its own melodies where and when it is desired. Or the *Benedicamus* may be borrowed from Vespers.

VIII. The customary benediction may be given;[56] or else the one from Numbers 6 [:24-27], which the Lord himself appointed:

"The Lord bless us and keep us. The Lord make his face shine upon us and be gracious unto us. The Lord lift up his countenance upon us, and give us peace."

Or the one from Psalm 67 [:6-7]:

"God, even our own God shall bless us. God shall bless us; and all the ends of the earth shall fear him."

I believe Christ used something like this when, ascending into heaven, he blessed his disciples [Luke 24:50-51].

The bishop should also be free to decide on the order in which he will receive and administer both species. He may choose to bless both bread and wine before he takes the bread. Or else he may, between the blessing of the bread and of the wine, give the bread both to himself and to as many as desire it, then bless the wine and administer it to all. This is the order Christ seems to have observed, as the words of the Gospel show, where he told them to eat the bread before he had blessed the cup [Mark 14:22-23]. Then is said expressly, "Likewise also the cup after he supped" [Luke 22:20; I Cor. 11:25]. Thus you see that the cup was not blessed until after the bread had been eaten. But this order is [now] quite new and allows no room for those prayers which heretofore were said after the blessing,[57] unless they would also be changed.

Thus we think about the mass. But in all these matters we will want to beware lest we make binding what should be free, or make sinners of those who may do some things differently or omit

---

54 "Go, mass is ended," the closing versicle of the Roman canon.
55 "Bless we the Lord," the closing versicle of the Roman canon for Advent and Lent. Vespers also closed with this versicle.
56 In the Roman mass: "May Almighty God bless you: the Father, and the Son, and the Holy Ghost."
57 The prayers listed under sections IV and V.

others. All that matters is that the Words of Institution[58] should be kept intact and that everything should be done by faith. For these rites are supposed to be for Christians, i.e., children of the "free woman" [Gal. 4:31], who observe them voluntarily and from the heart, but are free to change them how and when ever they may wish. Therefore, it is not in these matters that anyone should either seek or establish as law some indispensable form by which he might ensnare or harass consciences. Nor do we find any evidence for such an established rite, either in the early fathers or in the primitive church, but only in the Roman church. But even if they had decreed anything in this matter as a law, we would not have to observe it, because these things neither can nor should be bound by laws. Further, even if different people make use of different rites, let no one judge or despise the other, but every man be fully persuaded in his own mind [Rom. 14:5]. Let us feel and think the same, even though we may act differently. And let us approve each other's rites lest schisms and sects should result from this diversity in rites—as has happened in the Roman church. For external rites, even though we cannot do without them—just as we cannot do without food or drink—do not commend us to God, even as food does not commend us to him [I Cor. 8:8]. Faith and love commend us to God. Wherefore here let the word of Paul hold sway, "For the kingdom of God is not meat and drink; but righteousness and peace and joy in the Holy Ghost" [Rom. 14:17]. So the kingdom of God is not any rite, but faith within you, etc.

We have passed over the matter of vestments. But we think about these as we do about other forms. We permit them to be used in freedom, as long as people refrain from ostentation and pomp. For you are not more acceptable for consecrating in vestments. Nor are you less acceptable for consecrating without vestments. But I do not wish them to be consecrated or blessed—as if they were to become something sacred as compared with other garments—except that by general benediction of word and prayer by which every good creature of God is sanctified.[59] Otherwise,

---

58 Benedicationis verba.
59 Cf. I Tim. 4:4-5.

31

it is nothing but the superstition and mockery which the priests of Baal[60] introduced together with so many other abuses.

The Communion of the People

So far we have dealt with the mass and the function of the minister or bishop. Now we shall speak of the proper manner of communicating the people, for whom the Lord's Supper was primarily instituted and given this name. For just as it is absurd for a minister to make a fool of himself and publicly preach the Word where no one hears or to harangue himself in an empty room[61] or under the open sky, so it is equally nonsensical if the ministers prepare and embellish the Lord's Supper, which belongs to all, without having guests to eat and drink it, so that they who ought to minister to others eat and drink by themselves alone at an empty table and in a vacant room. Therefore, if we really want to cherish Christ's command, no private mass should be allowed in the church, except as a temporary concession for the sake of necessity or for the weak in faith.

Here one should follow the same usage as with baptism, namely, that the bishop be informed of those who want to commune. They should request in person to receive the Lord's Supper so that he may be able to know both their names and manner of life. And let him not admit the applicants unless they can give a reason for their faith and can answer questions about what the Lord's Supper is, what its benefits are, and what they expect to derive from it. In other words, they should be able to repeat the Words of Institution from memory and to explain that they are coming because they are troubled by the consciousness of their sin, the fear of death, or some other evil, such as temptation of the flesh, the world, or the devil, and now hunger and thirst to receive the word and sign of grace and salvation from the Lord himself through the ministry of the bishop, so that they may be consoled and comforted; this was Christ's purpose, when he in priceless love gave and instituted this Supper, and said, "Take and eat," etc.

---

[60] *Abominationis pontifices,* "the pontiffs of abomination."
[61] Literally, *inter saxa et ligna,* "between stones and wood."

But I think it enough for the applicants for communion to be examined or explored once a year. Indeed, a man may be so understanding that he needs to be questioned only once in his lifetime or not at all. For, by this practice, we want to guard lest the worthy and unworthy alike rush to the Lord's Supper, as we have hitherto seen done in the Roman church. There they seek only to communicate; but the faith, the comfort, the use and benefit of the Supper are not even mentioned or considered. Nay, they have taken pains to hide the Words of Institution, which are the bread of life itself, and have furiously tried to make the communicants perform a work, supposedly good in itself, instead of letting their faith be nourished and strengthened by the goodness of Christ. Those, therefore, who are not able to answer in the manner described above should be completely excluded and banished from the communion of the Supper, since they are without the wedding garment [Matt. 22:11-12].

When the bishop has convinced himself that they understand all these things, he should also observe whether they prove their faith and understanding in their life and conduct. For Satan, too, understands and can talk about all these things. Thus if the pastor should see a fornicator, adulterer, drunkard, gambler, usurer, slanderer, or anyone else disgraced by a manifest vice, he should absolutely exclude such person from the Supper—unless he can give good evidence that his life has been changed. For the Supper need not be denied to those who sometimes fall and rise again, but grieve over their lapse. Indeed, we must realize that it was instituted just for such people so that they may be refreshed and strengthened. "For in many things we offend all" [Jas. 3:2]. And we "bear one another's burdens" [Gal. 6:2], since we are burdening one another. But I was speaking of those arrogant people who sin brazenly and without fear while they boast glorious things about the gospel.

When mass is being celebrated, those to receive communion should gather together by themselves in one place and in one group. The altar and the chancel were invented for this purpose. God does not care where we stand and it adds nothing to our faith. The communicants, however, ought to be seen and known openly, both by those who do and by those who do not commune, in order that their lives may be better observed, proved, and tested. For participation in the Supper is part of the confession by which they confess before God, angels, and men that they are Christians. Care must therefore be taken lest any, as it were, take the Supper on the sly and disappear in the crowd so that one cannot tell whether they live good or evil lives. On the other hand, even in this matter I do not want to make a law, but simply want to demonstrate a decent and fitting order to be used in freedom by free Christian men.

Now concerning private confession before communion, I still think as I have held heretofore, namely, that it neither is necessary nor should be demanded. Nevertheless, it is useful and should not be despised; for the Lord did not even require the Supper itself as necessary or establish it by law, but left it free to everyone when he said, "As often as you do this," etc. [I Cor. 11:25-26]. So concerning the preparation for the Supper, we think that preparing oneself by fasting and prayer is a matter of liberty. Certainly one ought to come sober and with a serious and attentive mind, even though one might not fast at all and pray ever so little. But the sobriety I speak of is not that superstitious practice of the papists. I demand it lest people should come belching their drink and bloated with overeating. For the best preparation is—as I have said—a soul troubled by sins, death, and temptation and hungering and thirsting for healing and strength. Teaching these matters to the people is up to the bishop.

It remains to be considered whether both forms,[62] as they call them, should be administered to the people. Here I say this: Now that the gospel has been instilled among us these two whole years, we have humored the weak in faith long enough. Hereafter we shall act according to the words of St. Paul, "If any man be ignorant, let him be ignorant" [I Cor. 14:38]. For if after all this time they have not understood the gospel, it matters little whether they receive either form. If we continue to make allowance for their weakness, we only run the risk of confirming their obstinacy and

---

[62] Both elements, i.e., bread and wine.

34

of making rules contrary to the gospel. Wherefore, both forms may be requested and shall be offered in simple compliance with the institution of Christ. Those who refuse them will be left alone and receive nothing. For we are devising this order of the mass for those to whom the gospel has been proclaimed and by whom it has been at least partly understood. Those who have not yet heard or understood it are also not ready to receive advice concerning this matter [of liturgical forms].

Nor is it necessary to wait for a council—as they prate—in order to have this practice sanctioned. We have the law of Christ on our side and are not minded to be delayed by or to listen to a council in matters which manifestly are part of the gospel. Nay, we say more: If by chance a council should establish and permit this practice, then we would be the last to partake of both forms. Nay, in contempt both of the council and of its statute, we should then wish to partake either of one or of neither, but never of both; and we would hold those to be wholly anathema who on the authority of such a council and statute would partake of both.

You wonder why and ask for a reason? Listen! If you know that the bread and wine were instituted by Christ and that both are to be received by all—as the Gospels and Paul testify so clearly that even our adversaries themselves are forced to admit it—and if you still dare not believe and trust in Him enough to receive both forms, but dare to do so after men decide this in a council, are you not preferring men to Christ? Do you not extol sinful men over Him who is named God and worshiped as such [II Thess. 2:3-4]? Do you not trust in the words of men more than in the words of God? Nay rather, do you not utterly distrust the words of God and believe only the words of men? And how great a rejection and denial of God the most high is that? What idolatry can be compared to the superstitious regard in which you hold the council of men? Should you not rather die a thousand deaths? Should you not rather receive one or no form at all, than [both] in the name of an obedience which is a sacrilege and of a faith that amounts to apostasy?

Therefore, let them stop prating of their councils. First, let them do this: Let them restore to God the glory which they have denied him. Let them confess that with Satan their master they have held back one form, that they have lifted themselves up above God, that they have condemned his word, and have led to perdition so many people for so long a time. And let them repent of this unspeakably cruel and godless tyranny. Then, let them solemnly declare that we have done right when on our part and even against their dogma we have taught and received both forms and have not waited for their council. And let them give thanks, because we have refused to follow their perditious abomination. When they have done this, we shall gladly and willingly honor and obey their council and [its] statute. In the meantime, while they fail to do so and instead continue to demand that we should await their authorization, we shall listen to nothing. Rather, we shall continue to teach and act against them, particularly where we know it displeases them most. For what do they require with their diabolical demand except that we should exalt them above God and their words above his, and that we should receive the phantoms of their fancy as idols in the place of God? It is our concern, however, that the whole world be completely subjected and obedient to God.

I also wish that we had as many songs as possible in the vernacular which the people could sing during mass, immediately after the gradual and also after the Sanctus and Agnus Dei. For who doubts that originally all the people sang these which now only the choir sings or responds to while the bishop is consecrating? The bishops may have these [congregational] hymns sung either after the Latin chants, or use the Latin on one [Sun]day and the vernacular on the next, until the time comes that the whole mass is sung in the vernacular. But poets are wanting among us, or not yet known, who could compose evangelical and spiritual songs, as Paul calls them [Col. 3:16], worthy to be used in the church of God. In the meantime, one may sing after communion, "Let God be blest, be praised, and thanked, Who to us himself hath granted,"[63] omitting the line, "And the holy sacrament, At our last end, From the consecrated priest's hand," which

---

[63] See pp. 252-254.

was added by some devotee of St. Barbara[64] who, having neglected the sacrament all his life, hoped that he would on his deathbed be able to obtain eternal life through this work rather than through faith. For both the musical meter and structure prove this line to be an interpolation.[65] Another good [hymn] is "Now Let Us Pray to the Holy Ghost"[66] and also *"Ein Kindelein so löbelich."*[67] For few are found that are written in a proper devotional style. I mention this to encourage any German poets to compose evangelical hymns for us.

This is enough for now about the mass and communion. What is left can be decided by actual practice, as long as the Word of God is diligently and faithfully preached in the church. And if any should ask that all these [forms] be proved from Scriptures and the example of the fathers, they do not disturb us; for as we have said above, liberty must prevail in these matters and Christian consciences must not be bound by laws and ordinances. That is why the Scriptures prescribe nothing in these matters, but allow freedom for the Spirit to act according to his own understanding as the respective place, time, and persons may require it. And as for the example of the fathers, [their liturgical orders] are partly unknown, partly so much at variance with each other that nothing definite can be established about them, evidently because they themselves used their liberty. And even if they would be perfectly definite and clear, yet they could not impose on us a law or the obligation to follow them.

As for the other days which are called weekdays,[68] I see nothing that we cannot put up with, provided the [weekday] masses be

---

[64] St. Barbara was called upon as intercessor to assure people that they would be able to receive the sacraments of penance and the eucharist in the hour of death.

[65] It was sung to the same melody which had already served the two previous lines: "Let God be blessed," etc., and "That his own flesh and blood," etc. The line censured by Luther is lacking in one of the two pre-Reformation sources for this hymn.

[66] See pp. 263-264.

[67] A pre-Reformation Christmas hymn to the melody *"Dies est laetitiae."* See Julian, *Dictionary of Hymnology,* p. 325. For text and melody of this hymn, see Wilhelm Bäumker, *Das katholische deutsche Kirchenlied* (Freiburg: Herder, 1886), I, 286-289.

[68] *Feriae.*

discontinued. For Matins with its three lessons, the [minor] hours, Vespers, and Compline *de tempore* consist—with the exception of the propers for the Saints' days—of nothing but divine words of Scripture. And it is seemly, nay necessary, that the boys should get accustomed to reading and hearing the Psalms and lessons from the Holy Scripture. If anything should be changed, the bishop may reduce the great length [of the services] according to his own judgment so that three Psalms may be sung for Matins and three for Vespers with one or two responsories.[69] These matters are best left to the discretion of the bishop. He should choose the best of the responsories and antiphons and appoint them from Sunday to Sunday throughout the week, taking care lest the people should either be bored by too much repetition of the same or confused by too many changes in the chants and lessons. The whole Psalter, Psalm by Psalm, should remain in use, and the entire Scripture, lesson by lesson, should continue to be read to the people. But we must take care—as I have elsewhere explained—[70] lest the people sing only with their lips, like sounding pipes or harps [I Cor. 14:7], and without understanding. Daily lessons must therefore be appointed, one in the morning from the New or Old Testament, another for Vespers from the other Testament with an exposition in the vernacular. That this rite is an ancient one is proven by both the custom itself and by the words *homilia* in Matins and *capitulum*[71] in Vespers and in the other [canonical] hours, namely, that the Christians as often as they gathered together read something and then had it interpreted in the vernacular in the manner Paul describes in I Corinthians 14 [:26-27].[72] But when evil times came and there was a lack of prophets and interpreters, all that was left after the lessons and *capitula* was the

---

[69] Ordinarily, Matins had nine Psalms and eight responsories, Vespers and Compline eight Psalms and one responsory.
[70] See pp. 11-14.
[71] *Homilia*, i.e., "sermon," was the name of the lessons in Matins, which were taken both from Scripture and the writings of the church fathers. *Capitulum*, i.e., "chapter," is the name for the diminutive one-verse lesson read in Vespers. On this basis, Luther argues that Scripture readings had originally been longer—"chapter" rather than "verse"—and were followed by interpretative sermons.
[72] Cf. p. 11, n. 2.

response, "Thanks be to God."[73] And then, in place of the interpretation, lessons, Psalms, hymns, and other things were added in boring repetition. Although the hymns and the *Te Deum laudamus* at least confirm the same thing as the *Deo gratias,* namely, that after the exposition and homilies they used to praise God and give thanks for the revealed truth of his words. That is the kind of vernacular songs I should like us to have.

This much, excellent Nicholas, I have for you in writing about the rites and ceremonies which we either already have instituted in our Wittenberg church or expect to introduce, Christ willing, at an early date. If this example pleases you and others, you may imitate it. If not, we will gladly yield to your inspiration[74] and are prepared to accept corrections from you or from others. Nor should you or anyone else be deterred by the fact that here in Wittenberg the idolatrous "Topheth" [Jer. 7:31-32; 19:6] still continues as a shameless, ungodly source of revenue for the princes of Saxony. I am speaking of the Church of All Saints.[75] For by the mercy of God, we have so great an antidote among us in the riches of his Word that this plague languishes in its own little corner and can only contaminate itself. There are scarcely three or four swinish gluttons left to serve mammon in that house of perdition. To all others and to the whole populace, it is a loathsome and abominable thing. But we dare not proceed against them by force or by law, for Christians—as you know—should not fight except with the power of the sword of the Spirit. This is how I restrain the people every day. Otherwise, that house of all the saints—or rather of all the devils—would long be known by another name in all the earth. I have not used the power of the Spirit which the Lord has given me [II Cor. 13:10] against it, but patiently have borne this reproach if perchance God may give them repentance. Meanwhile,

---

[73] *Deo gratias.*
[74] Literally, "unction."
[75] This was the same church on the doors of which Luther had nailed the *Ninety-five Theses* six years earlier. It contained a famous collection of more than seventeen thousand relics which the Elector had amassed and which by attracting the seekers of indulgences were a lucrative revenue for the church. In 1522 they had once again been on exhibition, but on All Saints' Day, 1523, the custom was discontinued.

I am content that our house, which is more truly the house of all saints, reigns and stands here as a tower of Lebanon against the house of the devils [Song of Sol. 7:4]. Thus we torment Satan with the Word, even though he pretends to laugh. But Christ will grant that his hope will fail him and that he will be overthrown in the sight of all. Pray for me, you saint of God. Grace be with you and with us all. Amen.

A CHRISTIAN EXHORTATION
TO THE LIVONIANS
CONCERNING PUBLIC WORSHIP
AND CONCORD

1525

Translated by Paul Zeller Strodach

Revised by Ulrich S. Leupold

INTRODUCTION

This exhortation was prompted by internal dissensions in the Baltic city of Dorpat, Livonia.[1] Since 1521 the gospel had had a foothold in this city, and under Luther's own guidance and encouragement the Reformation in Livonia developed favorably. This trend, however, had been interrupted by the arrival of Melchior Hoffmann, a furrier from Swabia who believed he had a call to preach the gospel. He had been deeply influenced by the writings of Luther, but like so many others he also toyed with chiliastic-mystical phantasmagorias. Expelled from Wolmar, he came to Dorpat late in 1524, and on January 10, 1525, his adherents stormed churches and monasteries, destroying pictures and statues. When the city council grew suspicious of the new arrival and insisted that Hoffmann should bring proper recommendations, he went to Wittenberg in person and persuaded both Luther and Bugenhagen to direct letters to the Livonians, to which he also added one of his own.[2]

But in the ensuing years he leaned more and more toward the enthusiasts, and within a few years Luther was prompted to call him a dreamer and false prophet who should return to his furrier's trade.[3] Actually, Luther's letter, or exhortation, to the Livonians is so far from recommending Hoffmann that it does not even mention him. In this exhortation we see Luther applying the basic insights of his treatise on *The Freedom of a Christian*[4] to the field of worship. He tries to show how the church may tread the narrow path of liberty without falling prey either to license or to legalism.

---

[1] Livonia no longer exists as a political unit. It was divided between Estonia and Latvia in 1918. Dorpat is the German name for the Estonian city of Tartu, now in the Soviet Union.
[2] The letters of Bugenhagen and Hoffmann are in WA 18, 421-430. The title given Luther's exhortation is not Luther's own, but the title originally given the pamphlet containing all three.
[3] See the letter to Amsdorf, May 17, 1527. WA, Br 4, No. 1105.
[4] *LW* 31, 333-377.

The German text, *Eyne Christliche vormanung von eusserlichem Gottis dienste vnde eyntracht, an die yn lieffland,* is given in *WA* 18, 417-421; the following translation is a revision of P. Z. Strodach's translation in *PE* 6, 144-150.

A CHRISTIAN EXHORTATION
TO THE LIVONIANS
CONCERNING PUBLIC WORSHIP
AND CONCORD

June 17, 1525

To all beloved Christians in Livonia with their pastors and preachers, grace and peace from God our Father and our Lord Jesus Christ.

We should thank God the Father of all mercy greatly and at all times on account of you, dear sirs and friends, who according to the unsearchable riches of his grace has brought you to the treasure of his Word, in which you possess the knowledge of his dear Son, i.e., a sure pledge of the life and salvation which awaits you in heaven and has been prepared for all who steadfastly persevere in true faith and fervent love unto the end—even as we hope and pray that the merciful Father will preserve you and us, and perfect us in one mind, according to the likeness of his dear Son, Jesus Christ, our Lord. Amen.

However, I have heard from reliable witnesses that faction and disunion have arisen among you, because some of your preachers do not teach and act in accord, but each follows his own sense and judgment. And I almost believe this; for we must remember that it will not be any better with us than it was with the Corinthians and other Christians at the time of St. Paul, when divisions and dissension arose among Christ's people. Even as St. Paul himself acknowledges and says, "There must be factions and sects among you so that those who are genuine become known" [I Cor. 11:19]. For Satan is not satisfied with being the prince and god of the world. He also wants to be among the children of God, Job 1 [:6], and "prowls about like a roaring lion seeking some one to devour," I Peter 5 [:8].

45

This causes confusion among the people. It prompts both the complaint, "No one knows what he should believe or with whom he should side," and the common demand for uniformity in doctrine and practice. In times gone by, councils were held for this purpose and all sorts of rulings and canons made in order to hold all the people to a common order. But in the end these rulings and canons became snares for the soul and pitfalls for the faith. So there is great danger on either side. And we need good spiritual teachers who will know how to lead the people with wisdom and discretion.

For those who devise and ordain universal customs and orders get so wrapped up in them that they make them into dictatorial laws opposed to the freedom of faith. But those who ordain and establish nothing succeed only in creating as many factions as there are heads, to the detriment of that Christian harmony and unity of which St. Paul and St. Peter so frequently write. Still, we must express ourselves on these matters as well as we can, even though everything will not be done as we say and teach that it should be.

And first of all, I hope that you still hold pure and unblemished the teachings concerning faith, love, and cross-bearing and the principal articles of the knowledge of Christ. Then you will know how to keep your consciences clear before God, although even these simple teachings will not remain unassailed by Satan. Yes, he will even use external divisions about ceremonies to slip in and cause internal divisions in the faith. This is his method, which we know well enough from so many heresies.

Therefore, we will deal with factions in our time as St. Paul dealt with them in his. He could not check them by force. Nor did he want to compel them by means of commands. Rather, he entreated them with friendly exhortations, for people who will not give in willingly when exhorted will comply far less when commanded. Thus he says in Philippians 2 [:1-4]: "So if there is any encouragement in Christ, any incentive of love, any participation in the Spirit, any affection and sympathy, complete my joy by being of the same mind, having the same love, being in full accord and of one mind. Do nothing through strife or conceit, but in humility count others better than yourselves. Let each of you look not only to his own interests, but also to the interests of others." Then he adds the example of Christ, who in obedience to the Father made himself the servant of all.

Accordingly, I also shall exhort. First, I exhort your preachers with the same words as St. Paul, that they would consider all the good we have in Christ, the comfort, the encouragement, the Spirit, the love, the mercy, and in addition the example of Christ. In praise and thanksgiving for all these gifts, let them so conduct themselves that they establish and preserve unity of mind and spirit among themselves. They should be on their guard lest the devil sneak in through vainglory, which is especially dangerous and chiefly attacks competent men who hold the office of the Word. There is no better way to do this than for each not to take himself too seriously and to think little of himself, but very highly of the others, or—as Christ teaches in the Gospel—to seat himself in the lowest place among the guests at the wedding [Luke 14:7-10].

Now even though external rites and orders—such as masses, singing, reading, baptizing—add nothing to salvation, yet it is un-Christian to quarrel over such things and thereby to confuse the common people. We should consider the edification of the lay folk more important than our own ideas and opinions. Therefore, I pray all of you, my dear sirs, let each one surrender his own opinions and get together in a friendly way and come to a common decision about these external matters, so that there will be one uniform practice throughout your district instead of disorder—one thing being done here and another there—lest the common people get confused and discouraged.

For even though from the viewpoint of faith, the external orders are free and can without scruples be changed by anyone at any time, yet from the viewpoint of love, you are not free to use this liberty, but bound to consider the edification of the common people, as St. Paul says, I Corinthians 14 [:40], "All things should be done to edify," and I Corinthians 6 [:12], "All things are lawful for me, but not all things are helpful," and I Corinthians 8 [:1], "Knowledge puffs up, but love builds up." Think also of what he says there about those who have a knowledge of faith and of freedom, but who do not know how to use it; for they use it not for the edification of the people but for their own vainglory.

Now when your people are confused and offended by your lack of uniform order, you cannot plead, "Externals are free. Here in my own place I am going to do as I please." But you are bound to consider the effect of your attitude on others. By faith be free in your conscience toward God, but by love be bound to serve your neighbor's edification, as also St. Paul says, Romans 14 [15:2], "Let each of us please his neighbor for his good, to edify him." For we should not please ourselves, since Christ also pleased not himself, but us all.

But at the same time a preacher must watch and diligently instruct the people lest they take such uniform practices as divinely appointed and absolutely binding laws. He must explain that this is done for their own good so that the unity of Christian people may also find expression in externals which in themselves are irrelevant. Since the ceremonies or rites are not needed for the conscience or for salvation and yet are useful and necessary to govern the people externally, one must not enforce or have them accepted for any other reason except to maintain peace and unity between men. For between God and men it is faith that procures peace and unity.

This I said to the preachers so that they may consider love and their obligation toward the people, dealing with the people not in faith's freedom but in love's submission and service, preserving the freedom of faith before God. Therefore, when you hold mass, sing and read uniformly, according to a common order—the same in one place as in another—because you see that the people want and need it and you wish to edify rather than confuse them. For you are there for their edification, as St. Paul says, "We have received authority not to destroy but to build up" [II Cor. 10:8]. If for yourselves you have no need of such uniformity, thank God. But the people need it. And what are you but servants of the people, as St. Paul says, II Corinthians 2 [1:24], "We are not lords over your faith, but rather your servants for the sake of Jesus Christ."

At the same time, I also ask the people to have patience and not to be astonished if differences in teaching and practice are

48

caused by factions and sects. For who can stop the devil and his legions? Remember that tares always grow amidst the good seed, as every field of God's work shows and Christ confirms, Matthew 13 [:24-30]. Again, no threshing floor can have only clean corn, but there must be also hulls and straw. And St. Paul says, "In a house there are not only vessels for noble use, but also vessels for ignoble uses" [II Tim. 2:20]. Some are for eating and drinking, others for carrying and cleaning out rubbish and filth. Thus among Christians there must also be factions and heretics who pervert faith and love and confuse the people.

Now if a servant should become disturbed because he found that not all the cups in the house were of silver, but that there were also chamber pots and garbage cans, and he could not endure this discovery, what would happen? Who can keep house without unclean vessels? The same thing is true in Christendom. We cannot expect only to find noble vessels, but we must tolerate the ignoble ones as well, as St. Paul says, "There must be factions among you" [I Cor. 11:19]. And indeed, my dear friends, from the very fact that you discover factions and disunity[1] among you, you can tell that God gave to you the true Word and knowledge of Christ. For when you were under the pope, Satan certainly left you in peace, and though you might have had none but false teachers, he did not cause much dissension among you. But now that the true seed of God's Word is with you, he cannot bear it; he must sow his seed there too, even as he does here among us through the enthusiasts. God also tests you thereby to discover if you will stand fast.

Nevertheless, both you and your preachers should diligently seek to promote unity and to hinder this work of the devil, because God appoints the devil to do this in order to give us occasion to prove our unity and in order to reveal those that have stood the test. For in spite of all our efforts, enough factions and disunity will remain. St. Paul also points this out when he says, II Timothy 2 [:20], that there are both noble and ignoble vessels in the same house, and immediately adds, "If a man purge himself

---

[1] WA reads *eynickeyt*. This appears to be a misprint.

of such people, he shall be a vessel sanctified for noble use, useful to his master and ready for every good work" [vs. 21].

Receive this my sincere exhortation kindly, dear friends, and do your part to follow it as well as you can. This will prove needful and good for you and be to the honor and praise of God, who called you to his light. Now may our Lord Jesus Christ, who has begun his work in you, increase the same with grace and fulfil it to the day of his glorious coming, so that you together with us may go to meet him with joy and remain forever with him. Amen. Pray for us.

At Wittenberg on the Saturday after Trinity, 1525.

THE GERMAN MASS
AND ORDER OF SERVICE

1526

Translated by Augustus Steimle

Revised by Ulrich S. Leupold

INTRODUCTION

In his *Order of Mass and Communion*, 1523, Luther had given a detailed description and documentation of the evangelical mass in Wittenberg.[1] This liturgy was essentially a purified version of the traditional mass and was held in the Latin language. The only German parts in it were the sermon and a few hymns. But Luther expressed the hope that ultimately a completely German service might be provided, and he called for poets to enlarge the scanty store of good German hymns.

Actually, a German liturgy was no longer a novelty. In 1522 Wolfgang Wissenburger in Basel and Johann Schwebel in Pforzheim had begun services in the vernacular. The same year Kaspar Kantz introduced and published a German mass. In 1523 Thomas Münzer followed with a German mass, Matins, and Vespers elaborately printed with all the original plain-chant melodies. Other orders were introduced in Reutlingen, Wertheim, Königsberg, and Strassburg during 1524. The multiplicity of German masses threatened to become confusing, and Luther's friends appealed to him to end the confusion and to submit his own blueprint of a German mass. But the Reformer dragged his feet and for several years shied away from fulfilling their request. He had several reasons for his hesitancy. When his friend Nicholas Hausmann proposed an evangelical council to enforce liturgical uniformity, Luther objected to the use of compulsion. He felt that each evangelical center should be free either to devise its own liturgy or to borrow from others.[2] At the same time he objected to the legalism of those who meant to abolish the Latin mass completely and acted as though the reformation of the church depended on the exclusive use of the German language. In his *Against the Heavenly Prophets*, 1524, he wrote: "I am happy the mass now is held

---

[1] See pp. 15-40.
[2] *WA*, Br 3, No. 793, pp. 373-374.

53

among the Germans in German. But to make a necessity of this, as if it had to be so, is again too much. This spirit cannot do anything else than continually create laws, necessity, problems of conscience, and sin."[3] But the strongest reason for Luther's dilatoriness was his artistic integrity. He realized much more clearly than his eager contemporaries that introducing a German mass was more than a matter of translating the text. It required the creation of new music adapted to the speech rhythm of the German language. In *Against the Heavenly Prophets* he wrote: "I would gladly have a German mass today. I am also occupied with it. But I would very much like it to have a true German character. For to translate the Latin text and retain the Latin tone or notes has my sanction, though it doesn't sound polished or well done. Both the text and notes, accent, melody, and manner of rendering ought to grow out of the true mother tongue and its inflection, otherwise all of it becomes an imitation in the manner of the apes."[4] These words were evidently directed against Thomas Münzer, who had tried to fit the German words to the traditional plain-chant melodies. But even of other German liturgies published, those that offered any music at all—such as the *Nürnberg Mass* and the *Strassburg Kirchenamt* of 1525—showed little more imagination. Luther sought a more creative solution of the musical problem. When Hans von Minkwitz sent him the order which had been introduced in Sonnenwalde, he said in his reply, "In time I hope to have a German mass in Wittenberg that has a genuine style."[5] When Hausmann in March of 1525 sent a few samples of German liturgies (probably from Nördlingen, Allstedt, Strassburg, or Nürnberg), Luther answered: "I am returning the masses and have no objection against having them sung in this manner. But I hate to see the Latin notes set over the German words. I told the publisher what the German manner of singing is. This is what I want to introduce here."[6]

---

[3] *LW* 40, 141.
[4] *LW* 40, 141.
[5] *WA*, Br 3, No. 812, p. 412.
[6] *WA*, Br 3, No. 847, p. 462. In the same letter he sent *An Exhortation to the Communicants*, intended to replace the Preface, which forms the beginning of the communion office proper; cf. pp. 104-105.

The Music

This concern for the proper musical dress for the liturgy prompted Luther to proceed with utmost care when he finally acceded to Hausmann's repeated request and began to devise a German mass. Not content with his own musicianship, he prevailed upon the Elector to send the two leading musicians of his chapel, Conrad Rupsch (d. 1525) and Johann Walter (1496-1570), to Wittenberg for consultation on the proposed German mass.[7] Walter's report that Luther composed the chants for the lessons and the Words of Institution and the Sanctus hymn is confirmed by the following notes from a loose leaf[8] on which Luther indicated some of the principles that ought to be observed in the music for the German mass:

For the introit we shall use a Psalm, arranged as syllabically as possible,[9] for example:

And since the German language is quite monosyllabic, the termination has to have its own form, as you well know.

---

[7] WA 19, 49; cf. Johann Walter's own report of the visit in Nettl, *Luther and Music*, pp. 75-76.
[8] The original (apparently written in 1525; cf. WA 19, 49) is a draft in Luther's own hand. The text is found in WA 19, 70-71. A facsimile of the original is found at the end of WA 19.
[9] *Auf's allerengste gefasst.*
[10] There is no clef in the original. Cf. the introit Psalm in the *German Mass*, pp. 70-71.

The notes for the Epistle[11]

must somehow follow the Eighth Tone, but way down:

There - fore be - ing jus - ti - fied by faith,

we have peace with God, through, etc.

The notes for the Gospel
in the Fifth Tone,[12] also low:

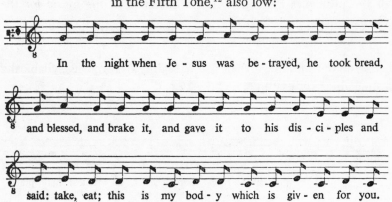

In the night when Je - sus was be - trayed, he took bread,

and blessed, and brake it, and gave it to his dis - ci - ples and

said: take, eat; this is my bod - y which is giv - en for you.

Question

Je - sus said to his dis - ci - ples:

---

[11] For a better comparison with the Epistle in the *German Mass*, we transposed Luther's music down one tone. Cf. the Epistle in the *German Mass*, pp. 72-74. Walter reports that Luther said to him, "Because Paul is a serious apostle, we want to arrange the eighth mode for the Epistle." Luther here followed contemporary esthetics which ascribed to every mode a certain "affect" or mood.

[12] The reciting note of the Fifth Tone should properly be *c*. Luther himself transposed this melody down a fourth.

Know ye that aft - er two days is the Pass - o - ver?

After that there is yet
The Sanctus and Agnus Dei
And the mass is complete.

In the original the music to Luther's *German Mass* is printed in German or hobnail notation. Only two notes are used: the punctum ◆ and the distropha in the form ◆◆ or ◆◆ . The first appears in our edition as an eighth note and the second as a quarter note. The distropha is used only at the end of a phrase. Both C and F clefs are used on a staff of four lines. The range implied is always that of the male voice. All of the music except the hymn "Isaiah 'Twas the Prophet" (the Sanctus) belongs to the category of liturgical recitative. It has therefore not been possible to reproduce it literally note by note. But our edition represents an attempt to fit the inflections of Luther's chants to the corresponding English words. This was all the more necessary because Luther's pointing shows a meticulous and extremely sensitive concern for the natural speech rhythm of the German language. We have tried to be equally considerate of the demands of the English texts. The reader will have to judge how far we succeeded.

The Individual Chants[13]

1. In the original the introit (Psalm 34) is printed out consecutively verse after verse with its music. In our edition we have arranged all the Psalm verses under one line of music to show the musical pattern that Luther used. The reader should observe that the whole note is being used for the reciting note and a small

---

[13] On the sources for the music in Luther's *German Mass*, cf. Friedrich Gebhardt, *Die musikalischen Grundlagen zu Luthers Deutscher Messe* (*"Luther-Jahrbuch,"* Vol. X [Munich: Chr. Kaiser Verlag, 1928]), pp. 56-169, and Christhard Mahrenholz, "Zur musikalischen Gestaltung von Luthers Gottesdienstreform," *Musicologica et Liturgica* (Kassel: Bärenreiter Verlag, 1960), pp. 154-168.

eighth note for optional notes which are used in some but not all verses. Luther developed this chant by recasting the first psalm tone. But whereas the original plain-chant psalm tone had two accented notes both in the mediation and termination, Luther provided for three in either place. Contrary to Gregorian usage, he also observed the word accent in the intonation. Due to these changes most of the text is sung to the intonation, mediation, and termination, and very little of it is left for the reciting note. Moreover, Luther takes many liberties with his cadences in the interest of better adapting the music to the text. His music is more flexible and follows the rhythm of speech more closely than Gregorian psalmody. On the other hand, it is less consistent and would therefore be more difficult to learn or to adapt to other Psalms.[14] This may be the reason why this introit Psalm was not taken over into other liturgies or hymnals.

2. The Kyrie is based on the first psalm tone.

3. The inflections for the Epistle are based on the eighth psalm tone. But the tonality is almost a modern F major. Here as in the introit Psalm, a certain emphasis on the inflections at the expense of the reciting note is quite evident. In comparison with the Gregorian tones for chanting the lessons, Luther's tone is far more "melodious." The range of the melody is greater (a seventh), the intervals used are larger, and most of the cadences (colon, period, and termination) provide for two accents.

The additional example for the Epistle at the end of the *German Mass*[15] seems to have been added to demonstrate the use of the proper inflection for questions. Strangely enough, this example uses a slightly modified and simplified version of the same tone. The melody hovers between *f* and *c* without rising to *a* and *b*-flat, as does the earlier example. On the whole, the pointing is simpler and more consistent. It has therefore been surmised that the "professional" musician, Johann Walter, was responsible for this version. In his report on the preparation of the music for the *German Mass*, Walter writes, "He [Luther] kept me for three weeks in Wittenberg to note down properly the chants of the Gos-

---

[14] Cf. Ameln *et al.* (eds.), *Handbuch der deutschen evangelischen Kirchenmusik*, I, 52°-57°.
[15] See pp. 84-86.

pels and the Epistles, until the first mass was sung in Wittenberg."[16] Luther's words to Justus Menius, "The last melody for the Epistle and Gospel pleases me better, although our people here do not use it; but I wish you and others would make use of it,"[17] need not contradict the assumption that Walter assisted in working out these examples.

4. For the Gospel Luther borrowed a feature from the traditional tone for the chanting of the passion.[18] In the latter it was customary to have the parts of the evangelist, of Christ, and of all other persons sung by different clerics and on different reciting notes. The evangelist's words were sung on middle c, the words of Christ on the lower f, and the words of all other persons on high f. Similarly, Luther used three levels: a for the evangelist, f for Christ, and c' for all other persons (e.g., John the Baptist and his interrogators in Luther's example). The tendency to make the whole chant more "melodious," to extend the cadences, and to allow for two accents in most of them is as evident here as in the Epistle tone. It has often been noted that Luther's introduction of this chant in the *German Mass* seems to contradict Walter's report on the preparation of this music. Luther says that the Gospel should be read "in the fifth tone." But Walter recalls that the Reformer assigned the sixth mode to the Gospel, for "Christ is a kind Lord and his words are sweet." Actually, these words need not imply any contradiction. The only difference between Lydian (the fifth mode) and Hypo-lydian (the sixth mode) is that the former gravitates toward c', while the latter gravitates toward f. Thus while the whole Gospel tone may be said to be in the fifth mode, the words of Christ certainly follow the sixth mode. In keeping with his frequent emphasis that the Words of Institution are the "gospel in a nutshell" or essentially proclamation,[19] Luther used the same melody for them as for the Gospel. The cadences are the same, and here as there Luther uses a different reciting note for the narration and for Christ.

---

[16] Cf. WA 19, 82 f.; cf. also Nettl, *op. cit.*, p. 76.
[17] *WA*, Br 4, No. 977, p. 27.
[18] See pp. 74-78.
[19] See U. S. Leupold (trans.), Vilmos Vajta's *Luther on Worship* (Philadelphia, 1958), p. 83.

The additional example at the end of the *German Mass*[20] for the chanting of the Gospel is as puzzling as that for the Epistle. Seemingly, it was added to illustrate the tone for the words of Jesus. But there is no distinction here between the reciting notes for the evangelist and for Jesus. The inflections are not the same. Especially the termination with its emphatic *b*-flat changes the whole character of the melody and makes it a modified first mode, very much like the introit Psalm and the Kyrie. Was Walter also the arranger of this example?

5. The text of the Sanctus[21] is a paraphrase of Isa. 6:1-4, and the melody is a free adaptation of a plain chant Sanctus (*In Dominicis Adventus et Quadragesimae* in the *Graduale Romanum*). Johann Walter vouches for Luther's authorship with the following words, ". . . among other [melodies] it is the German Sanctus which shows his [Luther's] perfect mastery in adapting the notes to the text."[22] And we will concur in this judgment if we note the expressive rise of the melody on "lofty throne," "six wings," "faces clear," "Holy is God," the climax on "loudly raised the shout," and the melodic dip on "clouds of smoke." Tonally, the melody is written in the Lydian mode. Since the Lydian Subdominant forms the awkward interval of an augmented fourth with the Tonic, it is always flatted, except when it serves as a quasi-leading note to the Dominant. This is the reason for the alternation of *f*-sharp and *f*-natural (since our edition offers the melody transposed from F-Lydian to C-Lydian). It should be mentioned that later sixteenth-century agendas had the "Holy, Holy," etc., in the chorale sung with special gravity and dignity. In city churches it was to be intoned by three boys kneeling before the altar.

The first completely German service in Wittenberg was held on October 29, 1525.[23] On Christmas Day of the same year it was definitively introduced and appeared in print early in 1526.

The text of the original Wittenberg print, *Deudsche Messe und ordnung Gottis diensts*, is given in WA 19, 72-113; the following translation is a revision of A. Steimle's translation in PE 6, 170-186.

---

[20] See pp. 86-89.
[21] See pp. 82-83.
[22] Michael Praetorius, *Syntagma Musicum*, I (Wittenberg, 1615), 451.
[23] WA, Br 3, No. 934, p. 591.

THE GERMAN MASS
AND ORDER OF SERVICE

Martin Luther's Preface

In the first place, I would kindly and for God's sake request all those who see this order of service or desire to follow it: Do not make it a rigid law to bind or entangle anyone's conscience, but use it in Christian liberty as long, when, where, and how you find it to be practical and useful. For this is being published not as though we meant to lord it over anyone else, or to legislate for him, but because of the widespread demand for German masses and services and the general dissatisfaction and offense that has been caused by the great variety of new masses, for everyone makes his own order of service. Some have the best intentions, but others have no more than an itch to produce something novel so that they might shine before men as leading lights, rather than being ordinary teachers—as is always the case with Christian liberty: very few use it for the glory of God and the good of the neighbor; most use it for their own advantage and pleasure. But while the exercise of this freedom is up to everyone's conscience and must not be cramped or forbidden, nevertheless, we must make sure that freedom shall be and remain a servant of love and of our fellow-man.

Where the people are perplexed and offended by these differences in liturgical usage, however, we are certainly bound to forego our freedom and seek, if possible, to better rather than to offend them by what we do or leave undone. Seeing then that this external order, while it cannot affect the conscience before God, may yet serve the neighbor, we should seek to be of one mind in Christian love, as St. Paul teaches [Rom. 15:5-6; I Cor. 1:10; Phil. 2:2]. As far as possible we should observe the same rites and ceremonies, just as all Christians have the same baptism and the same sacrament [of the altar] and no one has received a special one of his own from God.

That is not to say that those who already have good orders, or by the grace of God could make better ones, should discard theirs and adopt ours. For I do not propose that all of Germany should uniformly follow our Wittenberg order. Even heretofore the chapters, monasteries, and parishes were not alike in every rite. But it would be well if the service in every principality would be held in the same manner and if the order observed in a given city would also be followed by the surrounding towns and villages; whether those in other principalities hold the same order or add to it ought to be a matter of free choice and not of constraint. In short, we prepare such orders not for those who already are Christians; for they need none of them. And we do not live [and work] for them; but they live for us who are not yet Christians so that they may make Christians out of us. Their worship is in the spirit. But such orders are needed for those who are still becoming Christians or need to be strengthened, since a Christian does not need baptism, the Word, and the sacrament as a Christian—for all things are his—but as a sinner. They are essential especially for the immature and the young who must be trained and educated in the Scripture and God's Word daily so that they may become familiar with the Bible, grounded, well versed, and skilled in it, ready to defend their faith and in due time to teach others and to increase the kingdom of Christ. For such, one must read, sing, preach, write, and compose. And if it would help matters along, I would have all the bells pealing, and all the organs playing, and have everything ring that can make a sound. For this is the damnable thing about the popish services: that men made laws, works, and merits out of them—to the detriment of faith—and did not use them to train the youth and common people in the Scriptures and in the Word of God, but became so engrossed in them as to regard them as inherently useful and necessary for salvation. That is the [work of the] very devil. The ancients did not institute or order them to that intent.

Now there are three kinds of divine service or mass. The first is the one in Latin which we published earlier under the title *Formula Missae*.[1] It is not now my intention to abrogate or to change

---

[1] See *An Order of Mass and Communion for the Church at Wittenberg,* in this volume, pp. 15-40.

this service. It shall not be affected in the form which we have followed so far; but we shall continue to use it when or where we are pleased or prompted to do so. For in no wise would I want to discontinue the service in the Latin language, because the young are my chief concern. And if I could bring it to pass, and Greek and Hebrew were as familiar to us as the Latin and had as many fine melodies and songs, we would hold mass, sing, and read on successive Sundays in all four languages, German, Latin, Greek, and Hebrew. I do not at all agree with those who cling to one language and despise all others. I would rather train such youth and folk who could also be of service to Christ in foreign lands and be able to converse with the natives there, lest we become like the Waldenses in Bohemia,[2] who have so ensconced their faith in their own language that they cannot speak plainly and clearly to anyone, unless he first learns their language. The Holy Spirit did not act like that in the beginning. He did not wait till all the world came to Jerusalem and studied Hebrew, but gave manifold tongues for the office of the ministry, so that the apostles could preach wherever they might go. I prefer to follow this example. It is also reasonable that the young should be trained in many languages; for who knows how God may use them in times to come? For this purpose our schools were founded.

The second is the *German Mass and Order of Service,* which should be arranged for the sake of the unlearned lay folk and with which we are now concerned. These two orders of service must be used publicly, in the churches, for all the people, among whom are many who do not believe and are not yet Christians. Most of them stand around and gape, hoping to see something new, just as if we were holding a service among the Turks or the heathen in a public square or out in a field. That is not yet a well-ordered and organized congregation, in which Christians could be ruled according to the gospel; on the contrary, the gospel must be publicly preached [to such people] to move them to believe and become Christians.

The third kind of service should be a truly evangelical order and should not be held in a public place for all sorts of people.

---

[2] The Bohemian Brethren, a party that resulted from the movement started by John Huss. They had received episcopal ordination through the Waldenses and were dubbed "Waldenses" by their enemies.

But those who want to be Christians in earnest and who profess the gospel with hand and mouth should sign their names and meet alone in a house somewhere to pray, to read, to baptize, to receive the sacrament, and to do other Christian works. According to this order, those who do not lead Christian lives could be known, reproved, corrected, cast out, or excommunicated, according to the rule of Christ, Matthew 18 [:15-17]. Here one could also solicit benevolent gifts to be willingly given and distributed to the poor, according to St. Paul's example, II Corinthians 9. Here would be no need of much and elaborate singing. Here one could set up a brief and neat order for baptism and the sacrament and center everything on the Word, prayer, and love. Here one would need a good short catechism[3] on the Creed, the Ten Commandments, and the Our Father.

In short, if one had the kind of people and persons who wanted to be Christians in earnest, the rules and regulations would soon be ready. But as yet I neither can nor desire to begin such a congregation or assembly or to make rules for it. For I have not yet the people or persons for it, nor do I see many who want it. But if I should be requested to do it and could not refuse with a good conscience, I should gladly do my part and help as best I can. In the meanwhile the two above-mentioned orders of service must suffice. And to train the young and to call and attract others to faith, I shall—besides preaching—help to further such public services for the people, until Christians who earnestly love the Word find each other and join together. For if I should try to make it up out of my own need, it might turn into a sect. For we Germans are a rough, rude, and reckless people, with whom it is hard to do anything, except in cases of dire need.

On then, in the name of God. First, the German service needs a plain and simple, fair and square catechism. Catechism means the instruction in which the heathen who want to be Christians are taught and guided in what they should believe, know, do, and leave undone, according to the Christian faith. This is why the candidates who had been admitted for such instruction and learned the Creed before their baptism used to be called *catechumenos*. This instruction or catechization I cannot put better or more plainly

---

[3] The next paragraph indicates that the word "catechism" in this connection does not refer to a book, but to a catechization.

than has been done from the beginning of Christendom and retained till now, i.e., in these three parts, the Ten Commandments, the Creed, and the Our Father. These three plainly and briefly contain exactly everything that a Christian needs to know. This instruction must be given, as long as there is no special congregation, from the pulpit at stated times or daily as may be needed, and repeated or read aloud evenings and mornings in the homes for the children and servants, in order to train them as Christians. Nor should they only learn to say the words by rote. But they should be questioned point by point and give answer what each part means and how they understand it. If everything cannot be covered at once, let one point be taken up today, and tomorrow another. If parents and guardians won't take the trouble to do this, either themselves or through others, there never will be a catechism, except a separate congregation be organized as stated above.

In this manner they should be questioned:

What do you pray?

Answer: The Our Father.

What is meant when you say: Our Father in Heaven?

Answer: That God is not an earthly, but a heavenly Father who would make us rich and blessed in heaven.

What is meant by: Hallowed be thy name?

Answer: That we should honor his name and keep it from being profaned.

How do we profane or dishonor his name?

Answer: When we, who should be his children, live evil lives and teach and believe what is wrong.

And so on, what is meant by the kingdom of God, how it comes, what is meant by the will of God, by daily bread, etc., etc.

So in the Creed:

What do you believe?

Answer: I believe in God the Father, . . . to the end.

Thereafter from point to point, as time permits, one or two points at a time. For instance:

What does it mean to believe in God the Father Almighty?

Answer: It means to trust in him with all your heart and confidently to expect all grace, favor, help, and comfort from him, now and forever.

What does it mean to believe in Jesus Christ his Son?

Answer: It means to believe with the heart that we would all be eternally lost if Christ had not died for us, etc.

Likewise in the Ten Commandments, one must ask: What is meant by the First, the Second, the Third, and the other commandments? One may take these questions from our *Betbüchlein*[4] where the three parts are briefly explained, or make others, until the heart may grasp the whole sum of Christian truth under two headings or, as it were, in two pouches, namely, faith and love. Faith's pouch may have two pockets. Into one pocket we put the part [of faith] that believes that through the sin of Adam we are all corrupt, sinners, and under condemnation, Romans 5 [:12], Psalm 51 [:5]. Into the other we put the part [of faith that trusts] that through Jesus Christ we all are redeemed from this corruption, sin, and condemnation, Romans 5 [:15-21], John 3 [:16-18]. Love's pouch may also have two pockets. Into the one put this piece, that we should serve and do good to everyone, even as Christ has done for us, Romans 13. Into the other put this piece, that we should gladly endure and suffer all kinds of evil.

When a child begins to understand this it should be encouraged to bring home verses of Scripture from the sermon and to repeat them at mealtime for the parents, even as they formerly used to recite their Latin. And then these verses should be put into the pouches and pockets, just as pennies, groschen, and gulden[5] are put into a purse. For instance, let faith's pouch be for the gulden, and into the first pocket let this verse go: Romans 5 [:12], ". . . sin came into the world through one man and death through sin. . . ."

---

[4] Luther's *Booklet of Prayers* of 1522 contained the *Brief Explanation of the Ten Commandments, the Creed, and the Lord's Prayer*, which he had first published in 1520. See *WA* 10ᴵᴵ, 376-501.

[5] Pfennig, groschen, and gulden were coins of Luther's time, made of copper, silver, and gold respectively, and in their relative value they roughly correspond to the penny, dime, and (gold) dollar today. Hungarian gulden, however, were worth more than Rhenish gulden.

66

Also this one: Psalm 51 [:5], "Behold I was brought forth in iniquity, and in sin did my mother conceive me." These are two Rhenish gulden for the [first] pocket. Into the other pocket go the Hungarian gulden, for example this text, Romans 5 [4:25], "Jesus . . . was put to death for our trespasses and raised for our justification." Again John 3 [1:29], "Behold, the Lamb of God, who takes away the sin of the world!" These would be two good Hungarian gulden for the [second] pocket.

Let love's pouch be the pouch for silver. Into the first pocket shall go the texts concerning well doing, such as Galatians 4 [5:13], "Through love be servants of one another"; Matthew 25 [:40], "As you did it to one of the least of these my brethren, you did it to me." These would be two silver groschen for the [first] pocket. Into the other pocket shall go this verse: Matthew 5 [:11], "Blessed are you when men . . . persecute you . . . on my account"; Hebrews 12 [:6], "For the Lord disciplines him whom he loves, and chastises every son whom he receives." These are two *Schreckenberger*[6] for the [second] pocket.

And let no one think himself too wise for such child's play. Christ, to train men, had to become man himself. If we wish to train children, we must become children with them. Would to God such child's play were widely practiced. In a short time we would have a wealth of Christian people whose souls would be so enriched in Scripture and in the knowledge of God that of their own accord they would add more pockets, just as the *Loci Communes*,[7] and comprehend all Scripture in them. Otherwise, people can go to church daily and come away the same as they went. For they think they need only listen at the time, without any thought of learning or remembering anything. Many a man listens to sermons for three or four years and does not retain enough to give a single answer concerning his faith—as I experience daily. Enough has been written in books, yes; but it has not been driven home to the hearts.

---

[6] The *Schreckenberger* was a kind of silver groschen.
[7] *Loci Communes* were the basic principles and truths of any field of knowledge. The term was first applied to theology by Melanchthon, who used it as the title of his doctrinal handbook published in 1521. Luther thought highly of this book.

Concerning the Service

Since the preaching and teaching of God's Word is the most important part of divine service, we have arranged for sermons and lessons as follows: For the holy day or Sunday we retain the customary Epistles and Gospels and have three sermons. At five or six o'clock in the morning a few Psalms are chanted for Matins. A sermon follows on the Epistle of the day, chiefly for the sake of the servants so that they too may be cared for and hear God's Word, since they cannot be present at other sermons. After this an antiphon and the *Te Deum* or the Benedictus, alternately, with an Our Father, collects, and *Benedicamus Domino*. At the mass, at eight or nine o'clock, the sermon is on the Gospel for the day. At Vespers in the afternoon the sermon before the Magnificat takes up the Old Testament chapter by chapter. For the Epistles and Gospels we have retained the customary division according to the church year, because we do not find anything especially reprehensible in this use. And the present situation in Wittenberg is such that many are here who must learn to preach in places where this division is still being observed and may continue in force. Since in this matter we can be of service to others without loss to ourselves, we leave it, but have no objection to others who take up the complete books of the evangelists. This we think provides sufficient preaching and teaching for the lay people. He who desires more will find enough on other days.

Namely, on Monday and Tuesday mornings we have a German lesson on the Ten Commandments, the Creed, Lord's Prayer, baptism, and sacrament, so that these two days preserve and deepen the understanding of the catechism. On Wednesday morning again a German lesson, for which the evangelist Matthew has been appointed so that the day shall be his very own, seeing that he is an excellent evangelist for the instruction of the congregation, records the fine sermon of Christ on the Mount, and strongly urges the exercise of love and good works. But the evangelist John, who so mightily teaches faith, has his own day too, on Saturday afternoon at Vespers, so that two of the evangelists have their own days when they are being read. Thursday and Friday mornings have the weekday lessons from the Epistles of the apostles and the rest of the

68

New Testament assigned to them. Thus enough lessons and sermons have been appointed to give the Word of God free course among us, not to mention the university lectures for scholars.

This is what we do to train the schoolboys in the Bible. Every day of the week they chant a few Psalms in Latin before the lesson,[8] as has been customary at Matins hitherto. For as we stated above, we want to keep the youth well versed in the Latin Bible. After the Psalms, two or three boys in turn read a chapter from the Latin New Testament, depending on the length. Another boy then reads the same chapter in German to familiarize them with it and for the benefit of any layman who might be present and listening. Thereupon they proceed with an antiphon to the German lesson mentioned above. After the lesson the whole congregation sings a German hymn, the Lord's Prayer is said silently, and the pastor or chaplain reads a collect and closes with the *Benedicamus Domino* as usual.

Likewise at Vespers they sing a few of the Vesper Psalms in Latin with an antiphon, as heretofore, followed by a hymn if one is available. Again two or three boys in turn then read a chapter from the Latin Old Testament or half a one, depending on length. Another boy reads the same chapter in German. The Magnificat follows in Latin with an antiphon or hymn, the Lord's Prayer said silently, and the collects with the Benedicamus. This is the daily service throughout the week in cities where there are schools.

On Sunday for the Laity

Here we retain the vestments, altar, and candles until they are used up or we are pleased to make a change. But we do not oppose anyone who would do otherwise. In the true mass, however, of real Christians, the altar should not remain where it is, and the priest should always face the people as Christ doubtlessly did in the Last Supper. But let that await its own time.

To begin the service we sing a hymn or a German Psalm in the First Tone as follows:

---

[8] This lesson, as the rest of the paragraph shows, is the one from the catechism, the Gospels, and the Epistles mentioned in the preceding paragraph. In other words, the devotions of the schoolboys which he here describes are held in church and form part of the daily public Matins and Vespers.

[Intonation]   [Recitation] [Flex]   [Mediation]

	[Intonation]	[Recitation]	[Flex]	[Mediation]		
[1]	I will			bless the Lord	at all	times:
[2] My	soul shall	make her		boast	in the	Lord:
[3] O	mag - ni -			fy the	Lord with	me:
[4] I	sought the			Lord and	he heard	me:
[5] They looked un-				to him	and were	lightened:
[6] This	poor man			cried and the	Lord heard	him:
[7]	The an-	gel of				
	the Lord	en-camp-eth	round a - bout	them that	fear him:	
[8] O	taste and	see		that · the	Lord is	good:
[9] O	fear the			Lord,	ye his	saints:
[10]	The rich			lack and	suf - fer	hun-ger:
[11]	Come, ye	children,		heark-en	un - to	me:
[12] What	man is	he		that de -	sir - eth	life:
[13]	Keep thy			tongue	from	e - vil:
[14] De -	part from			e - vil	and do	good:
[15]	The eyes	of the		Lord are up-	on the	right-eous:
[16]	The face	of the				
	Lord is a-		gainst them	that do	e - vil:	
[17] The	righteous			cry and	the Lord	hear-eth:
[18] The	Lord is	nigh unto				
	them that	are the af-	are of a	bro - ken	heart:	
[19]	Man - y			flic-tions	of the	right-eous:
[20] He	keep - eth			all	his	bones:
[21] E -	vil shall			slay	the	god - less:
[22] The Lord re-				deem-eth the	soul of his	serv-ants:

[Recitation]   [Termination]

	Recitation			Termination			
[1] his praise shall continually			be	in	my		mouth.
[2] the humble shall hear	there-		of		and	be	glad.
[3] and let us exalt	his		name	to-	geth-		er.
[4] and deliver me			from		all	my	fears.
[5] and their fac-	es	were	not	a-	sham	-	ed.
[6] and saved him out	of		all	his	trou	-	bles.
[7] and	de-		liv - er-		eth	them	all.
[8] blessed is the man	that		trust - eth		in		him.
[9] for there is no want	to		them that		fear		him.
[10] but they that seek the Lord shall not	want		an - y		good		thing.
[11] I will teach you the fear			of		the		Lord.
[12] and loveth many days,	that		he	may	see		good.
[13] and	thy		lips	from	speak-ing		guile.
[14] seek peace			and	pur-	sue		it.
[15] and his ears are o-			pen	un-	to	their	cry.
[16] to cut off the remembrance			of	them	from the		earth.
[17] and delivereth them out	of		all	their	trou	-	bles.
[18] and saveth such as be of	a		con - trite		spir	-	it.
[19] but the Lord delivereth him			out		of	them	all.
[20] not one	of		them	is	bro	-	ken.
[21] and they that hate the right-	eous		shall	be	des - o - late.		
[22] and none of them that trust in	him		shall	be	des - o - late.		

71

Then follows the Kyrie eleison in the same tone, three times instead of nine, as follows:

Ky - ri - e   e - le - i - son.   Chris - te

e - le - i - son.   Ky - ri - e   e - le - i - son.

Thereupon the priest reads a collect in monotone on *F-fa-ut*,[9] as follows:

Almighty God, who art the protector of all who trust in thee, without whose grace no one is able to do anything, or to stand before thee: Grant us richly thy mercy, that by thy holy inspiration we may think what is right and by thy power may perform the same; for the sake of Jesus Christ our Lord. Amen.[10]

Thereafter the Epistle in the Eighth Tone, and let him for the reciting note remain on the same pitch as the collect.[11] The rules for it are these:

Period is the end of a sentence.
Colon is a part of a sentence.
Comma is a subdivision within the colon.

---

[9] In the medieval system of solmization the note *F-fa-ut* stands for the *f* on the second-highest line of the bass clef.

[10] This collect is given in the hymnals as the second collect after the *Te Deum*. It represents a conflation of the collects for the Third Sunday after Pentecost and for Rogate Sunday in the Roman rite.

[11] Luther offers the melody for the Epistle in the natural position of the Eighth Tone, i.e., with *c'* as the reciting note. Untransposed this melody would be far too high for the average male voice, going up to *e'* as it does. But with the instruction that the pitch should remain the same as in the collect, Luther indicates that the whole melody should be sung a fifth lower than written, with *f* as the reciting note. It is in this form that we reproduce the music for the Epistle.

Rules for this chant

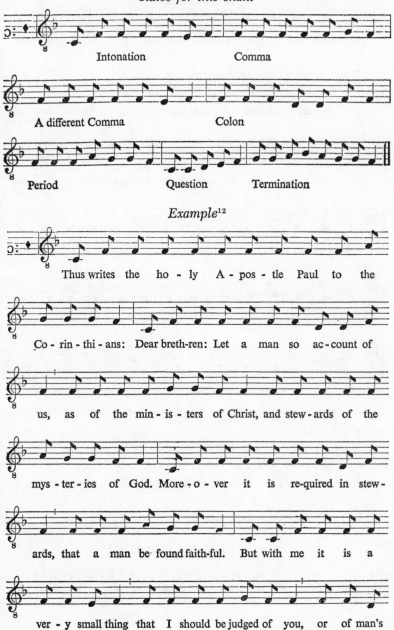

Intonation   Comma

A different Comma   Colon

Period   Question   Termination

Example[12]

Thus writes the   ho - ly   A - pos - tle   Paul   to   the

Co - rin - thi - ans: Dear breth-ren: Let   a   man   so   ac - count of

us,   as   of   the   min - is - ters   of Christ, and stew - ards   of   the

mys - ter - ies   of   God. More - o - ver   it   is   re-quired in   stew -

ards,   that   a   man   be found faith-ful.   But with me   it   is   a

ver - y   small thing   that   I   should be judged of   you,   or   of man's

---

[12] The example is from I Cor. 4:1-5.

73

judg-ment: yea, I judge not mine own self. For I know noth-ing

by my - self; yet am I not here - by jus - ti - fied: but he

that judg - eth me is the Lord. There - fore judge noth-ing be - fore

the time, un - til the Lord come, who both will bring to light the

hid - den things of dark-ness, and will make man - i - fest the coun -

sels of the hearts: and then shall ev - er - y man have praise of God.

He should read the Epistle facing the people, but the collect facing the altar.

After the Epistle a German hymn, either "Now Let Us Pray to the Holy Ghost"[13] or any other, is sung with the whole choir.

Then he reads the Gospel in the Fifth Tone, again facing the people.

The rules for this chant are these:

[The Voice of the Evangelist]

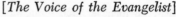

Intonation   Comma

[13] See pp. 263-264.

A different Comma   **Colon**

14   15

Period   **Termination**

The Voice of Persons

Comma   **A different Comma**

Colon   **Period**

Question   **Termination**

The Voice of Christ

Comma   **Colon**

Period   **Question**

16

Termination

---

[14] In this line all editions have the complete cadences a third higher. This is an obvious misprint, as the following example proves, and has been corrected in WA 19, 90.

[15] The original print has *b* instead of *a*, probably a misprint; cf. WA 19, 90.

[16] The original print has in this place *e, e, f, a, a*, which is obviously a misprint; cf. WA 19, 91.

Example

The Gospel for the Fourth Sunday in Advent would be chanted as follows:[17]

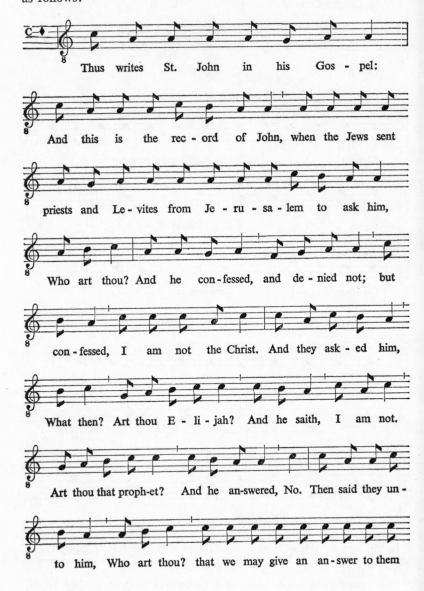

Thus writes St. John in his Gos - pel:

And this is the rec - ord of John, when the Jews sent

priests and Le - vites from Je - ru - sa - lem to ask him,

Who art thou? And he con - fessed, and de - nied not; but

con - fessed, I am not the Christ. And they ask - ed him,

What then? Art thou E - li - jah? And he saith, I am not.

Art thou that proph-et? And he an-swered, No. Then said they un -

to him, Who art thou? that we may give an an-swer to them

[17] John 1:19-28.

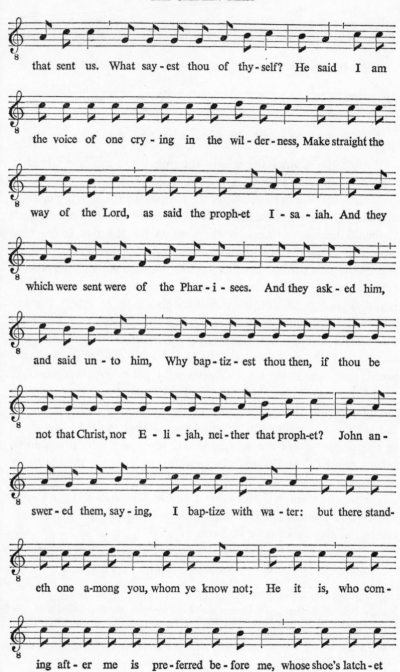

that sent us. What say - est thou of thy - self? He said I am

the voice of one cry - ing in the wil - der - ness, Make straight the

way of the Lord, as said the proph-et I - sa - iah. And they

which were sent were of the Phar - i - sees. And they ask - ed him,

and said un - to him, Why bap - tiz - est thou then, if thou be

not that Christ, nor E - li - jah, nei - ther that proph-et? John an -

swer - ed them, say - ing, I bap-tize with wa - ter: but there stand-

eth one a-mong you, whom ye know not; He it is, who com -

ing aft - er me is pre - ferred be - fore me, whose shoe's latch - et

77

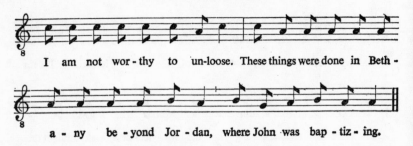

I am not wor-thy to un-loose. These things were done in Beth-
a-ny be-yond Jor-dan, where John was bap-tiz-ing.

After the Gospel the whole congregation sings the Creed in German: "In One True God We All Believe."[18]

Then follows the sermon on the Gospel for the Sunday or festival day. And I think that if we had the postil for the entire year,[19] it would be best to appoint the sermon for the day to be read wholly or in part out of the book—not alone for the benefit of those preachers who can do nothing better, but also for the purpose of preventing the rise of enthusiasts and sects. If we observe the homilies read at Matins, we note a usage similar to this.[20] For unless it is a spiritual understanding and the [Holy] Ghost himself that speaks through the preachers (whom I do not wish hereby to restrict; for the Spirit teaches better how to preach than all the postils and homilies), we shall ultimately get where everyone will preach his own ideas, and instead of the Gospel and its exposition we again shall have sermons on castles in Spain.[21] This is one of the reasons we retain the Epistles and Gospels as they are given in the postils—there are so few gifted preachers who are able to give a powerful and practical exposition of a whole evangelist or some other book of the Bible.

After the sermon shall follow a public paraphrase of the Lord's Prayer and admonition for those who want to partake of the sacrament, in this or a better fashion:

Friends in Christ: Since we are here assembled in the name of the Lord to receive his Holy Testament, I ad-

---

[18] Cf. pp. 271-273.
[19] Only half of Luther's *Kirchenpostille* with sermons on the Gospels of the church year had been published in 1522. The second half appeared in 1527; cf. *LW* 51, xiv f. The entire series is in *WA* 10¹, 1–2.
[20] According to the breviary, excerpts from the homilies of the church fathers were read at Matins.
[21] Literally, "blue ducks."

monish you first of all to lift up your hearts to God to pray with me the Lord's Prayer, as Christ our Lord has taught us and graciously promised to hear us.

That God, our Father in heaven, may look with mercy on us, his needy children on earth, and grant us grace so that his holy name be hallowed by us and all the world through the pure and true teaching of his Word and the fervent love of our lives; that he would graciously turn from us all false doctrine and evil living whereby his precious name is being blasphemed and profaned.

That his kingdom may come to us and expand; that all transgressors and they who are blinded and bound in the devil's kingdom be brought to know Jesus Christ his Son by faith, and that the number of Christians may be increased.

That we may be strengthened by his Spirit to do and to suffer his will, both in life and in death, in good and in evil things, and always to break, slay, and sacrifice our own wills.

That he would also give us our daily bread, preserve us from greed and selfish cares, and help us to trust that he will provide for all our needs.

That he would forgive our debts as we forgive our debtors so that our hearts may rest and rejoice in a good conscience before him, and that no sin may ever fright or alarm us.

That he would not lead us into temptation but help us by his Spirit to subdue the flesh, to despise the world and its ways, and to overcome the devil with all his wiles.

And lastly, that he would deliver us from all evil, both of body and soul, now and forever.

All those who earnestly desire these things will say from their very hearts: Amen, trusting without any doubt that it is Yea and answered in heaven as Christ has promised: Whatever you ask in prayer, believe that you shall receive it, and you will [Mark 11:24]. Amen.

Secondly, I admonish you in Christ that you discern

the Testament of Christ in true faith and, above all, take to heart the words wherein Christ imparts to us his body and his blood for the remission of our sins. That you remember and give thanks for his boundless love which he proved to us when he redeemed us from God's wrath, sin, death, and hell by his own blood. And that in this faith[22] you externally receive the bread and wine, i.e., his body and his blood, as the pledge and guarantee of this. In his name therefore, and according to the command that he gave, let us use and receive the Testament.

Whether such paraphrase and admonition should be read in the pulpit immediately after the sermon or at the altar, I would leave to everyone's judgment. It seems that the ancients did so in the pulpit, so that it is still the custom to read general prayers or to repeat the Lord's Prayer in the pulpit. But the admonition itself has since become a public confession. In this way, however, the Lord's Prayer together with a short exposition would be current among the people, and the Lord would be remembered, even as he commanded at the Supper.

I would, however, like to ask that this paraphrase or admonition follow a prescribed wording or be formulated in a definite manner for the sake of the common people. We cannot have one do it one way today, and another, another way tomorrow, and let everybody parade his talents and confuse the people so that they can neither learn nor retain anything. What chiefly matters is the teaching and guiding of the people. That is why here we must limit our freedom and keep to one form of paraphrase or admonition, particularly in a given church or congregation—if for the sake of freedom it does not wish to use another.

Thereupon the Office and Consecration to the following tune:

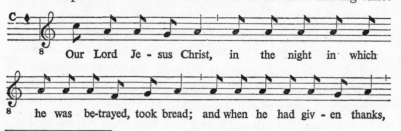

Our Lord Je - sus Christ, in the night in which he was be-trayed, took bread; and when he had giv - en thanks,

----

[22] *Darauf.*

80

he brake it and gave it to his dis - ci - ples, say - ing,

Take, eat; this is my bod - y, which is giv - en for you;

this do in re - mem-brance of me. Aft - er the same man -

ner al - so, he took the cup, when he had supped, and when he

had giv - en thanks, he gave it to them, say - ing, Drink ye all

of it; this cup is the New Tes - ta - ment in my blood,

which is shed for you, and for man - y,

for the re - mis - sion of sins; this do, as oft

as ye drink it, in re - mem - brance of me.

It seems to me that it would accord with [the institution of] the Lord's Supper to administer the sacrament immediately after the consecration of the bread, before the cup is blessed; for both Luke and Paul say: He took the cup after they had supped, etc. [Luke 22:20; I Cor. 11:25]. Meanwhile, the German Sanctus or the hymn, "Let God Be Blest,"[23] or the hymn of John Huss, "Jesus Christ, Our God and Savior,"[24] could be sung. Then shall the cup be blessed and administered, while the remainder of these hymns are sung, or the German Agnus Dei.[25] Let there be a decent and orderly approach, not men and women together, but the women after the men, wherefore they should also stand apart from each other in separate places. What should be done about private confession, I have written elsewhere, and my opinion can be found in the *Betbüchlein.*[26]

We do not want to abolish the elevation, but retain it because it goes well with the German Sanctus and signifies that Christ has commanded us to remember him.[27] For just as the sacrament is bodily elevated, and yet Christ's body and blood are not seen in it, so he is also remembered and elevated by the word of the sermon and is confessed and adored in the reception of the sacrament. In each case he is apprehended only by faith; for we cannot see how Christ gives his body and blood for us and even now daily shows and offers it before God to obtain grace for us.

The German Sanctus

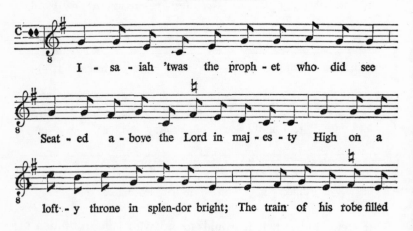

I - sa - iah 'twas the proph - et who did see

'Seat - ed a - bove the Lord in maj - es - ty High on a

loft - y throne in splen-dor bright; The train of his robe filled

---

[23] See pp. 252-254.
[24] See pp. 249-251.
[25] *"Christe, du Lamm Gottes";* cf. pp. 151-152.
[26] Cf. p. 34.
[27] The elevation was abolished in Wittenberg in 1542.

the tem - ple quite. Stand-ing be - side him were two ser - a - phim;

Six wings, six wings he saw on each of them. With twain they hid

in awe their fac - es clear; With twain they hid their feet in rev-

'rent fear. And with the oth - er twain they flew a - bout:

One to the oth - er loud - ly raised the shout: Ho - ly is God,

the Lord of Sab - a - oth, Ho - ly is God, the Lord of Sab -

a - oth, Ho - ly is God, the Lord of Sab - a - oth, Be - hold

his glo - ry fill - eth all the earth. The an - gels' cry made beams

and lin - tels shake; The house al - so was filled with clouds of smoke.

The collect follows with the benediction:

We give thanks to thee, Almighty God, that thou hast refreshed us with this thy salutary gift; and we beseech thy mercy to strengthen us through the same in faith toward thee, and in fervent love among us all; for the sake of Jesus Christ our Lord. Amen.

The Lord bless thee and keep thee.

The Lord make his face shine upon thee, and be gracious unto thee.

The Lord lift up his countenance upon thee, and give thee peace.

Exercise or Practice for the Intoning

For those who would like to become experienced and skilful in pointing the lesson, I give another example. Someone else may choose another.

The Epistle[28]

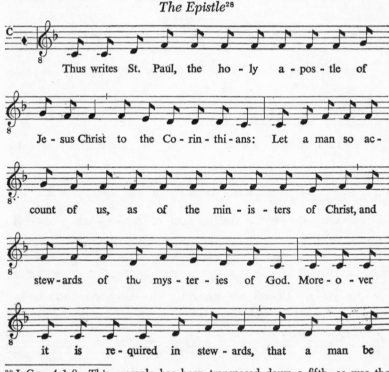

Thus writes St. Paul, the ho - ly a - pos - tle of
Je - sus Christ to the Co - rin - thi - ans: Let a man so account of us, as of the min - is - ters of Christ, and
stew - ards of the mys - ter - ies of God. More - o - ver
it is re - quired in stew - ards, that a man be

---

[28] I Cor. 4:1-8. This example has been transposed down a fifth, as was the Epistle on pp. 72-74.

84

found faith - ful. But with me it is a ver - y

small thing that I should be judg-ed of you, or of man's

judg-ment: yea, I judge not mine own self. For I know noth-ing

by my - self; yet am I not here - by jus - ti - fied: but he

that judg - eth me is the Lord. There - fore judge noth - ing be -

fore the time, un - til the Lord come, who both will bring to light

the hid - den things of dark-ness, and will make man - i - fest the

coun-sels of the hearts: and then shall ev - 'ry man have praise of God.

And these things, breth-ren, I have in a fig - ure trans-ferred to

my - self and to A - pol - los for your sakes; that ye might learn

85

in us not to think of men a - bove that which is writ - ten,

that no one of you be puffed up for one a - gainst an -

oth - er. For who mak - eth thee to dif - fer from an - oth - er?

and what hast thou that thou didst not re - ceive? now if

thou didst re - ceive it, why dost thou glo - ry as if thou

hadst not re - ceived it? Now ye are full, now ye are rich,

ye have reigned as kings with - out us: and I would to

God ye did reign, that we al - so might reign with you.

The Gospel[29]

Hear the ho - ly Gos - pel. Thus says Je - sus

---

[29] Matt. 6:24-34.

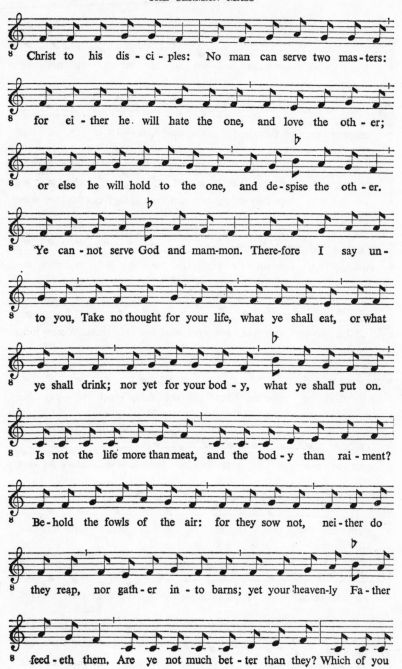

Christ to his dis - ci - ples: No man can serve two mas - ters:

for ei - ther he. will hate the one, and love the oth - er;

or else he will hold to the one, and de - spise the oth - er.

Ye can - not serve God and mam-mon. There-fore I say un -

to you, Take no thought for your life, what ye shall eat, or what

ye shall drink; nor yet for your bod - y, what ye shall put on.

Is not the life more than meat, and the bod - y than rai - ment?

Be - hold the fowls of the air: for they sow not, nei - ther do

they reap, nor gath - er in - to barns; yet your heaven-ly Fa - ther

feed - eth them. Are ye not much bet - ter than they? Which of you

by tak - ing thought can add one cu - bit un - to his stat - ure?

And why take ye thought for rai - ment? Con - sid - er the li - lies

of the field, how they grow; they toil not, nei - ther do they spin:

And yet I say un - to you, That e - ven Sol - o - mon in

all his glo - ry was not ar - rayed like one of these. Where - fore,

if God so clothe the grass of the field, which to - day is,

and to - mor - row is cast in - to the o - ven, shall he not

much more clothe you, O ye of lit - tle faith? There - fore take

no thought, say - ing, What shall we eat? or, What shall we drink?

or, Where - with - al shall we be cloth - ed? For aft - er all

these things do the Gen - tiles seek: for your heaven-ly Fa.- ther

know - eth that ye have need of all these things. But seek

ye first the king-dom of God, and his right - eous - ness;

and all these things shall be add - ed un - to you.

Take there - fore no thought for the mor - row: for the mor -

row shall take thought for the things of it - self.

Suf - fi - cient un - to the day is the e - vil there - of.

This is what I have to say concerning the daily service and instruction in the Word of God, which serves primarily to train the young and challenge the unlearned. For those who itch for new things will soon be sated and tired with it all, as they were heretofore in the Latin service. There was singing and reading in the churches every day, and yet the churches remained deserted and empty. Already they do the same in the German service. Therefore, it is best to plan the services in the interest of the young and such of the unlearned as may happen to come. With the others neither law nor order, neither scolding nor coaxing, will help. Allow them to leave those things in the service alone which they refuse to do willingly and gladly. God is not pleased with unwilling services; they are futile and vain.

But on the festivals, such as Christmas, Easter, Pentecost, St. Michael's, Purification, and the like, we must continue to use Latin until we have enough German songs. This work is just beginning; not everything has been prepared that is needed. We must arrive at a common standard to assess and control the profusion of orders.

Lent, Palm Sunday, and Holy Week shall be retained, not to force anyone to fast, but to preserve the Passion history and the Gospels appointed for that season. This, however, does not include the Lenten veil,[30] throwing of palms, veiling of pictures, and whatever else there is of such tomfoolery—nor chanting the four Passions, nor preaching on the Passion for eight hours on Good Friday. Holy Week shall be like any other week save that the Passion history be explained every day for an hour throughout the week or on as many days as may be desirable, and that the sacrament be given to everyone who desires it. For among Christians the whole service should center in the Word and sacrament.

In short, this or any other order shall be so used that whenever it becomes an abuse, it shall be straightway abolished and replaced by another, even as King Hezekiah put away and destroyed the brazen serpent, though God himself had commanded it be made, because the children of Israel made an abuse of it [II Kings 18:4]. For the orders must serve for the promotion of faith and love and not be to the detriment of faith. As soon as they fail to do this, they are invalid, dead and gone; just as a good coin, when counterfeited, is canceled and changed because of the abuse, or as new shoes when they become old and uncomfortable are no longer worn, but thrown away, and new ones bought. An order is an external thing. No matter how good it is, it can be abused. Then it is no longer an order, but a disorder. No order is, therefore, valid in itself—as the popish orders were held to be until now. But the validity, value, power, and virtue of any order is in its proper use. Otherwise it is utterly worthless and good for nothing. God's Spirit and grace be with us all. Amen. MARTIN LUTHER

---

[30] The Lenten veil, literally "hunger cloth," was a curtain which during Lent was rigged up in front of the altar to hide it (cf. *Der grosse Brockhaus*, Vol. V [Wiesbaden: Brockhaus, 1954], p. 583).

THE OCCASIONAL SERVICES

INTRODUCTION

In the course of reorganizing the church, Luther was also led tc revise some of the occasional services. He had no intention of creating a complete *Rituale Lutheranum*, but only issued formularies as they were called for by the demands of parishes or by the requests of his friends and co-workers. Orders for baptism, private confession, and marriage went out under his name in due course. But his formula for ordination, included in this volume, seems only to have been copied by hand and did not go into print during his lifetime. He failed to compose an order for burial.[1] And since he disapproved of confirmation as a special service,[2] he saw no need for a special order. He felt the same way about special ceremonies for blessings, dedications, and the like.[3]

---

[1] See his comments on Christian burials, pp. 325-331.
[2] Cf. Georg Rietschel, *Lehrbuch der Liturgik* (Göttingen: Vandenhoeck und Ruprecht), II (1952), 630-631.
[3] *Ibid.*, pp. 872-873.

The Order of Baptism

1523

Translated by Paul Zeller Strodach
~~*Revised by Ulrich*~~ *S. Leupold*

Very soon after the publication of his *Concerning the Order of Public Worship*, 1523,[1] Luther issued a German translation of the order for baptism. Here the need for a version in the vernacular was especially pressing, for his insistence on the intercession of the church as ground for the faith of the child called for prayers in which the parents and sponsors could intelligently participate.

This baptismal liturgy follows the traditional Roman rite, except that the exorcism has been abbreviated, the Creed moved from its place before the Lord's Prayer to the questions, and the collect *"Deus patrum nostrorum"* ("God of our Fathers") has been replaced by the so-called "flood prayer" (*Sintflutgebet*). The epilogue with Luther's comments on the meaning of the baptismal service was, in later editions, made into a preface to this order. The German text of the original Wittenberg print, *Das tauff buchlin verdeutscht*, is given in WA 12, 42-48; the following translation is a revision of P. Z. Strodach's translation in *PE* 6, 197-201.

In the same year, 1523, a brief baptismal liturgy supposedly by Luther appeared under the title *How One Shall Properly and Intelligibly Baptize a Person into the Christian Faith, Briefly Indicated by Doctor Martin Luther, at the Request of an Upright Burgomaster (Wie man recht und vorstendlich ein menschen tzum christen glauben tauffen sol, von Doc. Mar. Luther kurtz angetzeichent, auff bit einsz redlichen Burgemeysters")*. But that this document could be genuine is most unlikely. Although published in the same year as *The Order of Baptism*, it contradicts the latter in almost every respect. The baptismal prayers that Luther valued so highly are not even mentioned. Instead of immersion, this order prescribes superfusion. The translation of the same phrases is dif-

---

[1] See pp. 7-14.

95

ferent in the two works. Moreover, no Wittenberg print of the latter is in existence. It seems to represent a rather violent reduction of the baptismal service from the *Bamberg Agenda* of 1491. Finally, while there are numerous references to *The Order of Baptism* in Luther's later writings, this rival order is nowhere mentioned. Since it is not likely that it is genuine, it was omitted in our edition. (The original German text of it is given in *WA* 12, 51-52; an English translation is in *PE* 6, 210-211.)

The Order of Baptism[1]

The officiant shall blow three times under the child's eyes and shall say:

Depart thou unclean spirit and give room to the Holy Spirit.

Then he shall sign him with a cross on his forehead and breast and shall say:

Receive the sign of the holy cross on both thy forehead and thy breast.

Let us pray.

O Almighty eternal God, Father of our Lord Jesus Christ, look upon this N., thy servant whom thou hast called to instruction in the faith, drive away from him all the blindness of his heart, break all the snares of the devil with which he is bound, open to him, Lord, the door of thy grace: So that marked with the sign of thy wisdom he may be free of the stench of all evil lusts and serve thee joyfully according to the sweet savor of thy commandments in thy church and grow daily and be made meet to come to the grace of thy baptism to receive the balm of life; through Christ our Lord. Amen.

Let us pray again.

O God, immortal Comfort of all who ask, Savior of all who cry to thee, and Peace of all who pray to thee, Life of the believers, Resurrection of the dead, I cry to thee for this N., thy servant, who

---

[1] Literally, "Baptismal booklet put into German."

prays for the gift of thy baptism and desires thine eternal grace through spiritual regeneration: Receive him, Lord, and as thou hast said, "Ask and ye shall receive, seek and ye shall find, knock and it shall be opened unto you," so give now the reward to him that asketh and open the door to him that knocketh: so that he may obtain the eternal blessing of this heavenly bath and receive the promised kingdom of thy grace; through Christ our Lord. Amen.

He shall now take the child, put salt into his mouth, and say:

N., receive the salt of wisdom. May it aid thee to eternal life. Amen. Peace be with thee.

Let us pray.

Almighty eternal God, who according to thy righteous judgment didst condemn the unbelieving world through the flood and in thy great mercy didst preserve believing Noah and his family, and who didst drown hardhearted Pharaoh with all his host in the Red Sea and didst lead thy people Israel through the same on dry ground, thereby prefiguring this bath of thy baptism, and who through the baptism of thy dear Child, our Lord Jesus Christ, hast consecrated and set apart the Jordan and all water as a salutary flood and a rich and full washing away of sins: We pray through the same thy groundless mercy that thou wilt graciously behold this N. and bless him with true faith in the spirit so that by means of this saving flood all that has been born in him from Adam and which he himself has added thereto may be drowned in him and engulfed, and that he may be sundered from the number of the unbelieving, preserved dry and secure in the holy ark of Christendom, serve thy name at all times fervent in spirit and joyful in hope, so that with all believers he may be made worthy to attain eternal life according to thy promise; through Jesus Christ our Lord. Amen.

Therefore, thou miserable devil, acknowledge thy judgment and give glory to the true and living God, give glory to his Son Jesus Christ and to the Holy Ghost, and depart from this N., his servant; for God and our Lord Jesus Christ has of his goodness called him to his holy grace and blessing, and to the fountain of baptism so that thou mayest never dare to disturb this sign of the

97

holy cross ✠ which we make on his forehead; through him who cometh again to judge, etc.

So hearken now, thou miserable devil, adjured by the name of the eternal God and of our Savior Jesus Christ, and depart trembling and groaning, conquered together with thy hatred, so that thou shalt have nothing to do with the servant of God who now seeks that which is heavenly and renounces thee and thy world, and shall live in blessed immortality. Give glory therefore now to the Holy Ghost who cometh and descendeth from the loftiest castle of heaven in order to destroy thy deceit and treachery, and having cleansed the heart with the divine fountain, to make it ready, a holy temple and dwelling of God, so that this servant of God, freed from all guilt of former sin, may always give thanks to the eternal God and praise his name forever and ever. Amen.

I adjure thee, thou unclean spirit, by the name of the Father ✠ and of the Son ✠ and of the Holy Ghost ✠ that thou come out of and depart from this servant of God, N., for he commands thee, thou miserable one, he who walked upon the sea and stretched forth his hand to sinking Peter.

Let us pray.

Lord, holy Father, almighty eternal God from whom cometh all the light of truth, we beseech thine eternal and most tender goodness that thou wilt shed thy blessing upon this N., thy servant, and enlighten him with the light of thy knowledge, cleanse and sanctify him, and give him right understanding: that he be made worthy to come to the grace of thy baptism, that he may hold fast to a sure hope, true counsel, and holy teaching, and be made meet for the grace of thy baptism; through Jesus Christ our Lord. Amen.

The Lord be with you.

Response: And with thy spirit.

The Gospel of St. Mark [10:13-16].

Response: Glory be to thee, O Lord.

And they brought young children to him, that he should touch them: and his disciples rebuked those that brought them. But when Jesus saw it, he was much displeased, and said unto them, Suffer the little children to come unto me, and forbid them not: for of such is the kingdom of God. Verily I say unto you, Whosoever

98

shall not receive the kingdom of God as a little child, he shall not enter therein. And he took them up in his arms, put his hands upon them, and blessed them.

Then the priest shall lay his hand on the head of the child and pray the Our Father together with the sponsors kneeling.

Then he shall take spittle with his finger, touch the right ear therewith and say:

Ephphatha, that is, Be thou opened [Mark 7:34].

Then the nose and the left ear [and say]:

But thou, devil, flee; for God's judgment cometh speedily.

Then the child shall be led into the church, and the priest shall say:

The Lord preserve thy coming in and thy going out now and for evermore.

Then the priest shall have the child renounce the devil through his sponsors and say:

N., dost thou renounce the devil?
Response: Yes.
And all his works?
Response: Yes.
And all his ways?
Response: Yes.

Then he asks:

Dost thou believe in God the Father Almighty, Maker of heaven and earth?
Response: Yes.
Dost thou believe in Jesus Christ, his only Son our Lord, who was born and suffered?
Response: Yes.
Dost thou believe in the Holy Ghost, one holy Christian church, the communion of saints, the forgiveness of sins, the resurrection of the body, and after death an eternal life?
Response: Yes.

99

*Then he shall anoint the child on the breast and
between the shoulders with holy oil, and say:*

And I anoint thee with the oil of salvation in Jesus Christ our
Lord.

And he shall ask:

Wilt thou be baptized?

Response: Yes.

Then he shall take the child and dip[2] him in the font and say:

And I baptize thee in the name of the Father and of the Son
and of the Holy Ghost.

*Then the sponsors shall hold the little child in the font[3] and
the priest shall make the sign of a cross with
oil on the crown of his head and say:*

The almighty God and Father of our Lord Jesus Christ who
hath regenerated thee through water and the Holy Ghost and hath
forgiven thee all thy sin, anoint thee with the salutary oil to eternal
life. Amen.

Peace be with thee.

Response: And with thy spirit.

*And while the sponsors continue to hold the child in the font,
the priest shall put on him the christening hood[4] and say:*

---

[2] There were three modes of administering baptism in use at this period: *immersio*, i.e., total immersion of the child in the font; *superfusio*, i.e, holding the naked child over the font and pouring water over him profusely; and *infusio*, i.e., dipping only the head of the child in the font. Luther strongly favored immersion; cf. *LW* 35, 29. One of the early editions of *The Order of Baptism* has an interesting cut on the title page depicting the baptism of a child. The administrator is holding the infant on his left over the font and is pouring water over his head from his right hand. Two sponsors, a man and a woman, stand to the right of the font, and a server, holding an open book toward the administrator, stands to the left. In the lower left-hand corner the date '24 is quite plain; the artist's initials are undecipherable. The mode authorized in the *Rituale Romanum* (p. 18) is pouring on the infant's head in the sign of the cross, but where customary the child may be immersed (*PE* 6, 203).

[3] I.e., over the font.

[4] *Hauben*, "hood," in this order; *Westerhemd*, "christening robe," in the revised order (in this volume, pp. 106-109). The term *Westerhemd* is derived from *vestis*, the white robe placed over the naked child immediately after it

Receive the white, holy, and spotless robe which thou shalt bring before the judgment seat of Christ so as to receive eternal life. Peace be with thee.

Then he shall be lifted from the font and the priest shall put a candle in his hand:

Receive this burning torch and preserve thy baptism blameless, so that when the Lord cometh to the wedding thou mayest go to meet him to enter with the saints into the heavenly mansion and receive eternal life. Amen.

Martin Luther to All Christian Readers Grace and Peace in Christ our Lord

Martin Luther

As I daily see and hear the carelessness and disrespect—not to say frivolity—with which the high, holy, and comforting sacrament of baptism is being administered to little children (which I feel is partly because those present cannot understand a word of what is said and done), I have come to the conclusion that it would not only be profitable, but also is necessary to administer this sacrament in the German language. And I have, therefore, begun to do in German what was heretofore done in Latin, namely, to baptize in German, in order that the sponsors and others present may be stirred to greater faith and more earnest devotion, and that the priests who administer the baptism should show greater concern for the good of the hearers.

In all Christian earnestness I would ask all those who administer baptism, who hold the children, or witness it, to take this wonderful work to heart in all its seriousness. For here, in the words of these prayers, you hear how meekly and earnestly the Christian church concerns itself about the little child and how it confesses before God in plain undoubting words that he is possessed by the devil and is a child of sin and wrath, and prays very diligently for aid and grace through baptism that he may become a child of God.

---

had been baptized. Cf. *The Catholic Encyclopedia* (16 vols.; New York, 1907-1914), II, 273. Dressing those who have been baptized in white is an ancient Christian custom (*PE* 6, 203).

Remember, therefore, that it is no joke to take sides against the devil and not only to drive him away from the little child, but to burden the child with such a mighty and lifelong enemy. Remember, too, that it is very necessary to aid the poor child with all your heart and strong faith, earnestly to intercede for him that God, in accordance with this prayer, would not only free him from the power of the devil, but also strengthen him, so that he may nobly resist the devil in life and death. And I suspect that people turn out so badly after baptism because our concern for them has been so cold and careless; we, at their baptism, interceded for them without zeal.

Now remember, too, that in baptism the external things are the least important, such as blowing under the eyes, signing with the cross, putting salt into the mouth, putting spittle and clay into the ears and nose, anointing the breast and shoulders with oil, signing the crown of the head with the chrism, putting on the christening robe, placing a burning candle in the hand, and whatever else has been added by man to embellish baptism. For most assuredly baptism can be performed without all these, and they are not the sort of devices and practices from which the devil shrinks or flees. He sneers at greater things than these! Here is the place for real earnestness.

See to it, therefore, that you are present in true faith, listen to God's Word, and earnestly join in prayer. For when the priest says, "Let us pray," he is exhorting you to unite with him in prayer. And all sponsors and the others present should repeat with him the words of his prayer in their hearts to God. For this reason the priest should say these prayers very clearly and slowly so that the sponsors may hear and comprehend them and also pray with him with one accord in their hearts, carrying the little child's need before God most earnestly, setting themselves against the devil with all their strength on behalf of the child, and showing that they realize this is no joke as far as the devil is concerned.

For this reason it is right and proper not to permit drunken and boorish priests to baptize or such people to serve as sponsors. But decent, moral, earnest, and pious priests and sponsors ought to be chosen who can be expected to treat the matter with seriousness and true faith, lest the holy sacrament be made a mockery for the devil and an insult to God, who through it showers us with the abundant and infinite riches of his grace. He himself calls it a new birth by which we are being freed from all the devil's tyranny, loosed from sin, death, and hell, and become children of life, heirs of all the gifts of God, God's own children, and brethren of Christ. Ah, dear Christians, let us not value and administer this unspeakable gift so indolently and indifferently; for baptism is our only comfort and admits to every blessing of God and to the communion of all the saints. To this may God help us. Amen.

For the time being I did not want to make any marked changes in the order of baptism. But I would not mind if it could be improved. Its framers were careless men who did not sufficiently appreciate the glory of baptism. However, in order to spare the weak consciences, I am leaving it unchanged, lest they complain that I want to institute a new baptism and criticize those baptized in the past as though they had not been properly baptized. For as I said, the human additions do not matter very much, as long as baptism itself is administered with God's Word, true faith, and serious prayer. Herewith we commit you to the Lord. Amen.

An Exhortation to the Communicants

1525

Translated by Paul Zeller Strodach
Revised by Ulrich S. Leupold

In March, 1525, Nicholas Hausmann, a pastor in Zwickau and Luther's friend, the man to whom Luther had dedicated *An Order of Mass and Communion*,[1] sent Luther copies of a number of German masses for review. In his reply, dated March 26, 1525, Luther primarily criticized the music.[2] The only textual revision he suggested was this *Exhortation to the Communicants* to replace the preface with its versicles in the Roman mass. Luther sketched out this short exhortation on a sheet of paper and enclosed it with his reply to Hausmann.[3]

The German text, *Allerliebsten freunde ynn Christo*, is given in *WA*, Br 3, No. 847, pp. 462-463; the following translation is a revision of P. Z. Strodach's translation in *PE* 6, 137-138.

An Exhortation to the Communicants

Dearest friends in Christ: You know that our Lord Jesus Christ, out of unspeakable love, instituted at the last this his Supper as a memorial and proclamation of his death suffered for our sins. This commemoration requires a firm faith to make the heart and conscience of everyone who wants to use and partake of this Supper sure and certain that Christ has suffered death for all his sins. But whoever doubts and does not in some manner feel such faith should know that the Supper is of no avail to him, but will rather be to his hurt, and he should stay away from it. And since we cannot see such faith and it is known only to God, we leave it to

---

[1] See pp. 15-40.
[2] See p. 54.
[3] This exhortation is not an occasional service, but is a part of the mass. It has been placed here as one of the briefer formularies that Luther wrote.

the conscience of him who comes and admit him who requests and desires it. But those who cling to open sins, such as greed, hatred, anger, envy, profiteering, unchastity, and the like and are not minded to renounce them, shall herewith be barred [from the Supper] and be warned faithfully not to come lest they incur judgment and damnation for their own souls, as St. Paul says [I Cor. 11:29]. If however someone has fallen because of weakness and proves by his acts that he earnestly desires to better himself, this grace and communion of the body and blood of Christ shall not be denied to him. In this fashion each must judge himself and look out for himself. For God is not mocked [Gal. 6:7], nor will he give that which is holy unto the dogs or cast the pearls before swine [Matt. 7:6].

The Order of Baptism
Newly Revised

1526

Translated by Paul Zeller Strodach
Revised by Ulrich S. Leupold

In his earlier baptismal order of 1523,[1] Luther, in order not to offend weak consciences, had retained as many of the traditional ceremonies as possible. But both he and his friends grew more and more impatient with a host of man-made usages which were apt to becloud the essentials of the sacrament. In 1526 he yielded to the urging of his friend Nicholas Hausmann in Zwickau and published a revised form of *The Order of Baptism* which introduced some important changes. Omitted were the exsufflation, the first of the two opening prayers, the giving of salt, the first of the two exorcisms, the prayer after the exorcism, the salutation before the Gospel, the Ephphatha, the two anointings before and after baptism, and the placing of a lighted candle in the child's hands.[2]

The new order became immensely popular. Luther appended it to the *Small Catechism* (following *The Order of Marriage*),[3] and it was included in many of the Lutheran church orders which were published.

The preface is practically word-for-word the same as Luther's epilogue in *The Order of Baptism* of 1523. Only the last paragraph had become obsolete with the revision and was omitted. The reader is therefore referred to pp. 101-103 for the text of Luther's preface to *The Order of Baptism Newly Revised*.

The text of the oldest available Wittenberg print, of 1526, *Das tauffbuchlin verdeudscht, auffs new zu gericht*, is given in WA 19, 537-541; the following translation is a revision of P. Z. Strodach's translation in *PE* 6, 207-211.

---

[1] See pp. 95-103.
[2] The first collect was also revised from its form in the order of 1523; cf. pp. 96-97, 107.
[3] See pp. 110-115.

The Order of Baptism[1]
Newly Revised

The officiant shall say:

Depart thou unclean spirit and make room for the Holy Spirit.

*Then he shall sign him with a cross on
his forehead and breast and shall say:*

Receive the sign of the holy cross on both thy forehead and
thy breast.

Let us pray.

O Almighty eternal God, Father of our Lord Jesus Christ, I
cry to thee for this N., thy servant, who prays for the gift of thy
baptism and desires thine eternal grace through spiritual regeneration: Receive him, Lord, and as thou hast said, "Ask and ye shall
receive, seek and ye shall find, knock and it shall be opened unto
you," so give now the good to him that asketh and open the door
to him that knocketh: so that he may obtain the eternal blessing of
this heavenly bath and receive the promised kingdom of thy grace;
through Christ our Lord. Amen.

Let us pray.

Almighty eternal God, who according to thy righteous judgment didst condemn the unbelieving world through the flood and
in thy great mercy didst preserve believing Noah and his family,
and who didst drown hardhearted Pharaoh with all his host in the
Red Sea and didst lead thy people Israel through the same on dry
ground, thereby prefiguring this bath of thy baptism, and who
through the baptism of thy dear Child, our Lord Jesus Christ, hast
consecrated and set apart the Jordan and all water as a salutary
flood and a rich and full washing away of sins: We pray through
the same thy groundless mercy that thou wilt graciously behold
this N. and bless him with true faith in the spirit so that by means
of this saving flood all that has been born in him from Adam and
which he himself has added thereto may be drowned in him and

---

[1] Literally, "Baptismal booklet put into German, newly revised."

107

engulfed, and that he may be sundered from the number of the unbelieving, preserved dry and secure in the holy ark of Christendom, serve thy name at all times fervent in spirit and joyful in hope, so that with all believers he may be made worthy to attain eternal life according to thy promise; through Jesus Christ our Lord. Amen.

I adjure thee, thou unclean spirit, by the name of the Father ✠ and of the Son ✠ and of the Holy Ghost ✠ that thou come out of and depart from this servant of Jesus Christ, N. Amen.

Let us hear the holy Gospel of St. Mark [10:13-16].

And they brought young children to him, that he should touch them: and his disciples rebuked those that brought them. But when Jesus saw it, he was much displeased, and said unto them, Suffer the little children to come unto me, and forbid them not: for of such is the kingdom of God. Verily I say unto you, Whosoever shall not receive the kingdom of God as a little child, he shall not enter therein. And he took them up in his arms, put his hands upon them, and blessed them.

Then the priest shall lay his hands on the head of the child and pray the Our Father together with the sponsors kneeling.

Our Father, who art in heaven, hallowed be thy name, thy kingdom come, thy will be done, on earth as it is in heaven. Give us this day our daily bread; and forgive us our debts,[2] as we forgive our debtors; and lead us not into temptation, but deliver us from evil. Amen.

Thereupon the little child shall be brought to the font, and the priest shall say:

The Lord preserve thy coming in and going out now and for evermore.

Then the priest shall have the child, through his sponsors, renounce the devil and say:

N., dost thou renounce the devil?
Response: Yes.

---

[2] *Schulde.*

And all his works?
Response: Yes.
And all his ways?
Response: Yes.

Then he shall ask:

Dost thou believe in God the Father Almighty, Maker of heaven and earth?
Response: Yes.
Dost thou believe in Jesus Christ, his only Son our Lord, who was born and suffered?
Response: Yes.
Dost thou believe in the Holy Ghost, one holy Christian church, the communion of saints, the forgiveness of sins, the resurrection of the body, and after death an eternal life?
Response: Yes.
Dost thou desire to be baptized?
Response: Yes.

Then shall he take the child, dip it in the font, and say:

And I baptize thee in the name of the Father and of the Son and of the Holy Ghost.

Then the sponsors shall hold the little child in the font, and the priest shall say, while he puts the christening robe on the child:

The almighty God and Father of our Lord Jesus Christ, who hath regenerated thee through water and the Holy Ghost and hath forgiven thee all thy sin, strengthen thee with his grace to life everlasting. Amen.
Peace be with thee.
Answer: Amen.

109

The Order of Marriage
for Common Pastors

1529

Translated by Paul Zeller Strodach
Revised by Ulrich S. Leupold

Marriage, according to Luther, is an institution both secular and sacred.[1] It is secular because it is an order of this earthly life. In fact, it is the basic order for the preservation and propagation of the human race. It is not essential for the kingdom of God. It has not been instituted by Christ and is no sacrament, for it has no special command or promise from him. But as Jesus pointed out, its institution goes back to the beginning of the race and to the first human couple, when God himself joined Adam and Eve in wedlock.

To Luther, it is this institution by God that makes marriage sacred, a divine and holy order. It does not—like the sacraments—nourish and strengthen faith or prepare men for the life to come; but it is a secular order in which men can prove their faith and love, even though they are apt to fail without the help of the Word and the sacrament.

This two-sided but in no wise contradictory view prompted Luther, on the one hand, to dispense with the whole canon law on marriage. Laws and ordinances governing the external form of marriage were to him a matter for secular authority. Of course, in a Christian country they should be consonant with the Christian view on marriage, but detailed regulations were the concern not of the church but of the state. On the other hand, the church should be ready to bless the newly married, to pray for them, and to remind them of the true meaning of marriage.

But the parish visitations of 1528 opened Luther's eyes to the pitiful inadequacy of most of the clergy. In the following year he composed the *Large Catechism* and *Small Catechism* to build up

---

[1] See, e.g., WA 12, 92-142; LW 45, 35-49.

faith and order at the grass-roots level. And even before the *Small Catechism* appeared, he published in the early spring of 1529 his *Order of Marriage for Common Pastors*, to provide a simple and worthy order to replace the nuptial mass. Later in the same year he incorporated this form in the *Small Catechism* following Part V and preceding *The Order of Baptism Newly Revised*.[2]

Luther followed tradition in dividing the rite into three distinct but related actions, namely, the publication of the banns, the marriage proper in front of the church, and the benediction by God's word and prayer in the church before the altar. Not mentioned here, but taken for granted by Luther, was a public betrothal in which the bride and bridegroom with the consent of their parents would announce their intent to be married. This betrothal was the real foundation of marriage and was confirmed by the marriage in front of the church. It should also be added that Luther was wont, following the lessons, to preach a wedding sermon, in which he dwelt more extensively on the Christian meaning of marriage.

The German text, *Ein Traubüchlein für die einfältigen Pfarrherr*, is given in *WA* 30[III], 74-80; the following translation is a revision of P. Z. Strodach's translation in *PE* 6, 225-230.

The Order of Marriage
for Common Pastors

Many lands, many customs, says the proverb. Since marriage and the married estate are worldly matters, it behooves us pastors or ministers of the church not to attempt to order or govern anything connected with it, but to permit every city and land to continue its own use and custom in this connection. Some lead the bride to the church twice, both evening and morning, some only once. Some announce it formally and publish the banns from the pulpit two or three weeks in advance. All such things and the like I

---

[2] See pp. 106-109.

111

leave to the lords and the council[1] to order and arrange as they see fit. It does not concern me.

But when we are requested to bless them before the church or in the church, to pray over them, or also to marry them, we are in duty bound to do this. For this reason I have desired to offer this advice and form to those who do not know anything better, in case they should desire to follow our custom in this matter. The others who know all about it, that is, who do not know anything, but think that they know all about it—well, they do not need this service of mine, except to correct and improve it. But let them take good care lest they do anything the same as others, or they may be thought to have to learn from others. And wouldn't that be a pity?

Since hitherto it has been customary to surround the consecration of monks and nuns with such great ceremonial display (even though their estate and organization are an ungodly and purely human invention which does not have any foundation in the Scriptures), how much more should we honor this divine estate and gloriously bless and embellish it and pray for it. For though it is a worldly estate, yet does it have God's word in its favor and was not invented or instituted by men, as was the estate of the monks and nuns. Therefore, it should be accounted a hundred times more spiritual than the monastic estate, which in truth should be considered the most worldly and fleshly of all, because it was invented and instituted by flesh and blood, out of worldly reasons and considerations.

We must also do this so as to teach the young people to take this estate seriously, to honor it as a divine creation and command, and not to act so disgracefully at weddings, making fools of themselves with laughing, jeering, and other nonsense, as has been common till now, just as though it was a joke or child's play to enter into the married estate or to have a wedding. Those who first instituted the practice of leading the bride and bridegroom to church certainly did not regard it as a joke, but as a very serious matter; for there is no doubt that they desired the blessing of God and common prayer, but not tomfoolery or a pagan spectacle.

---

[1] I.e., the city council or town council.

112

This is proved by the rite itself. For whoever desires prayer and blessing from the pastor or bishop indicates thereby—even if he does not express it in so many words—into what peril and need he enters and how greatly he stands in need of the blessing of God and common prayer for the estate which he enters. For every day we see marriages broken by the devil through adultery, unfaithfulness, discord, and all manner of ill.

Therefore, we will deal in the following way with the bridegroom and bride (if they desire and ask it).

First, publishing the banns from the pulpit
with such words as these:

Hans N. and Greta N. purpose to enter into the holy estate of matrimony according to God's ordinance. They desire that common Christian prayer be made on their behalf so that they may begin it in God's name and prosper therein.

And should any one have anything to say against it, let him speak in time or afterward hold his peace. God grant them his blessing. Amen.

Marrying them at the entrance to the church
with words such as these:

Hans, dost thou desire Greta to thy wedded wife?
He shall say: Yes.
Greta, dost thou desire Hans to thy wedded husband?
She shall say: Yes.

Then let them give each other the wedding rings and
join their right hands together, and
say to them:

What God hath joined together, let not man put asunder [Matt. 19:6].

Then shall he say:

Since Hans N. and Greta N. desire each other in marriage and acknowledge the same here publicly before God and the world, in testimony of which they have given each other their hands and wedding rings, I pronounce them joined in marriage, in the name of the Father, and of the Son, and of the Holy Ghost. Amen.

Before the altar he shall read God's word over the bridegroom
and bride, Genesis, the second chapter [:18, 21-24]:[2]

And the Lord God said, It is not good that the man should be alone; I will make him a help meet for him. And the Lord God caused a deep sleep to fall upon Adam, and he slept; and he took one of his ribs, and closed up the flesh instead thereof; And the rib, which the Lord God had taken from man, made he a woman, and brought her unto the man. And Adam said, This is now bone of my bones, and flesh of my flesh: she shall be called Woman, because she was taken out of Man. Therefore shall a man leave his father and mother and shall cleave unto his wife: and they shall be one flesh.

Thereupon he shall turn to both of them and speak to them thus:

Since both of you have entered the married estate in God's name, hear first of all God's commandment concerning this estate. Thus speaketh St. Paul: Husbands, love your wives, even as Christ also loved the church, and gave himself for it; that he might sanctify and cleanse it with the washing of water by the word, that he might present it to himself a glorious church, not having spot, or wrinkle, or any such thing; but that it should be holy and without blemish. So ought men to love their wives as their own bodies. He that loveth his wife loveth himself. For no man ever yet hated his own flesh; but nourisheth and cherisheth it, even as the Lord the church [Eph. 5:25-29].

Wives, submit yourselves unto your own husbands, as unto the Lord. For the husband is the head of the wife, even as Christ is the head of the church: and he is the savior of the body. Therefore as the church is subject unto Christ, so let wives be to their own husbands in every thing [Eph. 5:22-24].

Second, hear also the cross which God has placed upon this estate. God spake thus to the woman [Gen. 3:16]: I will greatly multiply thy sorrow and thy conception; in sorrow thou shalt bring forth children; and thy desire shall be to thy husband, and he shall rule over thee.

---

[2] The entry into the church marks the beginning of the religious ceremony.

And God spake to the man [Gen. 3:17-19]: Because thou hast hearkened unto the voice of thy wife, and hast eaten of the tree, of which I commanded thee, saying, Thou shalt not eat of it: cursed is the ground for thy sake; in sorrow shalt thou eat of it all the days of thy life; thorns and thistles shall it bring forth to thee; and thou shalt eat the herb of the field; in the sweat of thy face shalt thou eat bread, till thou return unto the ground; for out of it wast thou taken: for dust thou art, and unto dust shalt thou return.

Third, this is your comfort that you may know and believe that your estate is pleasing to God and blessed by him. For it is written:

God created man in his own image, in the image of God created he him; male and female created he them. And God blessed them, and God said unto them, Be fruitful, and multiply, and replenish the earth, and subdue it: and have dominion over the fish of the sea, and over the fowl of the air, and over every living thing that moveth upon the earth. And God saw every thing that he had made, and, behold, it was very good [Gen. 1:27-28, 31].

Therefore, Solomon also says: Whoso findeth a wife findeth a good thing, and obtaineth favor of the Lord [Prov. 18:22].

Here he shall spread forth his hands over them and pray thus:

O God, who hast created man and woman and hast ordained them for the married estate, hast blessed them also with fruits of the womb, and hast typified therein the sacramental union[3] of thy dear Son, the Lord Jesus Christ, and the church, his bride: We beseech thy groundless goodness and mercy that thou wouldst not permit this thy creation, ordinance, and blessing to be disturbed or destroyed, but graciously preserve the same; through Jesus Christ our Lord. Amen.

---

[3] *Sakrament.* After 1520 Luther did not consider marriage a sacrament in the technical theological sense, but he often used the word "sacrament" from the Vulgate text of Eph. 5:32, where it is used to translate the Greek word *mystērion*, i.e., a revelation, formerly hidden. See *LW* 36, 92-95.

115

A Short Order of Confession Before the Priest
for the Common Man

1529

Translated by Paul Zeller Strodach
Revised by Ulrich S. Leupold

All through his life Luther was vitally concerned for the proper use of private confession. This concern started the Reformation. As father confessor of his flock, he opposed the sale of indulgences, and his *Ninety-five Theses* dealt with the true meaning of repentance, confession, and absolution. He returned to this theme again and again. In fact, all the major emphases of his theology come to the fore in his views on private confession. Two features in the Roman practice of private confession were especially objectionable to him. In the first place, he deplored the compulsion by which people were forced to go to confession regularly to give a complete catalog of their sins. Confession had become a burden, instead of a privilege, and, in the second place, the enforced enumeration of particular sins led to hypocrisy and a superficial understanding of sin.

Luther wanted Christians to go to confession not as a matter of ecclesiastical discipline, but for the benefit they would derive from it. In his view, confession was no requirement for the reception of holy communion, especially not for those spiritually mature enough to examine themselves, but rather a gracious provision of God for the relief of burdened consciences.

On the other hand, he constantly stressed that absolution offers forgiveness from God himself. He violently denounced the view of the Roman church which made absolution conditional upon the proper attitude and penance of the penitent. According to Luther, the absolution that one Christian offers to another in the name of God is absolutely valid. God forgives through the word of the brother. If a man fails to believe this word, so much the worse for him. But the fact that God's peace was offered to him remains unaffected whether he accepts the offer in faith or not. Thus Luther never thought of abolishing private confession. He knew and used its benefits in his own spiritual struggles, and he could not conceive of a Christian who could get along without it. He never designed an order of public confession, but in the *Small Catechism* he offered two forms of private confession.

The first of these appeared in the oldest extant Wittenberg edition of 1529 (actually the second or third edition of the *Small Catechism*) following the *Order of Baptism*, under the title, *A Short Order of Confession Before the Priest for the Common Man.* The German text, *Eine kurtze weise zu beichten für die einfeltigen, dem Priester*, is given in WA 30ᴵ, 343-345; the following translation is a revision of P. Z. Strodach's translation in *PE* 6, 215-216.

A Short Order of Confession Before the Priest for the Common Man

Reverend and dear sir: I beseech you, for God's sake, give me good counsel for the comfort of my soul.

What then do you desire?

Answer: Miserable man that I am, I confess and lament to you before God that I am a sinful and weak creature. I do not keep God's commandments; I do not really believe the gospel; I do nothing good; I cannot bear ill. Especially have I committed this and that[1] which burdens my conscience. I therefore ask that you, in God's stead, would declare unto me my sins forgiven and comfort me with the word of God.

Another Form of Confession

I confess before God and you that I am a miserable sinner, guilty of every sin, of unbelief and of blasphemy. I also feel that God's Word is not bringing forth fruit in me. I hear it, but I do not receive it earnestly. I do not show works of love toward my neighbor. I am full of anger, hate, and envy toward him. I am impatient, greedy, and bent on every evil. Therefore, my heart

---

[1] Here the penitent enumerates the particular sins which distress him.

117

and conscience are heavy, and I would gladly be freed of my sins. I ask you to strengthen my little faith and comfort my weak conscience by the divine word and promise.

Why dost thou desire to receive the sacrament?

Answer: Because I desire to strengthen my soul with God's Word and sign and to obtain grace.

But hast thou not found forgiveness of sins by absolution?

Answer: So what! I want to add the sign of God to his Word. To receive God's Word in many ways is so much better.

How One Should Teach Common Folk to Shrive Themselves

1531

Translated by Joseph Stump
Revised by Ulrich S. Leupold

In the 1531 edition of the *Small Catechism* Luther revised the order for confession. Instead of the rather brief outline that in 1529 appeared under the title *A Short Order of Confession Before the Priest for the Common Man*,[1] he gave a more detailed example of evangelical auricular confession. This he prefaced by a brief catechism on the meaning of confession, and he placed the whole between the fourth and fifth parts of the catechism. The German text, *Wie man die Einfeltigen sol leren Beichten*, is given in WA 30^I, 383-387; the following translation is a revision of Joseph Stump's translation in *An Explanation of Luther's Small Catechism* (Philadelphia, 1907), pp. 24-25.

How One Should Teach Common Folk to Shrive Themselves

What is confession?
Answer: Confession consists of two parts: one is that we confess our sins, the other that we receive absolution or forgiveness from the father confessor as from God himself, in no wise doubting, but firmly believing that our sins are thus forgiven before God in heaven.

What sins ought we to confess?
Answer: In the presence of God we should acknowledge ourselves guilty of all manner of sins, even of those we do not ourselves perceive, as we do in the Lord's Prayer. But in the pres-

---

[1] See pp. 116-118.

ence of the father confessor we should confess only those sins we know and feel in our hearts.

Which are these?

Answer: Here consider your calling according to the Ten Commandments, namely, whether you are a father or mother, a son or daughter, a master, mistress, or servant, if you have been disobedient, unfaithful, slothful, angry, unchaste, or quarrelsome, if you have injured any one by words or deeds, if you have stolen, neglected, or wasted aught, or done any other evil.

Please give me a brief order of confession.

Answer: Thus you shall say to the father confessor: Reverend and dear sir, I beseech you to hear my confession and to declare unto me the remission of sins in the name of God.

Then say: I, a poor sinner, confess before God that I am guilty of all sins. Especially do I confess that as a manservant, maidservant, etc., I am not faithfully serving my master; for here and there I have not done what I was told, I have angered and provoked them to curse, I have neglected my work and caused loss. I have been unchaste in word and deed, quarreled with my fellows, grumbled and cursed against my wife, etc. For all this I am sorry and ask for mercy. From now on I will do better.

Thus a master or mistress may speak:

Especially do I confess before you that I did not faithfully rule my children, servants, and wife to the glory of God. I have cursed, given a bad example with vulgar words and deeds, hurt and slandered my neighbor, sold at too much profit, given poor or underweight merchandise . . . , and whatever else he did against the commandments of God and his own calling.

But if someone should not be bothered by such or still greater sins, let him not try to find or feign other sins and thus make confession a torment. Let him tell one or two sins that he knows, e.g., especially do I confess that once I cursed, once I was inconsiderate in my words, once I neglected this N., etc. And let it remain at that.

But if you know of no sin at all (which seems almost impossible), don't confess any particular one, but receive forgiveness upon the general confession,[1] which you make to the father confessor before God.

Then the father confessor shall say: God be gracious unto thee and strengthen thy faith. Amen.

And further: Do you believe that my absolution is God's absolution?

Answer: Yes, dear sir.

Then let him [the father confessor] say: As thou believest, so be it done unto thee [Matt. 8:13]. And I, by the command of Jesus Christ our Lord, forgive thee all thy sin in the name of the Father and of the Son and of the Holy Ghost. Amen. Go in peace [Luke 7:50; 8:48; Mark 5:34].

But the father confessor will know how to comfort with additional Bible verses those who are greatly afflicted in conscience or who are grieved or tempted, and how to incite them to faith.

This is intended only to serve as the usual order of confession for the common people.

---

[1] Luther evidently thinks here of a general confession such as was customarily repeated by the congregation after the sermon (the so-called *Offene Schuld;* WA 19, 96), but which could also form the first part of private confession (cf. Luther's earlier *Short Order of Confession,* p. 117).

121

The Ordination of Ministers of the Word

1539

Translated by Paul Zeller Strodach
Revised by Ulrich S. Leupold

The rite of ordination Luther composed was an entirely new creation. It had no more than the name in common with the sacrament of ordination in the Roman church. Roman ordination was a sacrament, Lutheran ordination a rite. Roman ordination admitted a man to a special order or rank within Christendom. Lutheran ordination gave him certain functions. Roman ordination conferred on the candidate the power to conduct the sacrifice of the mass. Lutheran ordination set him aside for the work of preaching and administering the sacraments.

According to Luther every Christian was a priest, and baptism the true sacrament of ordination. But to exercise this priesthood publicly for the benefit of others, a man needed a call. That is why Luther often spoke of ordaining a minister in the sense of calling him. For a long time he was not too concerned about the public rite which might follow the call. He hesitated before he composed an order for it and did not even publish the one he devised, although it was ultimately printed in many church orders. Of course, in the beginning of the Reformation the need for an order of ordination was not very pressing. Most of the early preachers of the gospel were, like Luther himself, former priests, and the hope that the bishops would ultimately espouse the Protestant cause had not been given up. But as the gulf between Wittenberg and Rome deepened and most of the bishops sided with the pope, the need for an evangelical rite of ordination in which the ministers of the Word would have their call publicly attested became more and more urgent. The congregations had to know what men were qualified and properly certified to exercise the office of the Word, and the candidates needed a commissioning service on which to base their claim for authority.

The first evangelical ordination in Wittenberg had taken place as early as 1525, when Luther ordained Georg Rörer, but it was not until 1535 that the Elector John Frederick set out a definite order for the examination, calling, and ordination of candidates. Luther was frequently the ordinator, and the order he composed was soon accepted in Lutheran churches everywhere.[1]

This order has been preserved with slight variations in several sixteenth-century manuscripts. The following translation is a revision of the translation by P. Z. Strodach in PE 6, 237-239, which is based on a handwritten Wittenberg agenda of 1539, Ordinatio ministrorum verbi, which was discovered and published by Georg Rietschel (called "R"), as it appears in WA 38, 423-431. But we add in the footnotes the most significant alternate readings from two other texts, a Hamburg codex from about 1535 (called "H") and a Freyberg codex from 1538 (called "F").[2]

---

[1] The following account of an ordination is from Luther's Table Talk (WA, TR 5, 112, No. 5376): "When Doctor Martin ordained Magister Benedict Schumann on Jubilate Sunday, April 22, 1540 [actually in 1537], he read the passage, Acts 13 [:3], which relates how hands were laid upon the two apostles, Paul and Barnabas; also Acts 20 [:29] in which Paul warns the bishops and pastors at Miletus to guard themselves against the wolves; as well as the third chapter of I Timothy [:1-7] and Titus 1 [:7-9] on how a bishop should be called and conduct himself.

"In addition he said: 'My dear brother, you have been ordained by God to be a faithful servant of Jesus Christ in N. [Naumburg], to further his holy name by the pure teaching of the gospel, to which we call and send you by the power of God, just as God has sent us. Therefore, watch earnestly, be diligent, pray God that he may preserve you in this high calling, that you may not fall away by reason of false doctrine, heresy, sectarianism, or your own thoughts, but rather begin it in the fear of God, faithful diligence, and constant prayer and rightly accomplish it in Christ.' This was the main content of his prayer.

"Afterward he laid his hands upon him and, kneeling, prayed the Lord's Prayer aloud. When he had risen to his feet, he lifted up his eyes and hands to heaven and said: 'Lord God, heavenly, merciful Father, who hast commanded us to ask and seek and knock, and also promised to hear us when we call upon thee in the name of thy Son: In this promise we put our trust and pray: be thou pleased to send this thy servant of thy Word, Benedict, into thy harvest. Help him, bless his ministry and service, and open the ears of believers to the blessed course of thy Word, to the praise of thy name, the increase of thy kingdom, and the growth of thy church. Amen. Therefore, my dear brother, I wish for you, moreover, blessing and success, that you may walk in the fear of God and trust in the Lord!' Then 'Now Pray We All the Holy Ghost' was sung." Translated by John W. Doberstein in Minister's Prayer Book (Philadelphia: Muhlenberg Press, 1959), pp. 211-212.

[2] WA 38, 423-431, offers H, F, and R in parallel columns; a description of all the manuscripts is given in WA 38, 411. WA 38, 432-433, offers a Latin order which differs very little from the German form.

The Ordination of Ministers of the Word

First. The candidates shall be examined either on the same or on the preceding day. If they are worthy, the congregation after due admonition by the preacher shall pray for them and for the whole ministry, namely, that God would deign to send laborers into his harvest and preserve them faithful and constant in sound doctrine against the gates of hell, etc.[1]

Second. The ordinator and the minister or presbyters of the church shall place the ordinand in the center before the ordinator and all shall kneel before the altar. And the choir shall sing "*Veni sancte spiritus.*"[2]

V. Create in me a clean heart, O God.

R. And renew a right spirit within me.

The customary collect of the Holy Spirit shall be read.[3]

Third. After this the ordinator shall ascend the step of the predella and facing the ordinands shall recite with a clear voice I Timothy 3.[4] Thus writes St. Paul in the First Epistle to Timothy in the third chapter [:1-7]: This is a true saying, If a man desire the office of a bishop, he desireth a good work. A bishop then must be blameless, the husband of one wife, vigilant, sober, of good behavior, given to hospitality, apt to teach; not given to wine, no

---

[1] H continues: "and against the power of the world, because the ministry of the church is most important and necessary for all churches and is given and preserved by God alone."

[2] This is a departure from the Roman rite, where *Veni creator spiritus* is the traditional hymn for ordination. It is not clear whether Luther had in mind the Whitmonday sequence *Veni sancte spiritus et emitte coelitus* or the antiphon *Veni sancte spiritus, reple tuorum corda fidelium*, from which he later wrote the hymn "Come, Holy Spirit Lord and God"; see pp. 265-267.

[3] I.e., the collect *"Deus qui hodierna die corda fidelium"; see* Luther's version in translation, p. 135.

[4] H precedes the lessons from I Timothy and Acts with the following admonition: "St. Paul says: Every creature of God is good, etc., for it is sanctified by, etc. [I Tim. 4:4-5]. You are not only good creatures, sanctified by the Word and the sacrament of baptism, but in a second sanctification you have also been called to the holy and divine ministry, so that many others may be sanctified and reconciled to the Lord through your word and work. This goes to show how devoutly and worthily you ought to hold your holy office so that you may be sound in faith, pure in word, irreprehensible in conduct, and that you may be found good stewards in word and deed of the mysteries of God and useful ministers of Christ in the day of the Lord, as St. Paul teaches, I Timothy 3," etc.

striker, not greedy of filthy lucre; but patient, not a brawler, not covetous; one that ruleth well in his own house, having his children in subjection with all gravity (for if a man know not how to rule his own house, how shall he take care of the church of God?); not a novice, lest being lifted up with pride he fall into the condemnation of the devil. Moreover he must have a good report of them which are without; lest he fall into reproach and the snare of the devil.

Thus St. Paul admonishes the elders of the congregation at Ephesus: Take heed therefore unto yourselves, and to all the flock, over which the Holy Ghost hath made you overseers, to feed the church of God, which he hath purchased with his own blood. For I know this, that after my departing shall grievous wolves enter in among you, not sparing the flock. Also of your own selves shall men arise, speaking perverse things, to draw away disciples after them. Therefore watch, and remember, that by the space of three years I ceased not to warn every one night and day with tears [Acts 20:28-31].

Fourth. The ordinator addresses the ordinands in these or similar words:[5] Herein you hear that we bishops—i.e., presbyters and pastors—are called not to watch over geese or cows, but over the congregation God purchased with his own blood that we should feed them with the pure Word of God and also be on guard lest wolves and sects burst in among the poor sheep. This is why he calls it a good work. Also in our personal conduct we should live decently and honorably and rule our house, wife, children, and servants in a Christian way.

Are you now ready to do this?

Answer: Yes.[6]

Fifth. Then while the whole presbytery impose their hands on the heads of the ordinands, the ordinator says the Lord's Prayer in a clear voice. Let us pray. Our Father, etc.

---

[5] This admonition is lacking in H. F, which explicitly permits its omission, offers it in a slightly different form, beginning: "First, you hear here that the Holy Ghost called and ordained you bishops in his flock or church. Therefore, you must believe for certain that you were called by God, because the church sent you here and secular authority has called and desired you. For what the church and secular authorities do in these matters, God does through them, so that you may not be considered intruders."

[6] H omits this question and answer.

125

And if he desires or time permits, he may add this prayer which explains more fully the three parts of the Lord's Prayer: Merciful God, heavenly Father, thou hast said to us through the mouth of thy dear Son our Lord Jesus Christ: "The harvest truly is plenteous, but the laborers are few. Pray ye therefore the Lord of the harvest, that he will send forth laborers into his harvest" [Matt. 9:37-38]. Upon this thy divine command, we pray heartily that thou wouldst grant thy Holy Spirit richly to these thy servants, to us, and to all those who are called to serve thy Word so that the company of us who publish the good tidings may be great,[7] and that we may stand faithful and firm against the devil. the world, and the flesh, to the end that thy name may be hallowed, thy kingdom grow, and thy will be done. Be also pleased at length to check and stop the detestable abomination of the pope, Mohammed, and other sects which blaspheme thy name, hinder thy kingdom, and oppose thy will. Graciously hear this our prayer, since thou hast so commanded, taught, and promised, even as we believe and trust through thy dear Son, Jesus Christ our Lord, who liveth and reigneth with thee and the Holy Ghost, world without end. Amen.

Sixth. The ordinator shall address the ordinands with these words of St. Peter, I Peter 5 [:2-4]: Feed the flock of God which is among you, taking the oversight thereof, not by constraint, but willingly; not for filthy lucre, but of a ready mind; neither as being lords over God's heritage, but being ensamples to the flock. And when the chief Shepherd shall appear, ye shall receive a crown of glory that fadeth not away.

Seventh. The ordinator shall bless them with the sign of the cross and use these or other words: The Lord bless you that you may bring forth much fruit. After this each one shall return to his own place. And if it is desired, the congregation may sing "Now Let Us Pray to the Holy Ghost."[8]

This ended, the presbyter chants: Our Father, etc.[9] And first the ordinands shall commune with the congregation, then likewise the ordinator if he so desires.

---

[7] Cf. Ps. 68:11.
[8] Neither H nor F refer to the blessing. H also omits the hymn.
[9] Possibly a direct entrance into the consecration of communion.

126

THE COLLECTS

Translated by Paul Zeller Strodach
Revised by Ulrich S. Leupold

INTRODUCTION

In the course of his liturgical labors Luther wrote and translated a number of collects and formal prayers. Some of Luther's collects were parts of the orders for the mass, the Litany, baptism, ordination, and marriage; others were scattered in the hymnals that came out under his personal supervision.[1] His own hymns are often followed by appropriate versicles and collects, for example, a Christmas hymn by a Christmas versicle and collect or a communion hymn by a communion collect with its versicle(s). However, a given collect is frequently used in more than one connection. For example, the Christmas collect, "Help, Dear Lord God" is used with "All Praise to Thee, O Jesus Christ" and then with "From Heaven the Angel Troop Came Near," and the collect "Lord God, Heavenly Father, Thou Knowest" is used with the Litany and with the hymn "Our Father in the Heaven who Art."

Here we offer a complete repertory of Luther's collects intended for public worship, giving besides the text, a brief indication of the source and usage of each. Most of these collects are translations of traditional Latin collects. And—as in the case of some of the hymns—Luther may have used or adapted earlier translations. It is not possible to determine with certainty to what extent these collects can be credited to Luther, but at least he sanctioned their use and general acceptance in the Lutheran liturgy. Fuller liturgiological references are available in *PE* 6, the page numbers of which have been noted for every collect. The translations are revisions of P. Z. Strodach's translations in *PE* 6, 319-361.

---

[1] See pp. 193-194.

"Dear Lord God, Awaken Us"

In the older Lutheran hymnals this collect follows the Advent hymn "Come, the Heathen's Healing Light."[1] It is a translation of the traditional collect for the Second Sunday in Advent, "*Excita domine corda nostra*" (cf. PE 6, 342-343). The German text, "*Lieber HERR Gott wecke uns auff*," is given in WA 35, 552.

V. Prepare ye the way of the Lord:
R. Make his paths straight [Mark 1:3].

Dear Lord God, awaken us so that when thy Son cometh we may be prepared to receive him with joy and to serve thee with clean hearts; through the same thy Son Jesus Christ our Lord. Amen.

"Help, Dear Lord God, That We May Become and Remain Partakers"

In Klug's Wittenberg hymnal of 1533 this collect follows the hymn "All Praise to Thee, O Jesus Christ."[2] In the other early hymnals it is appended to "From Heaven the Angel Troop Came Near."[3] It is a free rendition of the proper collect for the third mass on Christmas Day (cf. PE 6, 344-346). The German text, "*Hilff, lieber HERR Gott, das wir der newen leiblichen Geburt*," is given in WA 35, 264.

V. Unto us a Child is born. Alleluia:
R. Unto us a Son is given. Alleluia [Isa. 9:6].

or:

V. The Word was made flesh. Alleluia:
R. And dwelt among us. Alleluia [John 1:14].

---

[1] See pp. 235-236.
[2] See pp. 240-241.
[3] See pp. 306-307.

131

or:

V. Unto you is born this day a Savior. Alleluia:

R. Which is Christ the Lord in the city of David. Alleluia [Luke 2:11].

Help, dear Lord God, that we may become and remain partakers of the new birth in the flesh of thy dear Son and be delivered from our old sinful birth; through the same thy Son Jesus Christ our Lord. Amen.

"Almighty Eternal God, We Heartily Pray Thee"

In the older hymnals this collect follows the hymn "In Peace and Joy I Now Depart."[4] This is an original collect by Luther and is noteworthy for its simplicity and the directness of its petition (cf. *PE* 6, 346-347). The German text, *"Allmechtiger ewiger Gott, wir bitten dich hertzlich,"* is given in *WA* 35, 553.

V. Lord, now lettest thou thy servant depart in peace:

R. For mine eyes have seen thy salvation [Luke 2:29-30].

Almighty eternal God, we heartily pray thee, grant that we may know and praise thy dear Son as did St. Simeon, who took him up in his arms and spiritually knew and confessed him; through the same thy Son Jesus Christ our Lord. Amen.

"Merciful Everlasting God, who Didst Not Spare Thine Own Son"

This is the first of two Lenten collects in the early Lutheran hymnals not connected with any hymn. It carries the caption "A Prayer on the Passion of Christ." Apparently, Luther wrote it, although it

---

4 See pp. 247-248.

reminds one of a number of Latin collects, in particular the proper collect of the mass in honor of the Holy Cross (cf. *PE* 6, 348-349). The German text, *"Barmhertziger ewiger Gott, Der du deines eigen Sones,"* is given in *WA* 35, 553.

V. Christ was wounded for our transgressions:
R. And bruised for our iniquities [Isa. 53:5].

Merciful everlasting God, who didst not spare thine own Son, but didst deliver him up for us all so that he might bear our sin upon the cross: Grant that our hearts may never be terrified or dismayed in this faith; through the same thy Son Jesus Christ our Lord. Amen.

"Almighty Father, Eternal God, who Didst Allow"

This is the second of two Lenten collects in the early Lutheran hymnals not connected with a hymn. It is a translation of the traditional collect *"Deus qui pro nobis filium tuum"* (cf. *PE* 6, 349-351). The German text, *"Allmechter Vater, ewiger Gott, der du fur uns deinen Son,"* is given in *WA* 35, 553.

V. The chastisement of our peace was upon him:
R. And with his stripes we are healed [Isa. 53:5].

Almighty Father, eternal God, who didst allow thy Son to suffer the agony of the cross so that thou mightest drive from us the enemy's power: Grant that we may so observe his passion and give thanks for it that we may thereby obtain forgiveness of sin and redemption from death eternal. Through the same thy Son, etc.

133

"Almighty God, who by the Death of Thy Son"

In the older hymnals this collect follows the hymn "Jesus Christ, Our Savior True."[5] It is an original collect by Luther and was adopted in nearly all of the Lutheran church orders, either as an Easter collect or to be used at the burial of the dead, or for both (cf. PE 6, 351-352). The German text, "*Allmechtiger Gott, der du durch den Tod deines Sons,*" is given in WA 35, 553-554.

V. Christ, being raised from the dead, dieth no more. Alleluia:

R. Death hath no more dominion over him. Alleluia [Rom. 6:9].

V. I know that my Redeemer liveth. Alleluia:

R. Who shall at the latter day wake me from the earth. Alleluia [Job 19:25].

Almighty God, who by the death of thy Son hast brought to naught sin and death and by his resurrection hast brought again innocence and everlasting life so that, delivered from the devil's power, we may live in thy kingdom: Grant us that we may believe this with all our heart and, steadfast in this faith, praise and thank thee always; through the same thy Son Jesus Christ our Lord. Amen.

"Almighty Lord God, Grant to Us who Believe"

This collect is a translation of the proper collect for the festival of the Ascension, "*Concede quaesumus omnipotens deus.*" In the older hymnals it follows the Easter collect "Almighty God, who by the Death of Thy Son"[6] (cf. PE 6, 360-362). The German text, "*Allmechtiger HERRE Gott, verleihe uns, die, wir gleuben,*" is given in WA 35, 554.

---

[5] See pp. 258-259.
[6] See above.

134

V. Christ ascended up on high. Alleluia:
R. And led captivity captive. Alleluia [Eph. 4:8].

or:

V. I ascend unto my Father, and your Father, Alleluia:
R. And to my God, and your God, Alleluia [John 20:17].

Almighty Lord God, grant to us who believe that thy only Son our Savior ascended this day into heaven that we, too, may spiritually walk and dwell with him in the life of the Spirit; through the same thy Son Jesus Christ our Lord. Amen.

"Lord God, Dear Father who Through Thy Holy Spirit"

In the older Lutheran hymnals this collect is appended to the hymn "Now Let Us Pray to the Holy Ghost."[7] It is a translation of the proper collect for Pentecost, *"Deus qui hodierna die corda fidelium"* (cf. PE 6, 353-354). The text, *"HErr Gott lieber Vater, der du (an diesem tage) deiner Gleubigen hertzen,"* is given in WA 35, 554.

V. Create in me a clean heart, O God:
R. And renew a right spirit within me [Ps. 51:10].

Lord God, dear Father, who (on this day) through thy Holy Spirit didst enlighten and teach the hearts of thy faithful people: Grant to us that we may have right understanding through the same Spirit and at all times rejoice in his comfort and power; through the same [sic] thy Son Jesus Christ our Lord. Amen.

---

[7] See pp. 263-264.

"Almighty Eternal God, who Hast Taught Us"

In the older hymnals this collect follows the hymn "God the Father with Us Be."[8] It is a translation of the proper collect for the festival of the Holy Trinity (cf. *PE* 6, 354-356). The text, *"Allmechtiger ewiger Gott, der du uns geleret hast,"* is given in WA 35, 554.

V. We laud God the Father, Son, and Holy Ghost. Alleluia:
R. And praise him now and for evermore. Alleluia.

Almighty eternal God, who hast taught us to know and confess in true faith that thou art one eternal God in three Persons of equal power and glory and to be worshiped as such: We beseech thee that thou wouldst at all times keep us firm in this faith in spite of whatever opposition we may incur; who livest and reignest, world without end. Amen.

"Almighty God, who Art the Protector"

This collect is found in the *German Mass*[9] (immediately after the Kyrie) and in the older hymnals as the second of two collects after the *Te Deum*.[10] It has been made by combining the address and a phrase of the petition from the proper collect for the Third Sunday after Pentecost with the last part of the proper collect for Rogate Sunday (cf. *PE* 6, 325-328). The German text, *"Almechtiger Gott, der du bist eyn beschutzer,"* is given in WA 19, 86.

V. Lord, I shall daily praise thee:
R. And glorify thy name forever and ever.

Almighty God, who art the protector of all who trust in thee, without whose grace no one is able to do anything, or to stand

---

8 See pp. 268-270.
9 See p. 72.
10 See pp. 171-175.

before thee: Grant us richly thy mercy, that by thy holy inspiration we may think what is right and by thy power perform the same; for the sake of Jesus Christ our Lord. Amen.

"O Thou Dear Lord God"

In Klug's Wittenberg hymnal of 1533 this collect follows the 111th Psalm set to a psalm tone;[11] in other hymnals it is appended to the hymn "Let God Be Blest."[12] It is a translation of the Corpus Christi collect, *"Deus qui nobis sub sacramento mirabili"* (cf. PE 6, 356-358). The German text, *"Ah du lieber HErr Gott,"* is given in WA 35, 556.

V. As often as ye eat this bread and drink this cup:
R. Ye shall show the Lord's death till he come [I Cor. 11:26].

O thou dear Lord God, who in connection with this wonderful sacrament hast commanded us to commemorate and preach thy passion: Grant that we may so use this sacrament of thy body and blood that daily and richly we may be conscious of thy redemption. Amen.

"We Give Thanks to Thee, Almighty God"

This is the postcommunion collect which Luther appointed in his *German Mass* and which was accepted in most of the subsequent Lutheran liturgies. A direct source for this collect has not been found, but it rephrases thoughts and expressions found in older traditional Latin collects (cf. PE 6, 329-332). The German text, *"Wyr dancken dir, almechtiger herr gott, das du uns durch dise heylsame gabe,"* is given in WA 19, 102.

---

[11] See pp. 181-183.
[12] See pp. 252-254.

137

We give thanks to thee, Almighty God, that thou hast refreshed us with this thy salutary gift; and we beseech thy mercy to strengthen us through the same in faith toward thee, and in fervent love among us all; for the sake of Jesus Christ our Lord. Amen.

"Lord God, Heavenly Father, who Createst Holy Desire"

In the older Lutheran hymnals this collect follows the hymn "Grant Peace in Mercy, Lord, We Pray."[13] It is a translation of the proper collect from the *Missa pro pace: Deus a quo sancta desideria* (cf. PE 6, 358-359), whence also the versicle. The German text, *"Herr Gott hymelischer Vater, der du heiligen mut,"* is given in WA 35, 233.

V. God, grant peace in all thy land:
R. Health and peace to every rank.

Lord God, heavenly Father, who createst holy desire, good counsel, and right works: Give to thy servants peace which the world cannot give so that our hearts may cling to thy commandments, and that by thy protection we may live our days quietly and secure from our enemies; through Jesus Christ thy Son our Lord. Amen.

"Lord God, Heavenly Father, from whom Without Ceasing We Receive"

This is the first of two collects that follow Luther's versification of the *Te Deum* in the earlier Lutheran hymnals.[14] It is an original prayer by Luther (cf. PE 6, 339-341). The German text, *"Herr*

---

[13] See pp. 286-287.
[14] The second is "Almighty God, who Art the Protector"; see p. 72.

Gott himelischer vater, von dem wir onn unterlas," is given in WA
35, 249.

V. O give thanks unto the Lord, for he is good:
R. For his mercy endureth forever [I Chron. 16:34].

Lord God, heavenly Father, from whom without ceasing we
receive exceedingly abundantly all good gifts and by whom we are
guarded daily from every evil: Grant us we beseech thee by thy
Spirit that we in true faith may acknowledge this thy goodness
with our whole heart and may now and evermore thank and praise
thy loving-kindness and tender mercy; through Jesus Christ thy Son
our Lord. Amen.

"Lord God Almighty, who Dost Not Disdain"

This is the first collect in the *German Litany,*[15] 1529, and in the
Latin Litany Corrected, 1529.[16] In the older Lutheran hymnals it
is the first of two collects following the hymn "Our Father in the
Heaven who Art"[17] and is prefaced by the versicles given below. It
is a translation of the traditional collect, *"Deus qui contritorum
non despicis gemitum"* (cf. PE 6, 332-334). The German text,
"HERR Allmechtiger Gott, der du der Elenden säufftzen," is given
in WA 35, 555.

V. Ask and ye shall receive:
R. That your joy may be full [John 16:24].

or:

V. Call upon me in the day of trouble:
R. I will deliver thee, and thou shalt glorify me [Ps. 50:15].

---

[15] See p. 169.
[16] See p. 169.
[17] See pp. 295-298.

Lord God Almighty, who dost not disdain the sighs of the forlorn nor scorn the longing of troubled hearts: Behold our prayer which we bring before thee in our need and graciously hear us, so that all which striveth against us of both the devil and men may come to nought and be scattered by thy good counsel, to the end that unhurt by all temptation[18] we may thank thee in thy church and praise thee at all times; through Jesus thy Son our Lord. Amen.

"Lord God, Heavenly Father, who Hast No Pleasure"

This is the second collect in Luther's *German Litany*[19] and (after 1533) the third in his *Latin Litany Corrected.*[20] It is a free translation of the traditional collect *"Deus qui delinquentes perire non pateris"* (cf. *PE* 6, 334-336). The German text, *"Herr Gott Hymelischer Vater der du nicht lust hast,"* is given in *WA* 30[III], 35.

Lord God, heavenly Father, who hast no pleasure in the death of poor sinners and wouldst not willingly let them perish, but dost desire that they should return from their ways and live: We heartily pray thee graciously to avert the well-deserved punishment of our sins and tenderly to grant us thy mercy for our future amendment; for the sake of Jesus Christ our Lord. Amen.

"Lord God, Heavenly Father, Thou Knowest"

This is the third collect in Luther's *German Litany*[21] and (after 1533) the fourth in his *Latin Litany Corrected.*[22] In the older Lutheran hymnals it is also the second of two collects appended to the hymn "Our Father in the Heaven who Art."[23] It is a literal

---

[18] *Anfechtung.*
[19] See p. 169.
[20] See p. 169.
[21] See p. 169.
[22] See p. 169.
[23] See pp. 295-298.

translation of the traditional collect *"Omnipotens Deus, qui nos in tantis periculis"* (cf. *PE* 6, 336-337). The German text, *"Herr Gott hymelischer Vater, du weisest, das wir ynn so mancher und grosser fahr,"* is given in *WA* 30ᴵᴵᴵ, 36.

V. Lord, thou hast heard the desire of the humble:
R. Their heart is certain that thou wilt incline thine ear [Ps. 10:17].

or:

V. Before they call, I will answer:
R. And while they are yet speaking, I will hear [Isa. 65:24].

Lord God, heavenly Father, thou knowest that because of our human weakness we are not able to stand fast in so many and great dangers: Grant us strength both in body and soul, that by thy help we may overcome whatever troubles us because of our sins; for the sake of Jesus Christ our Lord. Amen.

"Almighty Everlasting God, who Through Thy Holy Spirit"

This collect was not included in the first printings of the *German Litany*[24] but appears as the fourth of the collects in Michael Blum's *Enchiridion* (Leipzig, 1529?). It entered all printings shortly thereafter and was also included in the *Latin Litany Corrected.* It is a translation of the traditional collect *"Omnipotens aeterne Deus, cuius spiritu"* (cf. *PE* 6, 338-339). The German text, *"Allmechtiger Ewiger Gott, der du durch deinen Heiligen Geist,"* is given in *WA* 30ᴵᴵᴵ, 36.

Almighty everlasting God, who through thy Holy Spirit sanctifiest and rulest the whole church: Hear our prayer and graciously grant that it with all its members, by thy grace, may serve thee in true faith; through Jesus Christ thy Son our Lord. Amen.

---

[24] See p. 170.

141

"O Almighty Eternal God, Father of Our Lord Jesus Christ, Look Upon This N."

This is the first collect in Luther's *Order of Baptism*, 1523.[25] It is a direct translation of the traditional baptismal collect, *"Omnipotens sempiterne deus, pater domini nostri Jesu Christi"* (cf. PE 6, 319-320). The German text, *"O almechtiger ewiger Gott, Vater unsers herrn Jhesu Christi, du wolltest sehew,"* is given in WA 12, 43.

O Almighty eternal God, Father of our Lord Jesus Christ, look upon this N., thy servant whom thou hast called to instruction in the faith, drive away from him all the blindness of his heart, break all the snares of the devil with which he is bound, open to him, Lord, the door of thy grace: So that marked with the sign of thy wisdom he may be free of the stench of all evil lusts and serve thee joyfully according to the sweet savor of thy commandments in thy church and grow daily and be made meet to come to the grace of thy baptism to receive the balm of life; through Christ our Lord. Amen.

"O Almighty Eternal God, Father of Our Lord Jesus Christ, I Cry to Thee"

In Luther's *Order of Baptism Newly Revised*, 1526, this is the first collect.[26] With a slightly different invocation ("O God, immortal Comfort of all who ask") (PE 6, 320-321), it forms the second collect in his earlier *Order of Baptism*, 1523.[27] The German text, *"O Almechtiger Ewiger Gott, vater unsers herrn Jhesu Christi ich ruf dich an,"* is given in WA 19, 539. We give the text in the later version of 1526 with variants of the earlier wording noted in the footnotes.

---

[25] See p. 96.
[26] See p. 107.
[27] See p. 96.

O Almighty eternal God, Father of our Lord Jesus Christ,[28] I cry to thee for this N., thy servant, who prays for the gift of thy baptism and desires thine eternal grace through spiritual regeneration: Receive him, Lord, and as thou hast said, "Ask and ye shall receive, seek and ye shall find, knock and it shall be opened unto you," so give now the good[29] to him that asketh and open the door to him that knocketh: so that he may obtain the eternal blessing of this heavenly bath and receive the promised kingdom of thy grace; through Christ our Lord. Amen.

"Almighty Eternal God, who According to Thy Righteous Judgment"

This collect is the third in Luther's *Order of Baptism*, 1523[30] and the second in the *Order of Baptism Newly Revised*, 1526.[31] In the absence of a comparable prayer in the Roman rite, we must consider it original with Luther (cf. however *PE* 6, 321-324). The German text, *"Almechtiger Ewiger Gott, der du hast durch die sindflutt,"* is given in *WA* 12, 43-44.

Almighty eternal God, who according to thy righteous judgment didst condemn the unbelieving world through the flood and in thy great mercy didst preserve believing Noah and his family, and who didst drown hardhearted Pharaoh with all his host in the Red Sea and didst lead thy people Israel through the same on dry ground, thereby prefiguring this bath of thy baptism, and who through the baptism of thy dear Child, our Lord Jesus Christ, hast consecrated and set apart the Jordan and all water as a salutary flood and a rich and full washing away of sins: We pray through the same thy groundless mercy that thou wilt graciously behold

---

[28] Version of 1523 reads, "O God, immortal Comfort of all who ask, Savior of all who cry to thee, and Peace of all who pray to thee, Life of the believers, Resurrection of the dead, I cry to thee," etc.
[29] Version of 1523 reads, "reward."
[30] See p. 97.
[31] See p. 107.

this N. and bless him with true faith in the spirit so that by means of this saving flood all that has been born in him from Adam and which he himself has added thereto may be drowned in him and engulfed, and that he may be sundered from the number of the unbelieving, preserved dry and secure in the holy ark of Christendom, serve thy name at all times fervent in spirit and joyful in hope, so that with all believers he may be made worthy to attain eternal life according to thy promise; through Jesus Christ our Lord. Amen.

"Lord, Holy Father, Almighty Eternal God"

This is the fourth collect in Luther's *Order of Baptism*, 1523.[32] It is a translation of the traditional baptismal collect *"Eternam ac mitissimam pietatem"* (cf. PE 6, 324-325). The German text, *"Herr heyliger vater, almechtiger ewiger Got,"* is given in WA 12, 44.

Lord, holy Father, almighty eternal God from whom cometh all the light of truth, we beseech thine eternal and most tender goodness that thou wilt shed thy blessing upon this N., thy servant, and enlighten him with the light of thy knowledge, cleanse and sanctify him, and give him right understanding: that he be made worthy to come to the grace of thy baptism, that he may hold fast to a sure hope, true counsel, and holy teaching, and be made meet for the grace of thy baptism; through Jesus Christ our Lord. Amen.

"O God, who Hast Created Man and Woman"

This is the final collect in Luther's *Order of Marriage*, 1529.[33] It is quite possibly an original Luther collect, although it contains remi-

---

[32] See p. 98.
[33] See p. 115.

144

niscences of current older prayer forms (cf. *PE* 6, 341-342). The German text, *"HERRE Gott, der du man und weib geschaffen,"* is given in *WA* 30^{III}, 80.

O God, who hast created man and woman and hast ordained them for the married estate, hast blessed them also with fruits of the womb, and hast typified therein the sacramental union[34] of thy dear Son, the Lord Jesus Christ, and the church, his bride: We beseech thy boundless goodness and mercy that thou wouldst not permit this thy creation, ordinance, and blessing to be disturbed or destroyed, but graciously preserve the same; through Jesus Christ our Lord. Amen.

"Merciful God, Heavenly Father, Thou Hast Said to Us"

This is the final collect in Luther's *Ordination of Ministers of the Word*, 1539.[35] It is to be considered original (cf. *PE* 6, 360). The German text, *"Barmhertziger Gott, Himlischer Vater, Du hast durch den mund,"* is given in *WA* 38, 429.

Merciful God, heavenly Father, thou hast said to us through the mouth of thy dear Son our Lord Jesus Christ: "The harvest truly is plenteous, but the laborers are few. Pray ye therefore the Lord of the harvest, that he will send forth laborers into his harvest" [Matt. 9:37-38]. Upon this thy divine command, we pray heartily that thou wouldst grant thy Holy Spirit richly to these thy servants, to us, and to all those who are called to serve thy Word so that the company of us who publish the good tidings may be great,[36] and that we may stand faithful and firm against the devil, the world, and the flesh, to the end that thy name may be hallowed, thy kingdom grow, and thy will be done. Be also pleased at length to check and stop the detestable abomination of the pope,

[34] See p. 115, n. 3.
[35] See p. 126.
[36] Cf. Ps. 68:11.

Mohammed, and other sects which blaspheme thy name, hinder thy kingdom, and oppose thy will. Graciously hear this our prayer, since thou hast so commanded, taught, and promised, even as we believe and trust through thy dear Son Jesus Christ our Lord, who liveth and reigneth with thee and the Holy Ghost, world without end. Amen.

THE LITURGICAL CHANTS

INTRODUCTION

Luther's contribution to hymnody is so significant and far reaching in its effects that it has tended to overshadow his interest in the chant. His hymns were readily accepted everywhere. They were translated into countless languages and became known and loved the world over. His chants remained largely unknown outside of Germany (though his principles of pointing influenced Archbishop Cranmer and John Merbecke),[1] and some of them passed from use by the end of the sixteenth century. Viewed from the present, his hymns seem to point forward, while his chants appear as relics of the past. But Luther himself would have felt no such distinction. Both in his hymns and in his chants he neither disdained the use of older traditional materials nor shrank from revolutionary changes in the interest of German speech rhythm and popular appeal. For he wanted hymns and chants to be sung by the congregation as well as by the choir. Actually, the difference in musical style between these two forms was much smaller than it is today; for the chorales with their modal tonality and floating rhythm were much closer to plain chant than are modern hymns,[2] while the chants with their extended intonations and mediations were more syllabic and melodious than proper Gregorian psalmody.[3] Indeed, some items, such as the Gloria in Excelsis, Sanctus, Agnus Dei, or *Te Deum*, could be classified either as chants or as hymns. But it was this basic simplicity and folklike character of Luther's chants that made it possible for the congregation actively to participate in the liturgy. The general principles he established deserve the attention

---

[1] Both Cranmer in his *Litany* of 1544 and Merbecke in his *Book of Common Prayer Noted* of 1550 followed Luther in the elimination of melisms and the reduction of plain chant to a syllabic style. See in this volume, pp. 53-60; Winfred Douglas, *Church Music in History and Practice* (New York: Scribner's, 1937), pp. 79-81, 124; J. Eric Hunt, *Cranmer's First Litany, 1544, and Merbecke's Book of Common Prayer Noted, 1550* (London: S. P. C. K., 1939).
[2] See p. 198.
[3] See pp. 55-56.

of anyone who would have the laity share in liturgical chant. On the following pages we offer all of Luther's liturgical chants for the congregation, except those from his *German Mass,* which can be found there.[4]

---

[4] For the introit psalm, see pp. 70-71; for the Kyrie eleison, see p. 72; for the Sanctus, see pp. 82-83.

The Agnus Dei

1528

Translated by Ulrich S. Leupold

Among the hymns that Luther in his *German Mass* of 1526[1] recommended for singing during the administration of the holy communion is the "German Agnus Dei." Since Nicholas Decius' paraphrase of the same liturgical chant, "*O Lamm Gottes unschuldig*,"[2] did not appear until 1531, Luther probably had the hymn "*Christe, du Lamm Gottes*" in mind. The earliest source for this hymn is a Braunschweig church order of 1528,[3] but it may have been known in Wittenberg a few years earlier. Luther's good friend and colaborer Johann Bugenhagen was the author of the Braunschweig church order, and it was printed in Wittenberg. In fact, it is not unlikely that Luther himself had a hand in arranging this hymn, for its melody is strongly reminiscent of the Kyrie in the *German Mass*.[4] Our edition follows the facsimile rendition of the Braunschweig print, *Christe du lam Gades*, in Ameln's *Handbuch der deutschen evangelischen Kirchenmusik*, I, 580.

---

[1] See pp. 81-82.
[2] Cf. Amlen *et al.* (eds.), *Handbuch der deutschen evangelischen Kirchenmusik*, I, 64; for an English translation, see the *Service Book and Hymnal of the Lutheran Church in America* (1958), No. 70.
[3] *Der Erbarn Stadt Brunswig Christlike ordeninge.*
[4] See p. 72.

The Agnus Dei

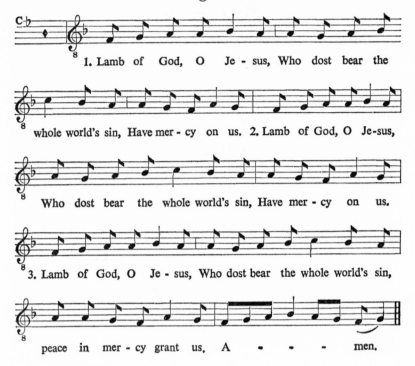

1. Lamb of God, O Je - sus, Who dost bear the whole world's sin, Have mer - cy on us. 2. Lamb of God, O Je-sus, Who dost bear the whole world's sin, Have mer - cy on us. 3. Lamb of God, O Je - sus, Who dost bear the whole world's sin, peace in mer - cy grant us. A - - - men.

The German Litany

and

The Latin Litany Corrected

1529

Translated by Paul Zeller Strodach
Revised by Ulrich S. Leupold

Luther had a deep appreciation for the Litany. Of course, he rejected the invocation of the saints that had become a part of it, and he wanted to have the Litany sung in the church rather than at processions, but as early as 1519 he expressed his approval of it.[1] During the reforms in Wittenberg under Karlstadt, 1521/22, it seems to have fallen into disuse. But the national emergency created when the Turks threatened the faith and freedom of all Christian lands prompted Luther to revive it. In his *On War Against the Turks*, begun in October, 1528, he insisted on the importance of believing prayer. "This might help if at Matins, Vespers, or after the sermon, we had the Litany sung or read in the church, especially by the young folk."[2] And shortly after, on February 13, 1529, he could report to Nicholas Hausmann, "We sing the Litany in church in Latin and in the vernacular; perhaps the music or melody of both versions will be published."[3] The same year saw the fulfilment of this promise. One month later he sent the first print of the *German Litany* with music to Hausmann. The accompanying letter referred to the fact that the *Latin Litany Corrected* had not yet been published,[4] but this too followed before the end of the summer.

Luther's Litanies with their appended collects are closely modeled after the *Roman Litany of All Saints*.[5] Nevertheless, there are significant differences between them:

---

[1] WA 2, 177-179.
[2] WA 30ᶦᶦ, 119.
[3] WA, Br 5, No. 1381, p. 17.
[4] WA, Br 5, No. 1395, p. 38.
Cf. *Graduale Romanum* (Düsseldorf: L. Schwann, 1921), pp. 250-253.

1. Luther omitted the invocations of the saints and the intercession for the pope and the departed.

2. Luther made the intercessions more specific than in the Roman form, as, e.g., in the petitions for faithful pastors, for the erring, for faithful laborers, etc.[6]

3. Luther simplified the music, especially for the responses.

Luther's two versions of the Litany are nearly the same, except for the following differences:

1. The *Latin Litany Corrected* has six more obsecrations than the German one.

2. The music of the *Latin Litany Corrected* derives from the traditional tune of the *Litany of All Saints*. The music of the *German Litany* is original with Luther.

3. The versicles and collects are not in the same order, and later editions of the *Latin Litany Corrected* have one additional collect.

Concerning the music of the Litanies, the following ought to be noted:

1. The original prints use semibreves, breves, and longas (for final notes) on a four-line staff with a C clef. Our edition substitutes eighth notes for the semibreves and quarter notes for the breves and longas. The reader should note the long notes on the Agnus Dei in the *German Litany*.

2. The prints of the *German Litany* can be divided into two groups.[7] The first, of which Blum's hymnal of 1529(?) is the earliest example, begins most of the responses on *a*. The second, of which the *Enchiridion*, Wittenberg, 1529, is the earliest extant print, has an *f* in the same place. WA 30^{III}, 29-34, offers the latter version. But since it is melodically more interesting, our edition is based on the former, following the reprint in Ameln's *Handbuch der deutschen evangelischen Kirchenmusik*, I[1], 415-417.

---

[6] For a complete table comparing Luther's Litanies with different Roman orders, cf. *PE* 6, 249-260.

[7] Cf. Christhard Mahrenholz, *"Zur musikalischen Gestaltung von Luthers deutscher Litanei," Musicologica et Liturgica*, pp. 169-195.

3. As indicated in the original texts, the Litany was supposed to be sung antiphonally by two choirs. The first choir was often made up of cantors or choir boys kneeling on the altar steps, the second by the choir whom the congregation could join. It should be noted that every petition was responded to; the modern practice of repeating a whole group of preces before the response is sung was unknown in Reformation times.

In this edition we offer first the *Latin Litany Corrected* without its collects, then the *German Litany* with the collects, giving in the notes the Latin variations from the German collects.

The German and Latin texts, *Die deudsch Litaney* and *Latina Litania correcta*, are given in *WA* 30^{III}, 29-42; the following translation is a revision of P. Z. Strodach's translation in *PE* 6, 262-266; 269-273.

The Latin Litany Corrected

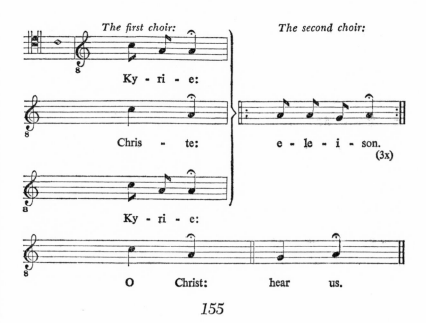

The first choir:

O God, the Fa -	ther	in	heav-	en: ⎫
O God, the Son, Redeem-		er	of	the world: ⎬
O God,		the	Ho -	ly Ghost: ⎭

Be gra -		cious	un - to	us: ⎫
Be gra -		cious	un - to	us: ⎬

From		ever -	y	sin: ⎫
From ever -		y	er -	ror: ⎬
From ever -		y	e -	vil: ⎭

From the snares	of	the	dev -	il: ⎫
From sudden and un -		ex -	pect - ed	death:
From plague		and	fam -	ine:
From war		and	blood-	shed: ⎬
From sedi -	tion	and	dis -	cord:
From light -	ning	and	tem -	pest:
From e -		ter -	nal	death: ⎭

By the mystery of the ho-	ly	in - car -	na -	tion: ⎫
By thy ho -	ly	na -	tiv -	ity:
By thy baptism, fast -	ing, and temp -		ta -	tion:
By thine ag -	ony	and	blood - y	sweat: ⎬
By thy cross		and	pas -	sion:
By thy death		and	bur -	ial:
By thy resurrec -	tion and	as -	cen -	sion:
By the advent of the Ho -		ly	Par -	aclete: ⎭

In all time of	our trib - u -		la -	tion: ⎫
In all time of	our	pros -	per -	ity: ⎬
In		the	hour	of death:
In the day		of	judg -	ment: ⎭

We sin -		ners:		

The second choir:

Have mer-　cy　up-　on us.
　　　　　　　　(3x)

Spare us,　　　good　　Lord.
　　　　　　　　　(2x)

Free us,　　　good　　Lord.
　　　　　　　　(3x)

Free us,　　　good　　Lord.
　　　　　　　　(7x)

Free us,　　　good　　Lord.
　　　　　　　　(8x)

Free us,　　　good　　Lord.
　　　　　　　　(4x)

Entreat　　thee　to　hear us.

157

The first choir:

That thou wouldst deign
to rule and govern
thy ho -   ly   cath - o - lic   church:
That thou wouldst deign
to preserve all bis -
hops, pastors, and
ministers of the
church in sound
word   and   ho - ly   life:
That thou wouldst deign
to remove all sects
and all   of -   fens-   es:
That thou wouldst deign
to lead back the err -
ing and deceived into the   way of truth:
That thou wouldst deign
to trample Satan un - der   our   feet:
That thou wouldst deign
to send faithful la -
borers in - to   thy   har -   vest:
That thou wouldst deign
to grant to all hearers
increase in the word
and in the fruit of the   Spir-   it:
That thou wouldst deign
to lift up the lapsed
and to strength - en   those who stand:
That thou wouldst deign
to encourage and as-
sist the tim - id and the tempt - ed:
That thou wouldst deign
to give peace and
concord to all kings and   princ- es:
That thou wouldst deign
to give to our emper-
or perpetual victory o - ver his en - emies:
That thou wouldst deign
to direct and protect
our ruler and   his   coun- selors:

The second choir:

We entreat   thee   to   hear us.

(12x)

The first choir:

That thou wouldst deign to bless and protect our magistrates	and	peo-	ple:
That thou wouldst deign to regard and deliver the afflicted and those	in	dan-	ger:
That thou wouldst deign to grant a safe deliv - ery to pregnant moth - ers and healthy ba - bies to	those	who	give suck:
That thou wouldst deign to cherish and guard the in -	fants	and the	sick:
That thou wouldst deign to liberate	the	cap-	tives:
That thou wouldst deign to protect and pro - vide for the or - phans	and	wid-	ows:
That thou wouldst deign to take pit - y	on	all	men:
That thou wouldst deign to forgive our ene - mies, persecutors, and slanderers and to	con-	vert	them:
That thou wouldst deign to give and preserve the fruits	of	the	earth:
That thou wouldst deign	to	hear	us:

The second choir:

We entreat   thee   to   hear us.
(10x)

161

The first choir: *The second choir:*

Lamb of God who bearest the sin of the world: Have mer-cy up-on us.

Lamb of God who bearest the sin of the world: Have mer-cy up-on us.

Lamb of God who bearest the sin of the world: Grant   us thy peace.

O   Christ: Hear us.

Ky - ri - e: e - le - i - son.

Christ - e: e - le - i - son.

Ky - ri - e   e - le - i - son.   A - - - - men.

162

The German Litany

The first choir:

Ky - ri - e:

Chris - te:

Ky - ri - e:

The second choir:

e - le - i - son. (3x)

O Christ: Hear   us.

The first choir:

Lord God,   Fa - ther   in   heav - en:
Lord God, Son, Re - deem - er   of   the   world:
Lord   God, Ho - ly   Ghost:

The second choir:

Have   mer - cy   up - on   us. (3x)

The first choir: The second choir:

Be   gra - cious   un - to   us: Spare us, good Lord.
Be   gra - cious   un - to   us: Help   us, good Lord.

From all   sins:
From all   er - ror: Good Lord, de - liv - er   us. (3x)
From all   e - vil:

163

The first choir:

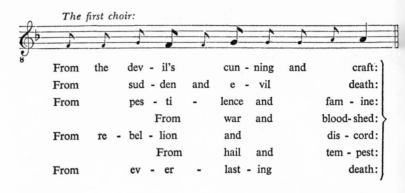

From	the	dev - il's		cun - ning	and	craft:
From		sud - den	and	e - vil		death:
From		pes - ti -		lence	and	fam - ine:
		From		war	and	blood- shed:
From	re -	bel - lion		and		dis - cord:
		From		hail	and	tem - pest:
From		ev - er -		last - ing		death:

By thy	ho -	ly	na - tiv - i - ty:
By thine	ag - o - ny	and blood - y	sweat:
	By	thy cross and	death:
By thy holy resur - rec -		tion and as -	cen - sion:
	In	our fi - nal	need:
	At	the last	judg-ment:

We poor sinners do	be - seech	thee:
And to rule and govern thy ho -	ly Chris -	tian church:
To preserve all bishops, pastors, and ministers of the church in the sound word and	ho - ly	life:
To curb all schisms and	of - fens -	es:
To restore the err -	ing and	mis - led:
To trample Satan un -	der our	feet:
To send faithful laborers into	thy har -	vest:
To accompany the Word with thy Spirit	and pow -	er:
To comfort and help the weakhearted and the	dis - tress -	ed:
To give to all kings and princes peace	and con -	cord:
To grant to our emperor perpetual victory over all	his en -	e - mies:

164

The second choir:

Good Lord, de - liv - er   us. (7x)

Help   us,   good Lord. (6x)

Thou wouldst hear   us, good Lord. (1x)

Hear   us,   good Lord. (10x)

165

The first choir:

To direct and defend our sovereign and all	his	coun -	sel - ors:
To bless and keep our magis -	trates	and	peo - ple:
To behold and succor all who are in danger and trib -	u -	la -	tion:
To rejoice the pregnant in the fruit of their womb and nursing mothers in the growth of	their	chil -	dren:
To cherish and guard all the sick	and	in -	fants:
To set free all	the	cap -	tives:
To defend and provide for all widows	and	or -	phans:
To take pity	on	all	men:
To forgive our enemies, persecutors, and slanderers, and to	con -	vert	them:
To give and preserve the fruits	of	the	earth:
And graciously	to	hear	us:

The second choir:

Hear   us,   good Lord. (11x)

The first choir: *The second choir:*

O Je - sus Christ, Son of God: Hear us, good Lord.

The first choir:

O Lamb of God who bar - est the sin of the world: (3x)

The second choir:

Have	mer - cy	up - on	us.
Have	mer - cy	up - on	us.
Grant	us	thy	peace.

The first choir: *The second choir:*

O Christ: Hear us.

Ky - ri - e: e - le - i - son.

Chris - te: e - le - i - son.

Both choirs together:

Ky - ri - e e - le - i - son. A - - men.

A Prayer upon the Litany[1]

V. Lord, deal not with us after our sins:

R. And reward us not according to our iniquities [Ps. 103:10].

or:[2]

---

[1] The *Latin Litany Corrected* prescribes the Lord's Prayer before the collects.
[2] In the *Latin Litany Corrected* this versicle is omitted here and used with the collect "Lord God, Heavenly Father, who Hast No Pleasure."

V. We have sinned with our fathers:

R. We have committed iniquity, we have done wickedly [Ps. 106:6].

Lord God Almighty, who dost not disdain the sighs of the forlorn nor scorn the longing of troubled hearts: Behold our prayer which we bring before thee in our need and graciously hear us, so that all which striveth against us of both the devil and men may come to nought and be scattered by thy good counsel, to the end that unhurt by all temptation[3] we may thank thee in thy church and praise thee at all times; through Jesus thy Son our Lord. Amen.

Another Prayer

V. The Lord's anger endureth but a moment:

R. And he taketh pleasure in life [Ps. 30:5].

or:

V. Call upon me, saith the Lord, in the day of trouble:

R. I will deliver thee, and thou shalt glorify me [Ps. 50:15].

Lord God, heavenly Father, who hast no pleasure in the death of poor sinners and wouldst not willingly let them perish, but dost desire that they should return from their ways and live: We heartily pray thee graciously to avert the well-deserved punishment of our sins and tenderly to grant us thy mercy for our future amendment; for the sake of Jesus Christ our Lord. Amen.[4]

Another Prayer

V. Lord, enter not into judgment with thy servant:

R. For in thy sight shall no man living be justified [Ps. 143:2].

Lord God, heavenly Father, thou knowest that because of our human weakness we are not able to stand fast in so many and great dangers: Grant us strength both in body and soul, that by thy help we may overcome whatever troubles us because of our sins; for the sake of Jesus Christ our Lord. Amen.

---

[3] *Anfechtung.*

[4] In the *Latin Litany Corrected* this collect uses the second versicle for the preceding collect.

169

Another Prayer[5]

V. Help us, O God of our salvation, for the glory of thy name:

R. Deliver us, and forgive us our sins, for thy name's sake [Ps. 79:9].

Almighty everlasting God, who through thy Holy Spirit sancti- fiest and rulest the whole church: Hear our prayer and graciously grant that it with all its members, by thy grace, may serve thee in true faith; through Jesus Christ thy Son our Lord. Amen.

Another:[6]

V. Call upon me in the day of trouble:

R. I will deliver thee, and thou shalt glorify me [Ps. 50:15]

Spare us Lord, spare us sinners, and although our increasing sins deserve continual punishment, be present, we pray thee, so that what we deserve to our eternal destruction may pass from us to aid in our correction. Through the Lord, etc.

---

[5] From 1533 on this is the second versicle and c   in the *Latin Litany Corrected.*
[6] This collect with its versicle appears only in the *Latin Litany Corrected* and not in the *German Litany.*

The Te Deum

1529?

Translation Composite

The *Te Deum* is one of the grandest hymns of Christendom. It combines a confession of faith with a song of praise and a prayer for help. Its beginnings go back to the first centuries of the Christian church. At one time it was credited to Ambrose and Augustine, supposedly improvised by them at Augustine's baptism. Modern research, however, suggests that it was not "composed" by a single author, but rather grew from many traditional strands, though possibly it received its final form from Nicetas, bishop of Remesiana in what is now Yugoslavia), a contemporary of Jerome. At any rate, the *Te Deum* was tremendously popular in the Middle Ages. It was regularly sung at Matins and at innumerable other occasions, such as the election of a pope, consecration of a bishop, coronation of a king, or the conclusion of a council. The saying went, "The church sings this hymn whenever she has been favored by God with a great blessing."[1]

Luther loved the *Te Deum*. In his book *The Three Symbols or Creeds of the Christian Faith,* 1538, he named the *Te Deum* in third place after the Apostles' Creed and Athanasian Creed and said: "The third symbol is said to be of SS. Augustine and Ambrose, and is supposed to have been sung at the baptism of Augustine. Whether that is true or not—and it does no harm whether one believes it or not—it is nevertheless a fine symbol or creed whoever the author) composed in the form of a chant, not only for the purpose of confessing the true faith, but also for praising and thanking God."[2]

In the same book he offered a prose translation of the *Te Deum*. But almost ten years earlier he had published a rimed paraphrase of the *Te Deum*. The earliest extant print of this version is in the Andrew Rauscher hymnal of 1531. Since Rauscher

---

Cf. Schlisske, *Handbuch der Lutherlieder,* p. 183.
LW 34, 202.

reprinted Klug's 1529 hymnal, it was probably the first hymnal to publish Luther's *Te Deum.*

Not that Luther's translation was the first. Several prose translations had been made during the Middle Ages, and a rimed version had appeared only a few years before Luther's. It is found in a Low-German prayer book published in 1536 by Ludwig Dietz in Rostock.

But here as elsewhere Luther proved more original and creative than any of his predecessors. Instead of clinging slavishly to the expressions of the Latin text, he recast the substance of the original in the new mold of a rimed chant for the people. Luther also recast the music. Doubtlessly the syllabic simplification of a florid Latin chant is Luther's own work, and the bold steps of the strongly Phrygian melody give almost more forceful expression to the archaic grandeur of the ancient canticle than the original plainchant melody.

The canticle consists of five stanzas, each with its own melodic pattern. The first stanza, having five verses and a concluding verse for both choirs, is the angelic song of praise, culminating in the *Ter Sanctus.* The second stanza, with six verses, adds praise of the Trinity by the apostles, prophets, martyrs, and all Christians. The third stanza, with five verses, is a confession of faith in Christ. The fourth stanza, with four verses, contains the prayer for salvation. The fifth stanza, again with five verses, returns to the melody of the first and contains petitions for the Christian life. It will be observed that the first, third, and fifth stanzas have the same number of verses. The first and last stanzas have an additional line to be sung by both choirs together. The fourth stanza begins and the fifth ends with a verse in half notes. The third stanza forms, as it were, the heart of the whole, with its confession of Christ preceded by praise and followed by prayer. And here again the verse on the incarnation forms the center of the whole; for it is both preceded and followed by twelve complete verses.

Luther wanted the two groups singing the *Te Deum* to alternate half-verse by half-verse instead of verse by verse as done in other antiphonal chants (e.g., the Gloria). This does not mean that two actual choirs were to sing the *Te Deum.* The Wittenberg church order of 1533 prescribes: "After the hymn let the choir intone the *Te Deum laudamus,* in Dr. Martin's German translation, and let one of the choristers in the schoolboys' pew[3] answer with the congregation at the half-verses. For the start he may also take a few boys into the pew to help him, until the congregation gets accustomed to singing along in this *Te Deum.*"[4] In other words, the first half-verse was to be sung by the choir, and the second by the congregation (reinforced by a few choir members).[5]

Luther's German *Te Deum* became as popular in the Lutheran church as the Latin version had been before. It was sung not only at Matins but also in the service for festival days, such as St. Michael's, All Saints', and Thanksgiving, and for occasional services such as confirmation and marriage.

The German text, *Herr Gott, dich loben wir,* is given in *WA* 35, 458-459. Our translation is a composite. Some verses are taken from the translation by George MacDonald in *Exotics* (London: Strahan, 1876), pp. 112-114, and others from the translation by Richard Massie in *Martin Luther's Spiritual Songs,* pp. 86-88.

WA 35, 521-524, offers the music following Klug 1535. We have chosen to follow the version of Babst 1545, given in Zahn, *Die Melodien der deutschen evangelischen Kirchenlieder,* V, No. 8562, which seems rhythmically a little more felicitous and has been generally accepted in modern hymnals. It was originally in mensural notation.

---

[3] The German word *Schülerstuhl* could also refer to the choir seats in the chancel, but in this context it seems to refer to a pew right in the nave where the chorister (i.e., one of the older choir members) and the boys would be able to help the singing of the congregation more effectively.

[4] This practice of infiltrating the congregation with a few choristers in order to teach the congregation new hymns and chants was quite common in the Reformation period.

[5] E. Sehling, *Die evangelischen Kirchenordnungen des XVI. Jahrhunderts,* I (Leipzig, 1902), 705; quoted in *WA* 35, 521, n. 1.

The Te Deum

The first choir: *The second choir:*

Lord God, thy praise we sing: Lord God, our thanks we bring.

Fa - ther in e - ter - ni - ty: all the world wor-ships thee.

An - gels and all heav'n-ly host: of thy glo - ry loud - ly boast.

Both cher - u - bim and ser - a-phim: sing ev - er with loud voice this hymn:

Ho - ly art thou, our God: ho - ly art thou, our God,

Both choirs together:

Ho - ly art thou, our God, the Lord of Sab - a - oth.

Thy god-like might and lord-ship go: wide o - ver heav'n and earth be-low.
The twelve a - pos - tles join in song: with the dear proph-ets' good-ly throng.
The mar-tyrs' no - ble ar - my raise: their voice to thee in hymns of praise.
All Chris-ten-dom with one ac-cord: ex-alt and praise their com-mon Lord.
Thee, God Fa-ther in heav-en's throne: and thine on - ly be-got-ten Son,
Al - so the Ho - ly Par - a - clete: we ev - er laud with prais-es meet.

O King of Glo-ry, thee we own: thou art the Fa-ther's on - ly Son.
Thou didst not spurn the vir-gin's womb: to save man-kind from sin and doom.
Thou on the might of death didst tread: and Chris-tians all to heav'n hast led.
Thou sit - test at thy Fa-ther's right: e - qual to him in pow'r and might.
To earth thou shalt re - turn a - gain: in maj - es - ty to judge all men.

174

Now come, Lord, to thy serv-ants' aid: who by thy blood thine own were made.

Let us in heav-en have our dole: and with the ho-ly e'er be whole.

Thy folk, Lord Je-sus Christ, ad-vance: and bless thine own in-her-it-ance.

Them watch and ward, Lord, ev'ry day: e-ter-nal-ly them raise, we pray.

Dai-ly, Lord God, we hon-or thee: and praise thy name con-tin-ual-ly.

Vouch-safe, O Lord, we hum-bly pray: to keep us safe from sin this day.
O   Lord, have mer-cy on us all: have mer-cy on us when we call.
Let shine on us, O God, thy face: our on-ly hope is in thy grace.

Our trust, O Lord, is all in thee: O let us ne'er con-found-ed be.

Both choirs together:

A - - - - - men.

175

The Magnificat
1533

Of the earlier Lutheran hymnals, Joseph Klug's Wittenberg hymnal of 1533 with its later editions and Valentin Babst's Leipzig hymnal of 1545 offer a wide variety of canticles from the Old and New Testaments, set to simple psalm tones. In Klug's hymnal, the fifth and last section begins with the following words:

"For a good example we have incorporated in this book the canticles from Holy Scripture which the patriarchs and prophets of old have made and sung, in order to show that we are no innovators, but have the example of all the saints on our side. For every Christian will be able to see that they—even as we—glorify only the grace of God and not the work of men. And of course no one would dare to condemn them, even though their example is no more respected than ours.

"But [we offer these canticles] mostly because we would want to have them sung with due sincerity and attention, i.e., with heart and mind, not as in the chapters and convents where they are made a fetish with such howling and bawling that no one can understand a thing. Of course, the people do not even want or try to understand them, let alone sing them with devotion and profit. Wherefore God is also angered rather than pleased."[1]

Following this introduction, Klug offers eleven Old Testament canticles, the 117th Psalm, and three New Testament canticles, set to simple psalm tones, mostly in *faux bourdon*. None of these show any distinctive features, except the Magnificat. Here is the only version of the *tonus peregrinus* in which the ligatures at the beginning of the first and second half-verse have been divided into two separate notes with their own syllables so as to provide a more melodious contour. In the light of Luther's other chants, it seems quite likely that the Reformer himself pointed this canticle, possibly also providing the following preface:

"First, she sings with a joyous heart of the grace and bless-

---

[1] Klug 1533, fols. 132b-133a.

ing which the merciful God had shown to her, praising and thanking him for it.

Second, she sings of the blessing and great and wonderful work which God continually does for all men in all the world, namely, that he takes mercy on the miserable and meek, that he raises the lowly and enriches the poor. Again, that he puts to nought the wisdom of the proud and arrogant, that he puts down the mighty who rely on their power and might, and that he turns rich men into beggars.

Third, she sings of the proper and highest work, namely, that God has visited and redeemed Israel through his only Son Jesus Christ."[2]

Klug's hymnal gives only the first verse with the music. The following arrangement is an attempt to set the whole Magnificat to this version of the *tonus peregrinus*. It will be noted that Luther here (as do most other early Lutheran sources) follows the so-called German chorale dialect when he substitutes *c* for *b*-flat in the intonations. The harmonization may be by either Luther or Johann Walter.

Our edition follows Ameln's facsimile edition of Klug's Wittenberg hymnal of 1533[3] (Konrad Ameln [ed.], Kassel: Bärenreiter Verlag, 1954), fols. 171v-172r. The original title is *Der lobesang Marie das Magnificat*.

---

[2] *Ibid.*, fols. 170a-170b. Luther also wrote a detailed commentary on the Magnificat; see *LW* 21, 297-358.
[3] This hymnal was originally entitled *Geistliche lieder auffs new gebessert zu Wittemberg. D. Mart. Luth. XXXiij.*

[Intonation]   [Recitation]   [Mediation]

[1] My   soul   doth   mag - ni - fy   the Lord:

[2] For he hath re - gard- ed the low
                              estate of   his   hand-   maid - en:

[3] For he that is might- y hath   done .to me   great things:

[4] And his   mer-   cy is on   them that   fear him:

[5] He   hath showed   strength with   his   arm:

[6] He hath put   down the   might - y from   their seats:

[7] He hath   fill - ed the   hun - gry with   good things:

[8] He hath   hol - pen his serv-
                              ant Israel in
                              remem -
                              brance of   his   mer - cy:

[9] Glory be   to   the   Fa - ther and to the Son:

[10] As it was in the
      be - gin - ning, is now,
                              and   ev -   er   shall be:

178

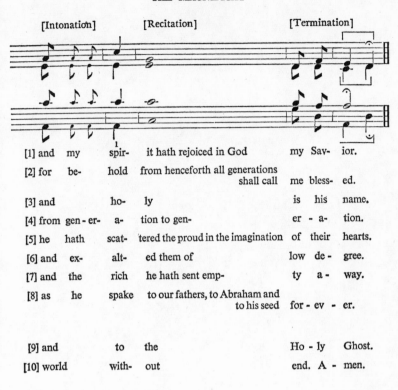

[Intonation]   [Recitation]   [Termination]

[1] and   my   spir-   it hath rejoiced in God   my   Sav-   ior.

[2] for   be-   hold   from henceforth all generations
                                              shall call   me bless- ed.

[3] and   ho-   ly   is   his   name.

[4] from gen - er- a-   tion to gen-   er - a-   tion.

[5] he   hath   scat- tered the proud in the imagination of their hearts.

[6] and   ex-   alt-   ed them of   low de - gree.

[7] and   the   rich   he hath sent emp-   ty   a -   way.

[8] as   he   spake to our fathers, to Abraham and
                                              to his seed   for - ev - er.

[9] and   to   the   Ho - ly   Ghost.

[10] world   with- out   end. A - men.

The Communio

1533

Klug's Wittenberg hymnal of 1533 in its section of communion hymns offers also the 111th Psalm arranged "to be sung during the distribution of the sacrament." It is set to the first psalm tone in its solemn form (psalmody of the mass). While Luther's name does not appear with it, several facts seem to indicate that he selected and pointed this Psalm for holy communion. This is the Psalm quoted most frequently in his discussions of the Lord's Supper, for he translated the fourth verse, "He hath instituted a memorial of his wonders," and found in it a direct reference to the dominical words, "This do in remembrance of me." It was therefore no more than logical that he should appoint the 111th Psalm as a *communio*, even as in the *German Mass* he had substituted the 34th Psalm for the introit.[1] Furthermore, the style of pointing is as free as in the introit Psalm of the *German Mass*. Here as there, the intonation, mediation, and termination are given rhythmical stress and melodic emphasis at the expense of the reciting note.

In the original hymnal the whole Psalm is printed verse by verse with its music. In our edition all the verses have been arranged under one line of music to show more clearly the musical pattern that Luther used. As in the introit for the *German Mass*, we are using a whole note for the recitation, eighth notes for the punctum, quarter notes for the distropha, and small eighth notes for optional notes that are needed in some but not in all verses.[2]

This Psalm is not found in *WA* or *PE*. Our edition follows Ameln's facsimile edition of Klug's hymnal of 1533,[3] fols. 30v-34r. The original title is *Der cxj Psalm zusingen wenn man das Sacrament empfehet.*

---

[1] See pp. 70-71.
[2] See pp. 57-58.
[3] Cf. Philipp Wackernagel, *Bibliographie zur Geschichte des deutschen Kirchenliedes im XVI. Jahrhundert.* (Frankfurt-am-Main, 1855), p. 123, No. 315.

The Communio

[Recitation]   [Mediation]

[1] I will	praise	the	Lord	with my	whole		heart:
[2] The	works			of the Lord	are		great:
[3] Full of	hon-	or and	maj-	es - ty is	his		work:
[4] He hath made							
his	won-	der-ful	works	to be re-	mem-		bered:
[5] He hath giv-en	meat	un-to	them	that	fear		him:
[6] He hath	showed	his peo-ple					
		the	pow-	er of	his		works:
[7] The works of his	hands	are	ver-	i - ty	and	judg-	ment:
[8] They stand	fast	for-	ev-	er	and	ev-	er:
[9a] He sent re-	demp-	tion	un-	to	his	peo	- ple:
[9b] Ho-ly and	rev-	er-	end	is	his		name:
[10b] A good un-der-	stand-	ing have all					
		they that	do	his	com- mand-		ments:
Glo-ry	be	to the	Fa-	ther and to	the		Son:
As it	was			in the	be-	gin-	ning:

182

[Recitation]   [Termination]

[1] in the assembly of the	up-	right in the con-	gre-	ga-		tion.
[2] sought out of all	them	that have	pleas-	ure	there-	in.
[3] and his righteousness en-	dur-	eth	for-	ev-		er.
[4] The Lord is gracious and	full	of	com-	pas-		sion.
[5] he will ever be	mind-	ful of	his	cov-	e-	nant.
[6] that he may give them the	her-	it - age of	the	hea-		then.
[7] all	his	com-mand-	ments	are		sure.
[8] and are	done	in truth	and	up-	right-	ness.
[9a] he hath commanded his	cov-	e - nant	for-	ev-		er.
[10a] The fear of the Lord is the be-	gin-	ning	of	wis-		dom.
[10b] his praise en-	dur-	eth	for-	ev-		er.
and	to	the	Ho-	ly		Ghost,
and ever shall	be,	world	with-	out		end.

A - - - - - - - - - men.

The Gloria in Excelsis

1537

Translated by Ulrich S. Leupold

Two rimed versions of the Gloria in Excelsis appear in the early sources of the Reformation period, both of them based on the melody of the *Gloria tempore paschali* in the Roman rite. They show many similarities in content as well as in musical substance. But while the one, "All Glory Be to God on High" ("*Allein Gott in der Höh sei Ehr*")[1] by Nicholas Decius, is written in the form of an ordinary chorale in four stanzas, the other, "All Glory, Laud, and Praise Be Given," probably by Luther, has the structure of an antiphonal chant, much like Luther's Sanctus hymn "Isaiah 'Twas the Prophet"[2] or his German *Te Deum*.[3] Decius' ultimately won out and became the most widely accepted Gloria in the German agendas. But for the first hundred years after the Reformation Luther's chant also enjoyed widespread popularity. It made its first appearance in an order of worship Nicholas Medler drew up in 1537 for the Church of St. Wenceslaus in Naumburg; it has been preserved in several manuscripts. Luther's authorship is indicated not with the chant itself but in the preceding order of service, by the remark, "The German *Et in terra*[4] as Doctor Martin Luther made it." A similar remark is found in the Nördlingen church order of 1555; the Bonn hymnal of 1561 also credits it to Luther.

On the other hand, sources much closer to Wittenberg fail to include the chant or, if they have it, to assign it to Martin Luther. Schumann's hymnals of 1539 and 1540, Lotter's hymnal of 1540,

---

[1] *Service Book and Hymnal of the Lutheran Church in America* (1958), No. 132.
[2] See pp. 82-83.
[3] See pp. 171-175.
[4] *Et in terra* ("and on earth," etc.) was the common name for the choral Gloria in Excelsis, because the first line (i.e., "*Gloria in Excelsis Deo*") was always chanted by the officiant, and the choir did not come in until the response: "*et in terra*," etc. In this case it is somewhat of a misnomer since the opening line of the Gloria is included in the chant, but it is not impossible that the officiant nonetheless intoned the opening line to its plain-chant melody.

and others from the same period are evidently ignorant of it. Klug 1543 and Babst 1545 have it, but in the section devoted to "hymns by pious Christians who lived before our time." These facts have cast a shadow on it and have led to extended controversies about its authenticity.[5] Although it is not possible to assert Luther's authorship with absolute certainty, the following points in its favor should be considered.[6]

1. While it is puzzling that Klug and Babst did not include this chant with the other Luther hymns, but inserted it in a later section, the same fate befell Luther's hymn "Thou who Art Three in Unity."[7] This may be due to the fact that except for the preface, Luther had no direct part in the preparation of these hymnals.[8]

2. Neither the contemporary sources nor modern scholars ascribe this hymn to anyone other than Luther.

3. Both text and music point to Luther as the author. The forthright simplicity and vivid concreteness of the words accord with the folklike style of his hymns. The syllabic structure of the melody and the bold intervals are quite in keeping with his musical principles and temperament. Furthermore, the frequently used cadential formula a g g, d c c or the like is strongly reminiscent of similar cadences in his Sanctus,[9] Te Deum,[10] and in the liturgical chants of the German Mass.[11] The long notes on "Jesus Christ" also recall the long notes in two of the versicles of the Te Deum.

This chant, like other chants, was sung antiphonally. The oldest source, the Naumburg church order, gives the following rubric: "In public worship all the German songs are sung alternately, i.e., the boys' choir sings one verse and the congregation (having its own cantor) the others. But if the organ is played, three choirs are formed [i.e., the organ forms one choir, the boys the second, and the congregation the third] and the organ always

---

[5] Cf. WA 35, 56-69, 287-296, 627-631.
[6] Cf. Konrad Ameln and K. Gerhardt, "Die deutschen Gloria-Lieder," Monatsschrift für Gottesdienst und kirchliche Kunst.," XLIII (1938), 225-231.
[7] See pp. 308-309.
[8] See pp. 317-318; 332-334.
[9] See pp. 82-83.
[10] See pp. 171-175.
[11] See pp. 70-89.

begins, except for the *Et in terra* when the [altar] boys begin, then the organ, then the choir, and then the people. But if the girls also are singing, four choirs are formed and sing all verses of the German songs one after the other, etc."[12]

Similarly, Laurentius Stiphelius in 1607 indicated that the second verse should be played by the organ, the third sung by the choir, the fourth by the congregation, the fifth by the girls, the sixth by the choir, the seventh by the congregation, the eighth by the girls, the ninth played by the organ, the tenth and eleventh sung by the choirs, the twelfth by the congregation, the thirteenth by the girls, and the fourteenth by the choirs. Nothing is said about the first verse. Evidently it was taken for granted that it would be sung by the altar boys.[13]

We present the chant as given in the reprint in Ameln *et al.*, *Handbuch der deutschen evangelischen Kirchenmusik*, I, 42, No. 61,[14] but transposed to the lower fifth. The German text begins with the words *"All ehr und lob soll Gottes sein."* The original Naumburg manuscript is in hobnail chorale notation.

---

[12] Ameln *et al.*, *Handbuch der deutschen evangelischen Kirchenmusik*, I, 572.
[13] *Ibid.*
[14] Cf. also *WA* 35, 288, 530-531.

The Gloria in Excelsis

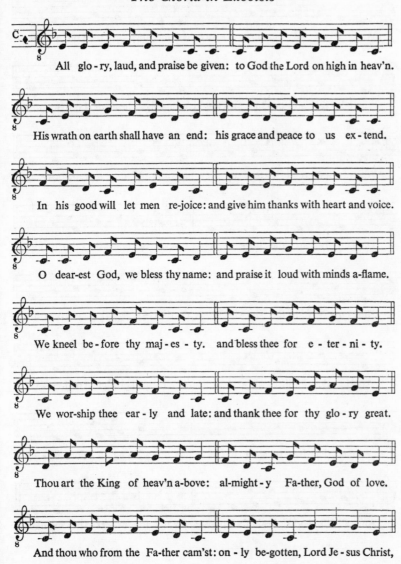

All glo - ry, laud, and praise be given: to God the Lord on high in heav'n.

His wrath on earth shall have an end: his grace and peace to us ex - tend.

In his good will let men re-joice: and give him thanks with heart and voice.

O dear-est God, we bless thy name: and praise it loud with minds a-flame.

We kneel be - fore thy maj - es - ty. and bless thee for e - ter - ni - ty.

We wor-ship thee ear - ly and late: and thank thee for thy glo - ry great.

Thou art the King of heav'n a-bove: al-might - y Fa-ther, God of love.

And thou who from the Fa-ther cam'st: on - ly be-gotten, Lord Je - sus Christ,

Thou Son of God, thou ten-der Lamb: thou art thy - self the great I Am.

187

Who tak-est all our sins a-way: have mer-cy on us, Lord, we pray.

Who tak-est all our sins a-way: vouch-safe to hear us, Lord, we pray.

Who at God's right sit-test for aye: have mer-cy on us, Lord, we pray.

Thou on-ly art the ho-ly One: o-ver all things the Lord a-lone,

Thou on-ly with the Ho-ly Ghost: O dear-est Sav-ior, Je-sus Christ,

Art in the Fa-ther's glo-ry high: of e-qual pow'r and maj-es-ty,

A-men, that is, so shall it be: as an-gels sing a-dor-ing-ly,

And all the world joins in their praise: now and for ev-er-last-ing days.

---

[1] According to the earliest manuscript, this note should be an eighth note.

THE HYMNS

Translated by George MacDonald

Revised by Ulrich S. Leupold

INTRODUCTION

The sudden bursting forth of the Lutheran chorale is one of the most thrilling chapters in the history of the Reformation. In December, 1523, Luther's *Order of Mass and Communion* appeared in print. Here Luther expressed his appreciation for some of the older German hymns from the Middle Ages and his desire to find poets who would write new hymns in a proper devotional style.[1] About the same time he wrote to court chaplain George Spalatin, asking him to render some of the Psalms in verse.[2] The letter indicates that he had sent similar letters to some of his other friends. It also mentions the enclosure by Luther of a Psalm paraphrase from his own pen, probably the hymn "From Trouble Deep I Cry to Thee."[3] But this apparently was not the only hymn he had written. Before the year was over, several of his hymns and those by his friends were printed and distributed in individual leaflets or broadsheets,[4] as, e.g., Luther's "From Trouble Deep I Cry to Thee,"[5] "Dear Christians, Let Us Now Rejoice,"[6] "A New Song Here Shall Be Begun,"[7] and Paul Speratus' *"Es ist das Heil."*[8] A chronicler of the city of Magdeburg gives a vivid account of a peddler who on May 6, 1524, sang the new Lutheran hymns on the market place and sold the leaflets to the people. The mayor had him clapped in jail, but the enthusiastic burghers saw that he was freed in short order to continue singing the hymns of Martin Luther.[9]

The Sources

Even before this event, in early January of the year 1524, an enterprising Nürnberg printer, Jobst Gutknecht, had begun to

---

[1] See p. 36.
[2] See p. 221.
[3] See pp. 221-224.
[4] For a list of these, see WA 35, 375-377.
[5] See pp. 221-224.
[6] See pp. 217-220.
[7] See pp. 211-216.
[8] "Salvation unto Us Has Come."
[9] *Chroniken der deutschen Städte vom 14. bis 16. Jahrh.* XXVII = *Die Chronik der niedersächsischen Städte.* Magdeburg II (Leipzig, 1899), p. 107; quoted in WA 35, 9.

compile into a hymnal a few of these broadsheets together with some other hymns he had obtained through a third person. In the sixteenth century, it must be remembered, there were no copyright laws. A hymn was in the public domain almost as soon as it was written, and every printer was free to print it, however faulty his copy might be. This oldest Lutheran hymnal is usually known in hymnological research as the *Achtliederbuch (Hymnal of Eight)*; it contains eight hymns, three by Paul Speratus, one by an unnamed author, and the following four by Luther: "Dear Christians, Let Us Now Rejoice,"[10] "Ah God, from Heaven Look Down,"[11] "Although the Fools Say with Their Mouth,"[12] and "From Trouble Deep I Cry to Thee."[13] Three different editions of it appeared early in 1524,[14] the first not later than the middle of January. The actual title page, "Some Christian hymns, canticles, and Psalms made according to the pure Word of God, from Holy Scripture by several very learned men, to sing in church as it is in part already practiced in Wittenberg," proves that by the end of 1523 Luther had begun to introduce some of the new hymns in the church services in Wittenberg.

This is also confirmed by the fact that Paul Speratus' German translation of *An Order of Mass and Communion*,[15] which appeared in January, 1524, had two chorales appended to it: Luther's "Would That the Lord Would Grant Us Grace"[16] and Johann Agricola's *"Fröhlich wollen wir Halleluja singen."*[17] In the summer of

---

[10] See pp. 217-220.
[11] See pp. 225-228.
[12] See pp. 229-231.
[13] See pp. 221-224.
[14] For a description of these, see WA 35, 336-337. Some scholars believe that the earliest edition (which on the title page bears the date MDXIIII, an obvious misprint) came out in 1523. This is the date that appears at the end of Luther's "Dear Christians, Let Us Now Rejoice" and Speratus' *"Es ist das Heil."* But Speratus' *"In Gott glaub ich"* bears the date 1524. These dates at the end of hymns have evidently been taken over from earlier broadsheets. In view of the evidence, the editor finds it easier to accept that the printer omitted one X on the title page, than that he set an I instead of an X.
[15] See p. 17.
[16] See pp. 232-234.
[17] See Zahn, *Die Melodien der deutschen evangelischen Kirchenlieder*, I, 627, No. 1625.

the same year the *Achtliederbuch* was followed by two hymnals called enchiridia[18] (handbooks), which were published by two different printers in Erfurt.[19] These collections, about three times as large as the *Achtliederbuch*, are practically identical, and each contains eighteen hymns by Luther. Evidently they were compiled by the same unnamed editor, though without authorization from Wittenberg.

The first hymnal prepared under Luther's own auspices is the *Geistliche Gesangbüchlein*,[20] edited by his friend and musical adviser Johann Walter and published in Wittenberg in late summer of the same year, 1524.[21] Actually, this is not a hymn book in the modern sense of the word, but a collection of polyphonic motets, based on Lutheran chorales. Primarily it was designed not for the congregation but for the choir. But it must be remembered that Luther wanted his hymns to be sung by the choir to familiarize the whole congregation with them. The hymn melody proper (in accordance with the older polyphonic style) is usually entrusted to the tenor. Of the thirty-eight German chorales in Walter's collection, twenty-four are by Luther. In other words, more than two-thirds of Luther's hymns were written between the late fall of 1523 and the summer of 1524.[22]

From 1524 on, every year witnessed the publication of more and larger hymn collections. Wherever the Reformation gained entrance, publishers vied in bringing out better and more comprehensive hymnals. Magdeburg, Zwickau, Leipzig, Erfurt, Nürnberg, Augsburg, Königsberg, and many other cities produced their own collections.[23] Especially important is Strassburg, where in 1525 the

---

18 Singular: enchiridion.
19 The one *in der Permenter Gassen*, the other *zcum Schwartzen Hornn;* see the description in WA 35, 338-345.
20 *Spiritual Hymn Booklet;* see the description in WA 35, 315-317.
21 See Luther's preface to this hymnal, in this volume, pp. 315-316.
22 With this conclusion we accept the results of the investigations of Walter Lucke, who in WA 35 refuted point-by-point the attempt of Friedrich Spitta ("*Ein feste Burg ist unser Gott,*" *Die Lieder Luthers in ihrer, Bedeutung für das evangelische Kirchenlied* [Göttingen, 1905]) to date the bulk of Luther's hymns much earlier.
23 For a description of these hymnals, see WA 35, 320, 325, 327-330, 332-334, 346-357, 362-366.

hymnals of Wolfgang Köpfel established a specific southwest German tradition in the selection and editing of texts and tunes.[24] In this volume it would lead too far afield to trace the family trees of all the hymnals that were published in Luther's lifetime, for the Reformation produced close to one hundred hymnals from 1524 until Luther's death in 1546.[25] Suffice it to list those hymnals that appeared under his own supervision. Besides Walter's collection, which appeared in four more and enlarged editions, Luther supervised the publication of the following hymnals:

The Lufft enchiridion, published in Wittenberg in 1526, offered the hymns from Walter's collection for the congregation.[26]

The Hans Weiss hymnal, published in Wittenberg in 1528, is lost. But its contents were the same as the Michael Blum hymnal, published in Leipzig in 1529(?).[27]

The Joseph Klug hymnal, published in Wittenberg in 1529, was also based on that of Hans Weiss. It is lost, but its contents can be reconstructed from the reprint by Rauscher (Erfurt, 1531)[28] and from the second edition of 1533, long lost but recently found again.[29]

The Valentin Schumann hymnal, published in Leipzig in 1539, is the source for some of Luther's later hymns.[30]

The Valentin Babst hymnal, published in Leipzig in 1545, was the finest hymnal of the Reformation period and the last to appear under Luther's own auspices.[31]

---

[24] For a description of the Strassburg hymnals, see WA 35, 357-363.

[25] In comparison, the English Reformation produced thirteen hymnals up to the end of the sixteenth century (Scottish hymnals included).

[26] See the description in WA 35, 317-318.

[27] See the description in WA 35, 318-319.

[28] See the description in WA 35, 320-321.

[29] See the description in WA 35, 321-322. For later editions of the Klug hymnal, see WA 35, 322, 331.

[30] See the description in WA 35, 325. For a later edition, see WA 35, 329-330.

[31] See the description in WA 35, 332-333, and Luther's preface, in this volume, pp. 332-334.

The Patterns

The rash of hymnals traced above is but one indication of the tremendous echo that Luther's hymns produced. A book with Lutheran hymns was sure to sell, for the chorales were the fanfare that opened many a Jericho to the advent of the Reformation.

The success of Luther's hymns was due not simply to the genius of the Reformer, but to the fact that his seed fell on fertile ground. He introduced no innovations, but only allowed the German hymn—long since existing—to come into its own and fulfil its destiny. In this, as in many other respects, the sixteenth century was a century of fulfilment.

From the early Middle Ages hymns in the vernacular had been, if not actively encouraged, at least tolerated by the church. They were sung at pilgrimages and processions and at special occasions, e.g., at the great festivals of the church year, and even at mass. Some of these folk hymns had grown from the response *Kyrie eleison* ("Lord, have mercy"), which the people continued to sing even when all other parts of the service had been taken over by choir and clergy. This refrain formed the end of every stanza and explains why these folk hymns were called *Leise(n)*. Luther enlarged some of the older *Leisen*, e.g., "Now Let Us Pray to the Holy Ghost" and "Let God Be Blest," and wrote several of his own hymns in the same style, e.g., the two hymns on the Ten Commandments.

Another form of sacred folk song, the carol, had come into vogue especially in connection with the liturgical dramas and mystery plays of the later Middle Ages. Luther did not alter any of the medieval carols, but several made their way into his hymnals. He also wrote some of his own hymns in the style of carols, e.g., "From Heaven on High I Come to You." Others again were simply translations of Latin verses. Luther used two German antiphons (i.e., one-stanza hymns) based on Latin originals, "In the Midst of Life We Are" and "Come, Holy Spirit Lord and God," and added additional stanzas. His procedure with the medieval Latin office hymns was less simple. Some of these had indeed been translated before him, but these earlier versions had been esoteric attempts by individual poets and had failed to gain acceptance among the common people. Thus Luther in his translations of the office hymns, e.g., "Come, God Creator Holy Ghost" and "Come, the Heathen's Healing Light," made an entirely new beginning. He used none of the earlier translations, but recast the sense of the Latin verses in a style as compact and terse as the original, yet simple enough to appeal to the feeling of the people.

The German folk song was the good earth from which all of Luther's hymns sprang. Its style textually and musically is evident everywhere, and its patterns are often clearly recognizable. The very first hymn by Luther, "A New Song Here Shall Be Begun," is modeled after the folk ballads, which told the stories of important events and personalities. Characteristic stock phrases and melodic turns of the folk song are found in all of Luther's hymns. This is particularly true of two offshoots of the German folk song, the *Meistersang* and the *Hofweise*. From the fourteenth century on, the trade guilds in the German cities had joined the heritage of the earlier German troubadours or *Minnesänger*. These singing schools maintained by coopers, cobblers, and candlemakers produced songs by the dozens and promoted their members from apprentices to journeymen and masters as they acquired the rules of the musical game. While the pedantry of these rules often quenched creativity and produced reams of poetry and music without spark, the *Meistersänger* did keep alive an interest in song and the initiative to write and to compose. Their brave attempts to tell whole biblical stories in song was not without influence on the early chorale.[32]

Another form of the German *Lied* which influenced Luther as a hymnist was the *Hofweise* or court air. The *Hofweise* was not a folk song proper. While the folk song is simple in structure, concrete in style, and of unknown authorship, the *Hofweisen* were the products of individual poet-composers who chose intricate metrical patterns to praise abstract concepts, such as virtue, patience, and beauty. They may often appear stilted and artificial,

---

[32] For an example of the *Meistersängers'* art, see Hans Sachs' (1494-1576) *Gülden Ton* in A. T. Davison and W. Apel, *Historical Anthology of Music* (Cambridge: Harvard University Press, 1949), I, 21, No. 24.

yet as the name indicates they were never without a certain refinement and nobility in the choice of words and musical cadences.[33] Luther's hymn on the church, "To Me She's Dear, the Worthy Maid," with its intricate structure of short and long verses and its ornate eulogy on the lady "church," is a typical example of the *Hofweise*.

The Style

To the modern ear Luther's verses sound awkward, if not uncouth. They lack the rich emotional overtones, the mellow flow of words, and the metric regularity that we commonly associate with poetry. Some of them sound more like prose than poetry. In short, the standards that govern the editing of modern hymnbooks are no help in understanding Luther as a hymnist. The hymns of the nineteenth century that form the bulk of today's hymnals were written according to the artistic canons of Romanticism. They use beautifully polished phrases and dance or march rhythms to create a certain mood and to give an ornate expression to personal religious feelings. But Luther's hymns were meant not to create a mood, but to convey a message. They were a confession of faith, not of personal feelings. That is why, in the manner of folk songs, they present their subject vividly and dramatically, but without the benefit of ornate language and other poetic refinements. They were written not to be read but to be sung by a whole congregation.

---

[33] The following love song by Paul Hofhaimer (1459-1537) is an example of the secular *Hofweise:*

Herzliebstes Bild
Beweis dich mild
Mit deiner Lieb und Gunst gen mir.
Desgleich will ich,
Wann ich han dich,
Nach Lust und Wunsch meins Herzen Gier.
Erwählt für all
In diesem Tal
Mit reichem Schall
Freu ich mich dein in Ehren.

Fritz Jöde, *Alte weltliche Lieder für gemischte Stimmen* (Wolfenbüttel: Georg Kallmeyer Verlag, 1927), pp. 42-44. For another example, see his *Meins traurens ist* in Davison and Apel, *op. cit.*, I, 96, No. 98.

197

The language and vocabulary are therefore simple and direct. Like the ancient Hebrew poets he knew so well, Luther used few adjectives and formed brief pungent lines consisting almost exclusively of verbs and nouns. Most of the words are monosyllables. The thought is condensed and concentrated. Frequently every line forms a sentence of its own. Enjambment, i.e., the carrying over of one or more words from one line to the next so as to bridge the break between verses, is quite uncommon. There is never a break in the middle of the verse. This again agrees with the nature of mass singing. A crowd sings a verse at a time, and so each verse must make sense as a unit.

Again, our modern hymns are iambic, trochaic, or dactylic, i.e., they observe a regular succession of metrical feet. The rhythmic structure, i.e., the succession of accented and unaccented syllables, is the same from stanza to stanza and often from verse to verse. If the first stanza begins with an upbeat, the second will never have a downbeat at the same place, and so forth.

But this tramping or tripping of metrical feet was foreign to Luther and was not in fact made a law of poetry until one hundred years later. Like the *Meistersänger*, Luther counted syllables, but the accents vary from line to line. Sometimes they are quite regular; other times they seem to clash with the rhythm or arbitrarily to change from trochaic to iambic and more complicated feet. This rhythmical freedom, however, is not necessarily a defect, as it may appear to the modern hymnologist. Instead of fitting sentences into the rigid mold of metrical feet, Luther was able to stress certain words irrespective of the tyranny of "light" and "heavy" accents. Of course, this would have been impossible with melodies in strict duple, triple, or quadruple time of the kind that are found in modern hymnals. But the modal melodies that Luther adapted to his words were far less rigid and much more flexible than modern hymn tunes written in 3/4 or 4/4 time and allowed a stress on different notes, as the rhythm of speech demanded.

Also in the matter of rime, Luther's hymns are much freer than those of later centuries. Often there is more of an assonance than a proper rime. On the other hand, there are many alliterations. Luther loved the ancient German *Stabreim* and used it freely.

That the hymns were not carelessly dashed off can be seen from their structure. Usually Luther followed a definite plan, the various stanzas forming one symmetric whole, as will be shown in the introductions to the individual hymns.

Unfortunately little of the original ruggedness of Luther's poetic style survived in the translations of his hymns that have found their way into modern English and American hymnals. With the mighty resurgence of English hymnody during the nineteenth century, many poets tried their hand at rendering Luther's verse into English. But most of them took considerable liberties with the originals. Frequently they changed irregular verse forms into more accepted meters.[34] Usually they aimed at a more polished and elegant style than was really justified in view of Luther's angularity. They tried to make him speak in the mellifluent accents of a Victorian churchman, with the result that both the literal sense and the original style often were lost.[35]

Of course, it is almost impossible to preserve in modern English the literal meaning of a sixteenth-century German hymn, together with its original meter and peculiar style. One always has to sacrifice either on the side of loyalty to the original or on the side of an English form that will sound convincing and make sense to the modern reader. In this edition faithfulness to the original wording, style, and meter seemed more important than a completely idiomatic English rendition. Perhaps the most felicitous attempt to translate Luther's hymns without loss of their original ruggedness was made by the Scottish theologian and writer George

---

[34] This is true, e.g., of John Anderson, *Hymns from the German by Dr. Martin Luther;* John Hunt, *The Spiritual Songs of Martin Luther;* Catherine Winkworth, *Lyra Germanica* (1855-1858) and *The Chorale Book for England* (1863); Richard Massie, *Martin Luther's Spiritual Songs.*

[35] Massie indeed says of Luther's style in his foreword: "There is no originality of thought, no splendid imagery, no play of fancy to attract the reader, whose taste has been formed on the productions of the nineteenth century" (*ibid.,* p. v), and also: "My first aim has been to give the meaning of the original with accuracy and fidelity. . . . My next aim has been to imitate the simple, idiomatic, biblical language of the original, for any attempt at finery or embellishment would mar the simplicity which constitutes their chief charm. I have also endeavoured, as far as I could do without affectation, to throw an air of archaic dignity over them by using language somewhat older and more quaint than in common use . . ." (*ibid.,* p. ix). But even Massie takes frequent liberties with the meter and sense of the originals.

MacDonald (1824-1905). MacDonald's translation,[36] used in this edition, has been completely passed by in common use, presumably because he consciously, and often successfully, tried to express Luther's robust lines in an English idiom of similar character. Obviously he took for a pattern the older English verse. He sought to preserve the vivid metaphors, metrical irregularity, and folk-song quality of Luther's hymns. He imitated Luther's preference for monosyllables by using mostly Anglo-Saxon words. Due to the prevalence of feminine rimes in German poetry and their scarcity in English with its lack of suffixes, many hymn translations from the German suffer from a tedious repetition of rimes on "-ation," such as creation, salvation, foundation, and justification. These words tend to make the English style more academic and pompous than the German. MacDonald almost completely avoided them.

Of course, his verse may strike the modern reader simply as something odd, if not "exotic." Perhaps the best retort to this impression is given by MacDonald himself in the following passage from his preface:

" 'Do you call this good English?'

" 'I hope it is good English,' I answer.

" 'It reads so like a translation! And good German should be translated into good English, you allow.'

" 'Yes. But if it be good English, a little flavor of the German is only an enrichment.'

" 'It is more than a little flavor.'

" 'Are you sure it is not the antiquated tone you mistake for a German one? Does it sound stranger than much of our own poetry of the same date?'

" 'The verse is rugged.'

" 'I am so glad you find it so. I have succeeded. Luther's verse is often very rugged: sometimes he seems to care only that the number of syllables should correspond with the number of the notes to which the line has to be sung.'

---

[36] *Exotics, A Translation of the Spiritual Songs of Novalis, the Hymn-Book of Luther, and Other Poems from the German and Italian* (London: Strahan and Co., 1876), pp. 38-116. MacDonald's titles are regularly omitted. The best brief introduction to MacDonald is C. S. Lewis, *George MacDonald, An Anthology* (New York: Macmillan, 1947).

" 'But should you do it badly because he does it carelessly?'

" 'Yes, I think so; seeing, in his case at least, the main object should be the man through the poetry.'

" 'But your rhymes are sometimes bad.'

" 'Not oftener, I hope, than Luther's. But I will confess to a certain pleasure, amidst the difficulties of translating, and the paramount desire to preserve first the spirit and next the meaning, when I came upon a bad rhyme which allowed me greater scope for being at once true to his faulty mode and his grand spirit. I consider a bad rhyme a fair advantage to the translator, where its reproduction happens to fall in with his ends.' "[37]

We offer most of the hymns in a slightly revised version of MacDonald's translation. Our edition would like to present Luther's hymns in an English form which is as close as possible to the original German text and at the same time singable to the original melodies. In cases where MacDonald's text seemed to be unclear, inaccurate, or unsingable, changes were therefore made by the editor, with an occasional assist from other standard translations. Minor variations in orthography and phraseology have not been noted. Major changes have been indicated in the introductions to the individual hymns.

The Music

The hymnals of the sixteenth century are filled with music. Later, when hymnals swelled to immense proportions and many texts were sung to the same melody, printers avoided the extra expense of adding music by issuing hymnals without a single tune. Not so in the sixteenth century. From the *Achtliederbuch*[38] on, the Lutheran hymnals provided music for most if not all of the hymns that they offered. Each hymn was given its own proper tune or tunes, though certain tunes were matched with several hymns. Excepting polyphonic collections, such as Walter's hymnal of 1524,

---

[37] MacDonald, *op. cit.*, pp. xiii-xiv. In this section of his preface, MacDonald quotes from his remarks on this translation published elsewhere. To avoid a confusing mass of quotation marks, the editor has omitted those by which MacDonald indicates he is quoting himself. The effect of this is to make the above text an exact duplication of MacDonald's own.

[38] See p. 192.

the hymnbooks offered only the melody line, usually in the range of the male voice. Although the music was included, the composer's name was never given.

All this is also true of Luther's hymns. While in the early sources—notably those printed without authorization and supervision from Wittenberg—some uncertainty prevailed about the proper melodies for his hymns, and a few of them had to subsist on borrowed tunes, ultimately at least one proper (and different) melody was agreed upon for each of his hymns. But who composed these melodies is often hard to ascertain. Of course, for the older German hymns which Luther enlarged and for Latin hymns which he translated, well-known tunes that had been sung for centuries were used, though often with significant alterations. But what about the music for Luther's new hymns? Did he write the stirring strains of "Our God He Is a Castle Strong," "From Trouble Deep I Cry to Thee," and of all the other hymns he created? Here opinions are divided. Luther's contemporaries and early biographers took it for granted that he composed both the words and the music of his hymns. This attitude prevailed up to the nineteenth century when historical scholarship began to subject every fond tradition to critical investigation and delighted in exposing one myth after another. Scholars pointed at the obvious anonymity of the tunes and would credit fewer and fewer melodies to Luther, until around the turn of the century a prominent hymnologist, Wilhelm Nelle,[39] could claim that not a single tune had been composed by Luther. But recent musicological research in and since the 1923 edition of Luther's hymns in WA 35 has reversed this judgment. Today musicologists are inclined to accept Luther as the composer of most if not all of the new melodies that appeared with his hymns, especially in the Wittenberg hymnals, and as the arranger of some of the older tunes.

This conclusion is almost inescapable for two reasons: first, Luther's musicianship and, second, the fact that poet and composer were almost always the same person in the sixteenth century. There can be no question regarding his musical competence. With a thorough musical grounding from school, university, and

---

[39] *Geschichte des deutschen evangelischen Kirchenliedes* (Hamburg, 1909).

cloister, he had not only a deep appreciation of and impeccable taste in music, but was capable of creative work.[40] With such gifts it is hard to imagine that he would have depended entirely on others to furnish music for his texts. It was then taken for granted that poet and composer were the same person. A man did not write a poem and then wait for a composer to come along and set it to music. The composition of text and tune were considered twin crafts that with industry and application could be mastered by anyone, especially since absolute originality of personal expression was not expected. The line between plagiarism and creativity was not drawn as sharply as today. A poet might make use of standing folk-song phrases in his verse[41] and arrange familiar melodies to fit the mood and meter of his words. Luther would have been an odd exception had he left the tuning of his hymns to others. Moreover, many of his tunes exhibit certain traits that agree with his known musical ideas and his whole temperament. The tendency toward syllabic style—in marked distinction from the hymnals of Münzer or the Bohemian brethren—points to his conviction that the melismatic style of plain chant is unsuitable for German verse. The preference for disjunct rather than conjunct movement, with bold fourths and fifths setting the tone, and the frequent defiant beginnings on the highest note of the scale are quite in keeping with what we know of his daring and dauntless temperament.[42] The introductions to individual hymns in this volume give further attention to the origin of the music.

The sixteenth century marks the transition from the ancient church modes, Dorian, Phrygian, Lydian, and Mixo-lydian, to the modern major and minor scales. Though some of Luther's melodies, e.g., "From Heaven on High I Come to You," savor strongly of the modern major scale, the majority are definitely modal in character. Some of the melodies, e.g., those for "Our God He Is a Castle Strong" or "To Me She's Dear, the Worthy Maid" are amazingly complicated in their rhythmical structure. They abound

---

[40] On Luther's musicianship, see also p. 55.
[41] See, for example, Luther's "A New Song Here Shall Be Begun," pp. 211-216.
[42] Cf. Rudolf Gerber, *Zu Luthers Liedweisen* (*"Festschrift. Max Schneider zum 60. Geburtstag"* [Halle: Ernst Schneider, 1935]), pp. 26-39.

in syncopations and rhythmical anticipations. Here we must ask whether the congregations of Luther's time, who before had hardly opened their mouths in the service, were able to execute rhythms as intricate as these and still keep together and in time. A dogmatic answer to this question is not possible.

On the one hand, it is a matter of record that the irregular rhythms of Luther's hymn melodies are part and parcel of the sixteenth-century polyphonic style. The homophonic arrangements in modern hymnals entrust the given melody to the sopranos so that it can be heard easily, while the other voices provide no more than a harmonic background. Rhythmically speaking, the four voices are completely synchronized, beginning every line and syllable on the same beat. This rhythmical homogeneity was something sixteenth-century composers did their best to avoid. They placed the given melody not in the soprano but in the tenor. And to make it stand out, they gave the tenor melody as much rythmical independence as possible. Either the tenor would sing in very long notes against lively runs in the other voices,[43] or the composer would syncopate the tenor melody so as to create suspensions and passing notes between it and the other voices, especially at the cadences. Even comparatively plain melodies could be "dressed up" in this way to serve as tenors in a polyphonic setting. So some of Luther's hymn tunes may have received their polyrhythmical form at the hand of Walter for the sake of polyphonic arrangement. The congregation may have sung them in far simpler rhythms. The hymnbook editors of the sixteenth century took great liberty with rhythm, so that most of Luther's hymns appear in more than one rhythmical form, as will be seen.[44] It is therefore hardly in keeping with the practice of the Reformation period to declare a certain rhythmical version of a given melody to be the only correct one.

On the other hand, we dare not judge the musical abilities of past generations by our own. The congregations of the sixteenth century, though unaware of the harmonic riches to which we have become accustomed, may have had a far subtler sense of rhythm than the average layman of today and may have taken the rhyth-

---

[43] Cf. Luther's telling description of this style, p. 324.
[44] In the footnotes we offer the significant melodic and rhythmic variations, but not obvious misprints which are quite common in the early hymnals.

204

mical hurdles of some of Luther's hymns in their stride. For example, the polyrhythmical version of "Our God He Is a Castle Strong" was published as a unison melody fifteen years before the earliest polyphonic setting appeared in print. The polyrhythmical version was reprinted with minor variations again and again for the following century and a half. Not until the eighteenth century did the isometric form of the melody in equal quarter or half notes supplant the polyrhythmical version.

But regardless of whether the congregations in Luther's time sang the chorales with or without all the syncopations and rhythmical intricacies found in the printed sources, one fact is clear—the beat of the music was fairly rapid.

The original sources are unanimous on this point. All of Luther's hymns except "Isaiah 'Twas the Prophet" are given in mensural notation. And in all of them the semibreve (◊) is the basic syllabic unit, that is, it marks the beat. This semibreve looks like our whole note in modern notation. That is why modern transcriptions have often printed the chorales in whole and half notes, leaving the familiar but mistaken impression that Luther's hymns were slow, stately dirges. Actually, the semibreve corresponds to our whole note only in shape; its time value was quite different. The musical textbooks of the time state definitely that the duration of the semibreve is equal to the pulse beat of a man with quiet respiration. We know therefore that around 1500 the semibreve represented about M.M. 60-80 (i.e., ♩ = one second or a little less).[45] This is why we have transcribed the semibreve by a quarter note and reduced all other notes proportionately. Historically speaking, there is no excuse for dragging the Reformation chorales. The notion of stately churchliness in whole and half notes is entirely a product of romanticist imagination and has no basis in historical fact.

Finally, it remains to be said that we have ordered the hymns as far as possible in chronological order and those of like vintage according to the church year. The following indexes classify them in various metrical, musical, liturgical, and topical categories.

[45] See Curt Sachs, "Some Remarks about Old Notation," *The Musical Quarterly*, XXXV (1948), 365-370.

Metrical Index

Four Lines

75.47 with Kyrieleison
Jesus Christ, unser Heiland — Jesus Christ, Our Savior True

77.77
Nun komm, der Heiden Heiland — Come, the Heathen's Healing Light

87.88 with Kyrioleis
Gelobet seist du Jesu Christ — All Praise to Thee, O Jesus Christ

88.78
Jesus Christus unser Heiland — Jesus Christ, Our God and Savior

88.87
Komm, Gott Schöpfer Heilger Geist — Come, God Creator Holy Ghost

88.87 with Kyrioleis
Dies sind die heiligen zehn Gebot — These Are the Holy Ten Commands
Mensch, willst du leben seliglich — Man, Wouldst Thou Live All Blissfully

L.M.
Christum wir sollen loben schon — Jesus We Now Must Laud and Sing
Der du bist drei in Einigkeit — Thou who Art Three in Unity
Erhalt uns, Herr, bei deinem Wort — Lord, Keep Us Steadfast in Thy Word
Vom Himmel kam der Engel Schar — From Heaven the Angel Troop Came Near

Vom Himmel Hoch — From Heaven on High I Come to You

Wohl dem der in Gottes Furcht — Happy who in God's Fear Doth Stay
Was fürchtst du, Feind Herodes sehr — Herod, Why Dreadest Thou a Foe

99.11 10 with Kyrioleis
Nun bitten wir den heiligen Geist — Now Let Us Pray to the Holy Ghost

Five Lines

8 7. 8. 7. 8
Verleih uns Frieden — Grant Peace in Mercy, Lord, We Pray

Six Lines

8 4. 8 4. 77
Mit Fried und Freud ich fahr dahin — In Peace and Joy I Now Depart

8 8. 8 8. 8 8
Vater unser im Himmelreich — Our Father in the Heaven who Art

Seven Lines

7 7. 7 7. 7 7 8 with Alleluia
Christ lag in Todesbanden — Death Held Our Lord in Prison

8 7. 8 7. 8 8 7
Ach Gott vom Himmel sieh darein — Ah God, from Heaven Look Down
Aus tiefer Not — From Trouble Deep I Cry to Thee

206

Es spricht der Unweisen Mund wohl	Although the Fools Say with Their Mouth
Nun freut euch liebe Christen	Dear Christians, Let Us Now Rejoice
Wär' Gott nicht mit uns	Were God Not with Us at This Time

Eight Lines
L. M. D. with Alleluia
Komm, Heiliger Geist, Herre Gott	Come, Holy Spirit Lord and God

Nine Lines
8 7. 8 7. 5 5. 5 6 7
Ein feste Burg	Our God He Is a Castle Strong

8 7. 8 7 D. 7
Christ unser Herr zum Jordan kam	To Jordan When Our Lord Had Gone
Ein neues Lied wir heben an	A New Song Here Shall Be Begun
Es wollt uns Gott	Would That the Lord Would Grant Us Grace

Ten Lines
L. M. D. 8 8
Wir glauben all an einen Gott	In One True God We All Believe

Irregular
Mitten wir im Leben sind	In the Midst of Life We Are
Gott sei gelobet	Let God Be Blest

Twelve Lines
8 7 D. 4 4 D. 7 8. 7 6
Sie ist mir lieb, die werte Magd	To Me She's Dear, the Worthy Maid

Fourteen Lines
7 7. 7 7. 7 7. 7 7. 7 7. 7 7. 7 8
Gott der Vater wohn uns bei	God the Father with Us Be

Sixteen Lines
10 10. 10 10. 10 10. 10 10. 10 10. 10 10. 10 10. 10 10
Jesaja dem Propheten das geschah	Isaiah 'Twas the Prophet

Sources of Melodies

Pre-Reformation Melody	Luther Hymn	
Latin Hymns:		
A solis ortus cardine	Christum wir sollen loben schon	Jesus We Now Must Laud and Sing
Hostis Herodes impie	Was fürchst du, Feind Herodes sehr	Herod, Why Dreadest Thou a Foe
O lux beata trinitas	Der du bist drei in Einigkeit	Thou who Art Three in Unity
Veni creator spiritus	Komm, Gott Schöpfer Heiliger Geist	Come, God Creator Holy Ghost
Veni redemptor gentium	Nun komm, der Heiden Heiland	Come, the Heathen's Healing Light
Latin Antiphons:		
Media vita in more sumus	Mitten wir im Leben sind	In the Midst of Life We Are
Da pacem domine	Verleih uns Frieden	Grant Peace in Mercy, Lord, We Pray
Veni sancte spiritus	Komm, Heiliger Geist, Herre Gott	Come, Holy Spirit Lord and God
German Leisen:		
In Gottes Namen fahren wir	Dies sind die heiligen zehn Gebot	These Are the Holy Ten Commands
Nun bitten wir den heiligen Geist	Nun bitten wir den heiligen Geist	Now Let Us Pray to the Holy Ghost
Gott sei gelobet	Gott sei gelobet	Let God Be Blest
Gelobet seist du, Jesu Christ	Gelobet seist du, Jesu Christ	All Praise to Thee, O Jesus Christ
Credo Hymn:		
Wir glauben all an einen Gott	Wir glauben all an einen Gott	In One True God We All Believe
Secular Folk song:		
Ich komm aus fremden Landen her	Vom Himmel kam der Engel Schar	From Heaven the Angel Troop Came Near
Sacred Folk song:		
Begierlich in dem Herzen mein	Ach Gott von Himmel sieh darein	Ah God, from Heaven Look Down
Gott der Vater wohn uns bei	Gott der Vater wohn uns bei	God the Father with Us Be
Erfreue dich, liebe Christengemein	Nun freut euch liebe Christen	Dear Christians, Let Us Now Rejoice
Maria du bist Gnuden roll	Es wollt uns Gott	Would That the Lord Would Grant Us Grace
John Huss:		
Jesus Christus nostra salus	Jesus Christus unser Heiland	Jesus Christ, Our God and Savior
Bohemian Brethren:		
Begehren wir mit Innigkeit	Vater unser im Himmelreich	Our Father in the Heaven who Art

Liturgical and Topical Index

The Service

Introit:	Nun bitten wir den heiligen Geist	Now Let Us Pray to the Holy Ghost
Gloria:	All Ehr und Lob soll Gottes sein	All Glory, Laud, and Praise Be Given
Credo:	Wir glauben all an einen Gott	In One True God We All Believe
After the Sermon:	Erhalt uns, Herr, bei deinem Wort	Lord, Keep Us Steadfast in Thy Word
	Verleih uns Frieden	Grant Peace in Mercy, Lord, We Pray
Sanctus:	Jesaja dem Propheten das geschah	Isaiah 'Twas the Prophet
Communion:	Jesus Christus unser Heiland	Jesus Christ, Our God and Savior
Post-Communion:	Gott sei gelobet	Let God Be Blest
Closing:	Es wollt uns Gott	Would That the Lord Would Grant Us Grace
Evening:	Der du bist drei in Einigkeit	Thou who Art T h r e e in Unity

Wedding

	Wohl dem der in G o t t e s Furcht	Happy who in God's Fear Doth Stay
	Gott der Vater wohn uns bei	God the Father with Us Be

Funeral

	Aus tiefer Not	From Trouble Deep I Cry to Thee
	Mitten wir im Leben sind	In the Midst of Life We Are
	Mit Fried und Freud ich fahr dahin	In Peace and Joy I Now Depart

The Church Year

Advent:	Nun komm, der H e i d e n Heiland	Come, the Heathen's Healing Light
Christmas:	Christum, wir sollen loben schon	Jesus We Now Must Laud and Sing
	G e l o b e t seist du, Jesus Christ	All Praise to Thee, O Jesus Christ
	Vom Himmel Hoch	From Heaven on High I Come to You
	Vom Himmel kam der Engel Schar	From H e a v e n the Angel Troop Came Near
Epiphany:	Was fürchtst du, F e i n d Herodes sehr	Herod, Why Dreadest Thou a Foe
	Wohl dem der in Gottes Furcht	Happy who in God's Fear Doth Stay
	Wär' Gott nicht mit uns	Were God Not with Us at This Time
Pre-Lent:	Es s p r i c h t der Unweisen Mund wohl	Although the Fools Say with Their Mouth

Lent:	Dies sind die heiligen zehn Gebot	These Are the Holy Ten Commands
	Mensch, willst du leben seliglich	Man, Wouldst Thou Live All Blissfully
Presentation:	Mit Fried und Freud ich fahr dahin	In Peace and Joy I Now Depart
Easter:	Christ lag in Todesbanden	Death Held Our Lord in Prison
	Jesus Christ, unser Heiland	Jesus Christ, Our Savior True
Pentecost:	Komm, Gott Schöpfer Heiliger Geist	Come, God Creator Holy Ghost
	Nun bitten wir den heiligen Geist	Now Let Us Pray to the Holy Ghost
	Komm, Heiliger Geist, Herre Gott	Come, Holy Spirit Lord and God
Trinity:	Gott der Vater wohn uns bei	God the Father with Us Be
	Wir glauben all an einen Gott	In One True God We All Believe
St. Michael and All Angels:	Sie ist mir lieb, die werte Magd	To Me She's Dear, the Worthy Maid

The Catechism

First Part:	Dies sind die heiligen zehn Gebot	These Are the Holy Ten Commands
	Mensch, willst du leben seliglich	Man, Wouldst Thou Live All Blissfully
Second Part:	Wir glauben all an einen Gott	In One True God We All Believe
Third Part:	Vater unser im Himmelreich	Our Father in the Heaven who Art
Fourth Part:	Christ unser Herr zum Jordan kam	To Jordan When Our Lord Had Gone
Fifth Part:	Jesus Christus unser Heiland	Jesus Christ, Our God and Savior

The Gospel of the Reformation

	Ein neues Lied wir heben an	A New Song Here Shall Be Begun
	Nun freut euch, liebe Christen	Dear Christians, Let Us Now Rejoice
	Ach Gott vom Himmel, sieh darein	Ah God, from Heaven Look Down
	Ein feste Burg	Our God He Is a Castle Strong
	Erhalt uns, Herr, bei deinem Wort	Lord, Keep Us Steadfast in Thy Word

"A New Song Here Shall Be Begun"

1523

Among Luther's most faithful followers were members of his own order. As early as 1519 Jakob Spreng, the prior of the Augustinian monastery in Antwerp, defended Luther's teachings. In 1521 the Diet of Worms put Luther under the ban, called him a devil in human form, and branded his teaching heretical. In the parts of Germany where Lutheranism was strongest, the terms of this edict were never carried out. Luther's own prince, Frederick the Wise, refused to set his name to it, and, instead of prosecuting Luther, he had him taken into protective custody on the Wartburg.

In the Netherlands, however, political conditions were different. These lands were directly under the emperor. Here the Edict of Worms was carried out to the letter. In Antwerp Jakob Spreng and his successor Henry von Zütphen were arrested and threatened with execution. The remaining Augustinians were undeterred and continued to preach with great success, and so the whole monastery was laid to the ground and all the monks imprisoned. When the scholastics of the famous University of Louvain made it known that the friars would either have to recant or be burned at the stake, all but three renounced Lutheran teaching. The three confessors were convicted of heresy and condemned to death at the stake. The fate of one of them, Lambert Thorn, is not quite clear. He remained in prison and was not executed until 1528. Luther sent him a letter of comfort in 1524.[1] But the other two, Heinrich Voes and Johann Esch, died martyrs' deaths at the market place in Brussels on July 1, 1523, the first blood witnesses of the Reformation.[2]

Naturally, Luther was deeply moved. Instead of pitying these men for the sacrifice which they had been forced to offer, he considered their faithfulness a victory and their martyrdom an honor. But he was incensed by the rumors quickly spread by his enemies who claimed that Heinrich and Johann had with their dying

---

[1] *WA*, Br 3, No. 707, pp. 238-239.
[2] See also *The Burning of Brother Henry*. LW 32, 261-283.

breath disavowed their own teaching and made their "peace with the church." He wanted the blood witness of these two men to be known and the lies of his enemies to be exposed. And so he availed himself of the mass media most commonly used in his day for broadcasting important news. In an age without newspapers, radio, or television, when many people were illiterate, the folk song was the most common form of mass communication. Folk ballads told the stories of kings and villains, of treason and heroism, of battles and banditry. They were printed on broadsheets and widely sold. Wandering minstrels sang them in the market place, the roadside, and the tavern. The ballads quickly made their way from town to town, and soon they were known by heart. Their style was dramatic and direct, their language simple. Often they began with an introductory verse, such as "What shall we now take up and sing?"[3]

Luther was thoroughly familiar with ballads such as these. In his student days he mastered the lute. On the way to the Diet of Worms he entertained the guests at an inn in Frankfurt, singing and accompanying himself on the lute.

It was this role Luther assumed when he wrote the ballad of the two Brussels martyrs, probably early in August, 1523. Beginning with the characteristic folk song phrase, "A new song here shall be begun," it became the first hymn of the Reformation. Overnight, as it were, Luther became aware of his gift as a hymnist, and the bulk of his hymns appeared within the next few months. Although Luther wrote no other hymns in the form of a ballad, his martyrs' hymn served as the pattern for countless Anabaptist hymns that appeared in the following years, describing the fate of their martyrs in as many as one hundred stanzas.

Luther's "A New Song Here Shall Be Begun" appeared first on a broadsheet of 1523. Subsequently it found its place in the enchiridia and in Walter's Wittenberg hymnal of 1524, but with a significant difference: the ninth and tenth stanzas in Walter's and all later versions are not found in the enchiridia. Lucke[4] stresses the inherent contradiction between stanzas nine-ten and stanzas

---

[3] *Was wollen wir singen und heben an?*
[4] WA 35, 93-94.

eleven-twelve. While the former accuse Luther's enemies of try
ing to hush up the case, the latter denounce them for spreading
falsehoods about an alleged retraction on the part of the martyrs.
Lucke believes that Luther intended stanzas nine and ten to replace eleven and twelve and that the printer mistakenly inserted
all four stanzas. However, assuming the truth of the conjecture, it
would seem strange that none of the later hymnals appearing
under Luther's supervision corrected the mistake. And the example of modern dictatorships shows that the same censor who
tries to suppress a certain news item will often at the same time
set his own version of the event afloat in order to confuse those
who might have heard of it in spite of the official suppression.

The music, too, is in the style of a folk ballad. Its similarity
to "Our God He Is a Castle Strong" both in structure and melodic
progression is evident. Luther's authorship can be taken for
granted. In this edition the melody has been transposed a fourth
lower. The German text, "*Eyn newes lyed wyr heben an*," is given
in *WA* 35, 411-415; the music is given in *WA* 35, 487-488. The
translation, with minor alterations,[5] is from MacDonald, *Exotics*,
pp. 71-76.

---

[5] The first and third lines in the third stanza are from Richard Massie, *Martin Luther's Spiritual Songs*, p. 41.

"A New Song Here Shall Be Begun"

ERFURT 1524

1. A new song here shall be be - gun—
The Lord God help our sing - ing! Of what our God himself hath done, Praise, hon - or to him bring - ing. At Brus - sels
in the Neth - er - lands By two boys, mar - tyrs youth - ful
He showed the won - ders of his hands, Whom he with
fa - vor truth - - ful So rich - ly hath a - dorn - ed.

2 The first right fitly John was named,
So rich he in God's favor;
His brother, Henry—one unblamed,
Whose salt lost not its savor.
From this world they are gone away,
The diadem they've gained;
Honest, like God's good children, they
For his word life disdained,
And have become his martyrs.

---

[1] Walter's Wittenberg hymnal of 1524 and most later hymnals have the final
cadence lead to the dominant instead of the tonic:

So rich - ly hath a - dorn - ed.

3 The old arch-fiend did them immure
   With terrors did enwrap them.
   He bade them God's dear Word abjure,
   With cunning he would trap them:
   From Louvain many sophists came,
   In their curst nets to take them,
   By him are gathered to the game:
   The Spirit fools doth make them—
   They could get nothing by it.

4 Oh! they sang sweet, and they sang sour;
   Oh! they tried every double;
   The boys they stood firm as a tower,
   And mocked the sophists' trouble.
   The ancient foe it filled with hate
   That he was thus defeated
   By two such youngsters—he, so great!
   His wrath grew sevenfold heated,
   He laid his plans to burn them.

5 Their cloister-garments off they tore,
   Took off their consecrations;
   All this the boys were ready for,
   They said Amen with patience.
   To God their Father they gave thanks
   That they would soon be rescued
   From Satan's scoffs and mumming pranks,
   With which, in falsehood masked,
   The world he so befooleth.

6 Then gracious God did grant to them
   To pass true priesthood's border,
   And offer up themselves to him,
   And enter Christ's own order,
   Unto the world to die outright,
   With falsehood made a schism,
   And come to heaven all pure and white,
   To monkery be the besom,
   And leave men's toys behind them.

7 They wrote for them a paper small,
   And made them read it over;
   The parts they showed them therein all
   Which their belief did cover.
   Their greatest fault was saying this:
   "In God we should trust solely;
   For man is always full of lies,
   We should distrust him wholly:"
   So they must burn to ashes.

8 Two huge great fires they kindled then,
   The boys they carried to them;
   Great wonder seized on every man,
   For with contempt they view them.
   To all with joy they yielded quite,
   With singing and God-praising;

The sophs had little appetite
For these new things so dazing.
Which God was thus revealing.

9 They now repent the deed of blame,[2]
Would gladly gloze it over;
They dare not glory in their shame,
The facts almost they cover.
In their hearts gnaweth infamy—
They to their friends deplore it;
The Spirit cannot silent be:
Good Abel's blood out-poured
Must still besmear Cain's forehead.

10 Leave off their ashes never will;
Into all lands they scatter;
Stream, hole, ditch, grave—nought keeps them still
With shame the foe they spatter.
Those whom in life with bloody hand
He drove to silence triple,
When dead, he them in every land,
In tongues of every people,
Must hear go gladly singing.

11 But yet their lies they will not leave,
To trim and dress the murther;
The fable false which out they gave,
Shows conscience grinds them further.
God's holy ones, e'en after death,
They still go on belying;
They say that with their latest breath,
The boys, in act of dying,
Repented and recanted.

12 Let them lie on for evermore—
No refuge so is reared;
For us, we thank our God therefore,
His word has reappeared.
Even at the door is summer nigh,
The winter now is ended,
The tender flowers come out and spy;
His hand when once extended
Withdraws not till he's finished.

---

[2] *WA* 35, 414-415, prints this verse and the next one at the end of the poem; cf. pp. 212-213.

"Dear Christians, Let Us Now Rejoice"

1523

If the ballad describing the martyrs' deaths of Johann Esch and Heinrich Voes was Luther's first hymn, this ballad of the believer's justification was most likely his second. With the former it shares a vivid, personal, dramatic style. But while in the martyrs' hymn two individuals served to illustrate the joy and confidence of faith, here the same theme is depicted in the struggles and victories of every believer. And while the first hymn described a historical event, the second takes its material from Luther's innermost experiences.[1]

The first source of Luther's hymn, the *Achtliederbuch*, seems to have reprinted it from an earlier broadsheet. The date 1523 still appears at the end of the hymn. Copies of this leaflet that remained extant to the nineteenth century are now lost, but two broadsheets from 1524 are in existence. From the *Achtliederbuch* the hymn passed into all Lutheran hymnals, beginning with the Erfurt enchiridia and Walter's Wittenberg hymnal of 1524. Three melodies have been associated with it. The *Achtliederbuch* gives a magnificent tune which, with its leaping fourths in the first, third, fifth, and seventh lines, graphically portrays the mood of the words. This is the proper tune for the hymn and is also found in Walter's Wittenberg hymnal and many later collections. Quite likely it is from Luther's own pen, even though here as elsewhere he made use of a well-known idiom. The two vigorous fourths in the opening line are found in other folk songs of the period. Besides

---

[1] Hans Joachim Moser in *"Nun freut euch, lieben Christen gmein," Gestalt und Glaube. Festschrift für . . . Oskar Soehngen* (Wittenberg: Luther-Verlag, 1960), pp. 137-144, seeks to prove that here too the Reformer makes use of older folk song patterns. *The Songbook of Ann of Cologne* (*ca.* 1500) has a hymn, *"Ervreue dich, lieve krystengemeyn,"* which shows striking similarities with "Dear Christians, Let Us Now Rejoice." The first four lines of the first two stanzas are identical with the corresponding lines in Luther's hymn, and the last three lines of Luther's seventh stanza are the same as its refrains for both the first and second stanzas. Paul Albers, however, comes to the opposite conclusion in Ameln *et al.* (eds.), *Jahrbuch für Liturgik und Hymnologie,* V, 132-133, as does Ludwig Wolff, *ibid.,* VII, 99-102. They both consider *"Ervreuwe dich"* a corrupted version of Luther's hymn that was subsequently entered on a blank page in the *Songbook of Ann of Cologne.*

this melody, two other tunes were also associated with this hymn in the Reformation hymnals. The Erfurt enchiridia prescribe for it the tune *"Es ist das Heil uns kommen her."*[2] This may be the tune that Luther originally had in mind when he wrote the hymn, for before the tune became associated with its present text it belonged to two pre-Reformation hymns: *"Freu dich, du werte Christenheit"* and *"Freut euch, ihr Frauen und ihr Mann."* Finally in Klug 1533 and subsequent hymnals the tune *"Es ist gewisslich an der Zeit"*[3] was assigned to it, evidently with the intention of providing a simpler melody. But neither this melody nor *"Es ist das Heil"* expresses the same exuberant joy as the proper tune. It is the latter that we offer in our edition. The German text, *"Nu freut euch, lieben Christen gmeyn,"* is given in WA 35, 422-425; all three melodies are given in WA 35, 493-495. The translation, with slight revisions, is that by MacDonald, *Exotics*, pp. 80-83.

---

[2] *Service Book and Hymnal of the Lutheran Church in America* (1958), No. 259.

[3] *Common Service Book of the Lutheran Church* (Philadelphia, 1917/18), No. 514. This melody is often, but improperly, called *"Nun freut euch"* in modern English and American hymnals.

"Dear Christians, Let Us Now Rejoice"

NÜRNBERG 1523

1. { Dear Chris - tians, let us now re - joice,
   { That of good cheer and with one voice,

And dance in joy - ous meas - ure: Of what to
We sing in love and pleas - ure.

us our God hath shown, And the sweet won - der

he hath done; Full dear - ly hath he wrought it.

2 Forlorn and lost in death I lay,
A captive to the devil,
My sin lay heavy, night and day,
For I was born in evil.
I fell but deeper for my strife,
There was no good in all my life,
For sin had all possessed me.

3 My good works they were worthless quite,
A mock was all my merit;
My will hated God's judging light,
To all good dead and buried.
E'en to despair me anguish bore,
That nought but death lay me before;
To hell I fast was sinking.

4 Then God was sorry on his throne
To see such torment rend me;
His tender mercy he thought on,
His good help he would send me.
He turned to me his father-heart;
Ah! then was his no easy part,
For of his best it cost him.

---

[1] Some of the later hymnals substitute here *d* for *f* to avoid the high note.
[2] Some hymnals simplify and corrupt this passage to read *c, b, d,* etc.

5 To his dear Son he said: "Go down,
'Tis time to take compassion.
Go down, my heart's exalted crown,
Be the poor man's salvation.
Lift him from out sin's scorn and scath,
Strangle for him that cruel Death,
That he with thee live ever."

6 The Son he heard obediently,
And by a maiden mother,
Pure, tender—down he came to me,
For he would be my brother.
Secret he bore his strength enorm,
He went about in my poor form,
For he would catch the devil.

7 He said to me: "Hold thou by me,
Thy matters I will settle;
I give myself all up for thee,
And I will fight thy battle.
For I am thine, and thou art mine,
And my place also shall be thine;
The enemy shall not part us.

8 "He will as water shed my blood,
My life he from me reave will;
All this I suffer for thy good—
To that with firm faith cleave well.
My life from death the day shall win,
My innocence shall bear thy sin,
So art thou blest forever.

9 "To heaven unto my Father high,
From this life I am going;
But there thy Master still am I,
My spirit on thee bestowing,
Whose comfort shall thy trouble quell,
Who thee shall teach to know me well,
And in the truth shall guide thee.

10 "What I have done, and what I've said,
Shall be thy doing, teaching,
So that God's kingdom may be spread—
All to his glory reaching.
Beware what men would bid thee do,
For that corrupts the treasure true;
With this last word I leave thee."

"From Trouble Deep I Cry to Thee"
[The 130th Psalm]
1523

n his *Order of Mass and Communion,* 1523, Luther had expressed
his desire to have more German hymns sung in the service and his
disappointment at the lack of poets.[1] Toward the end of the same
year, he wrote to his friend the court chaplain, George Spalatin,
and solicited his help. "Following the example of the prophets
and fathers of the church, I intend to make German Psalms for
the people, i.e., spiritual songs so that the Word of God even by
means of song may live among the people.

"Everywhere we are looking for poets. Now since you are so
skilful and eloquent in German, I would like to ask you to work
with us in this and to turn a Psalm into a hymn as in the enclosed sample of my own work. But I would like you to avoid
new-fangled, fancied words and to use expressions simple and
common enough for the people to understand, yet pure and fitting.
The meaning should also be clear and as close as possible to the
Psalm. Irrespective of the exact wording, one must freely render
the sense by suitable words. I myself am not sufficiently gifted
to do these things as I would. But you may be a Heman [I Chron.
6:33 and *passim*], Asaph [I Chron. 6:39 and *passim*], or Jeduthun
[I Chron. 16:41]. . . . Perhaps I may recommend to you the 6th
Psalm, *Domine, ne in furore,* or the 143rd, *Domine, exaudi,* and to
Johann Dolzig the 32nd, *Beati quorum;* for I have already translated the [130th] *De profundis,* and the [51st] *Miserere mei* I have
ordered from someone else. But if these are difficult to handle,
take *Benedicam Dominum* and *Exultate, justi, in Domino,* i.e., the
34th or 33rd, or else the 103rd, *Benedic, anima mea.* Answer,
please, if we may count on you. Farewell in the Lord."[2]

Spalatin apparently never fulfilled Luther's request. But the
sample Luther mentioned seems to have been his paraphrase of

---

[1] See pp. 36-37.
[2] WA, Br 3, No. 698, pp. 220-221.

the 130th Psalm, "From Trouble Deep I Cry to Thee." This would set the time of writing in the latter part of the year 1523. A broadsheet of Luther's hymn was known in Magdeburg as early as May 6, 1524.

"From Trouble Deep I Cry to Thee" is found in all the earliest hymnals, but with a significant difference. While Walter's Wittenberg hymnal of 1524 and all the later hymnals in Luther's sphere have the now-common five stanzas, a four-stanza version with slightly different lines and a conflation of the second and third stanzas is found in the *Achtliederbuch*, the Erfurt enchiridia and some later southwest German, especially Strassburg, hymnals. Jobst Gutknecht in Nürnberg, the printer of the *Achtliederbuch*, may have received this corrupted version from someone who had heard the hymn in Wittenberg, but did not know the exact words (or the tune). A six-stanza version (with a Gloria Patri), appearing first in a Low-German hymnal of 1525, is doubtlessly not by Luther.

In Wittenberg the hymn soon became a favorite for funerals. It was sung at the burials of Frederick the Wise and John of Saxony and also of Martin Luther.

A number of different melodies have been associated with it. The *Achtliederbuch* prescribes the tune *"Es ist das Heil uns kommen her"*;[3] one of the Erfurt enchiridia assigns the melody *"Ach Gott vom Himmel"*;[4] and the Strassburg hymnals since 1525 have the C major tune that is found in most American hymnals. But in the other enchiridion, in Walter's hymnal of 1524, and in subsequent Wittenberg hymnals, a Phrygian melody of great beauty became the proper tune for this text. Its plaintive character gives forceful expression to the words, and it may well be the work of Luther. We offer both this melody and the one from the Strassburg hymnals, the latter transposed to the lower fifth. The German text, *"Aus tieffer not schrey ich zu dyr,"* is given in WA 35, 419-420; both tunes are given in WA 35, 492-493. The translation, with minor revisions, is that by MacDonald, *Exotics*, pp. 101-102.

---

[3] *Service Book and Hymnal of the Lutheran Church in America* (1958), No. 259.
[4] See p. 226.

"From Trouble Deep I Cry to Thee"

Phrygian Melody

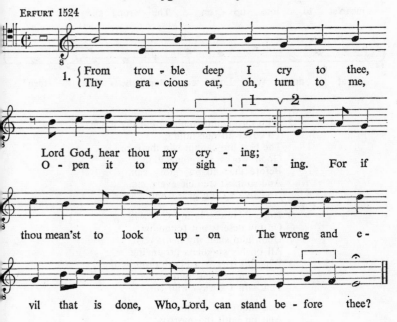

ERFURT 1524

1. From trou - ble deep I cry to thee,
   Thy gra - cious ear, oh, turn to me,

Lord God, hear thou my cry - ing;
O - pen it to my sigh - - - - ing. For if

thou mean'st to look up - on The wrong and e -

vil that is done, Who, Lord, can stand be - fore thee?

F major Melody

STRASSBURG 1525

1. From trou - ble deep I cry to thee,
   Thy gra - cious ear, oh, turn to me,

Lord God, hear thou my cry - ing;
O - pen it to my sigh - ing. For if thou

---

[1] Later Strassburg prints since 1559 have a half note here and at the asterisk.

mean'st to look up - on The wrong and e - vil

that is done, Who, Lord, can stand be - fore thee?

2 With thee counts nothing but thy grace
To cover all our failing.
The best life cannot win the race,
Good works are unavailing.
Before thee no one glory can,
And so must tremble every man,
And live by thy grace only.

3 Hope therefore in my God will I,
On my deserts not founding;
Upon him shall my heart rely,
All on his goodness grounding.
What his true Word doth promise me,
My comfort shall and refuge be;
That will I always wait for.

4 And though it last into the night,
And up until the morrow,
Yet shall my heart hope in God's might,
Nor doubt or take to worry.
Thus Israel must keep his post,
For he was born of [the] Holy Ghost,
And for his God must tarry.

5 Although our sin be great, God's grace
Is greater to relieve us;
His hand in helping nothing stays,
The hurt however grievous.
The Shepherd good alone is he,
Who will at last set Israel free,
From all and every trespass.

---

[2] *Ordnung des Herren Nachtmahl* (Strassburg, 1525) and later sources substitute *e* for *f.*

"Ah God, from Heaven Look Down"

[The 12th Psalm]

1523

This hymn is a paraphrase of Psalm 12. It probably was written about the same time as "From Trouble Deep I Cry to Thee," i.e., toward the end of 1523. Its earliest appearance is in the *Acht-liederbuch* of 1524, the editor of which used a handwritten manuscript.[1] The Erfurt enchiridia added a doxology, but it is stylistically too different to be ascribed to Luther. Also, it was not accepted by the editors of the Wittenberg hymnals.

The proper melody for this hymn is uncertain. The *Acht-liederbuch* assigns the tune *"Es ist das Heil"*[2] to Luther's three Psalm paraphrases ("Ah God, from Heaven Look Down," "Although the Fools Say with Their Mouth," and "From Trouble Deep I Cry to Thee"), probably for want of better information. The Erfurt enchiridia contain the Hypo-phrygian melody that ultimately won out. But Walter has a Dorian tune of great beauty. Klug 1533 has the melody from the enchiridia, but as second choice. His first tune is in the Phrygian mode and fell quickly into oblivion. The Strassburg hymnals give a fourth melody.

We offer the Dorian melody from Walter 1524 and the Hypo-phrygian melody from the enchiridia that became the proper tune for the hymn. One or both of these could be by the Reformer. The Dorian tune sounds somewhat like a minor counterpart to "Dear Christians, Let Us Now Rejoice."[3] But the Hypo-phrygian tune has a better claim to being Luther's. For although the first half has a close affinity to the fifteenth-century folk song *Begierlich in dem Herzen mein*," the whole melodic progression accentuates the main stresses of the text, and from Lufft's Wittenberg hymnal of 1526 on, it was in all hymnals produced under Luther.[4]

---

[1] Walter Lucke in WA 35, 14, has convincingly shown this by analyzing the editor's reading of the manuscript.
[2] *Service Book and Hymnal of the Lutheran Church in America*, No. 259.
[3] Cf. p. 219.
[4] Cf. Konrad Ameln, *"Ach Gott, vom Himmel sieh darein"* in *Jahrbuch für Liturgik und Hymnologie*, VI, 100-112.

W. A. Mozart found the Hypo-phrygian melody in a textbook on counterpoint by the Bach pupil, J. P. Kirnberger, and used it in his *Magic Flute* for the song of the "Two Men in Armor" (Second Act, Finale).

The German text, *"Ach Gott von hymel sich dar eyn,"* is given in *WA* 35, 415-417; all four melodies are given in *WA* 35, 488-490. The translation, with minor revisions, is that by MacDonald, *Exotics*, pp. 62-64.

"Ah God, from Heaven Look Down"

Hypo-phrygian Melody

ERFURT 1524

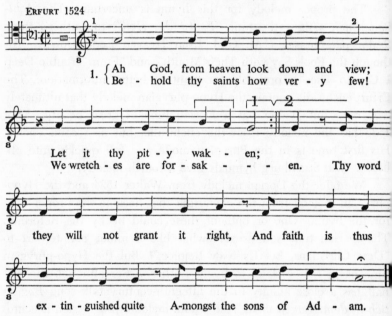

1. { Ah God, from heaven look down and view;
   { Be - hold thy saints how ver - y few!

Let it thy pit - y wak - en;
We wretch - es are for - sak - - - en. Thy word

they will not grant it right, And faith is thus

ex - tin - guished quite A-mongst the sons of Ad - am.

---

[1] The key signature *b*-flat is missing in the enchiridia, either through an oversight on the part of the printer or in accordance with the older custom of leaving altered notes to the discretion and understanding of the singer or player. From Lufft's Wittenberg hymnal of 1526 on, the key signature is regularly *b*-flat.

[2] Klug 1533 and later hymnals have a slightly different rhythm in this place: the last note of the first line is a quarter note, followed by an eighth rest and an eighth note upbeat.

Dorian Melody

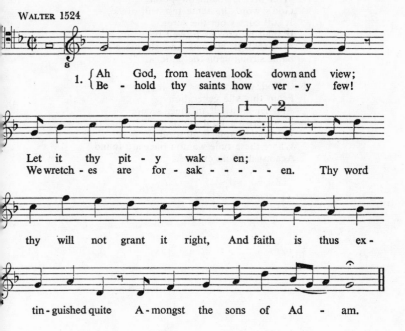

WALTER 1524

1. { Ah God, from heaven look down and view;
   { Be - hold thy saints how ver - y few!

Let it thy pit - y wak - en;
We wretch - es are for - sak - - - - - en. Thy word

thy will not grant it right, And faith is thus ex -

tin - guished quite A - mongst the sons of Ad - am.

2 They teach a cunning false and fine,
   In their own wits they found it;
   Their heart in one doth not combine,
   Upon God's word well grounded.
   One chooses this, the other that;
   Endless division they are at,
   And yet they keep smooth faces.

3 God will outroot the teachers all
   Whose false appearance teach us;
   Besides, their proud tongues loudly call—
   "What care we?—Who can reach us?
   We have the right and might in full;
   And what we say, that is the rule;
   Who dares to give us lessons?"

4 Therefore saith God: "I must be up;
   My poor ones ill are faring;
   Their sighs crowd up to Zion's top,
   My ear their cry is hearing.
   My healing word shall speedily
   With comfort fill them, fresh and free,
   And strength be to the needy."

227

5 Silver that seven times is tried
 With fire, is found the purer;
 God's word the same test will abide,
 It still comes out the surer.
 It shall by crosses proved be;
 Men shall its strength and glory see
 Shine strong upon the nations.

6 O God, we pray, preserve it pure
 From this vile generation
 And let us dwell in thee, secure
 From error's infiltration.
 The godless rout is all around
 Where these rude wanton ones are found
 Against thy folk exalted.

"Although the Fools Say with Their Mouth"

[The 14th Psalm]

1523

Since this hymn, together with "Ah God, from Heaven Look Down" and "From Trouble Deep I Cry to Thee," made its first appearance in the *Achtliederbuch*, it probably was written at the same time as they were, i.e., late in 1523. Here as in "Ah God, from Heaven Look Down," Luther may have been thinking of the enthusiasts. Liturgically, the hymn seems to have been assigned to the pre-Lenten season.[1]

As a tune for this hymn the *Achtliederbuch* prescribes "*Es ist das Heil*,"[2] i.e., the same tune it prescribes for the other two Luther Psalm paraphrases. The Erfurt enchiridia assign to it "*Salvum me fac*," i.e., the Hypo-phrygian melody of "Ah God, from Heaven Look Down." The Strassburg hymnals give it the Hypo-mixo-lydian tune "*Ach Gott, wie sind mein Sünd' so viel*."[3] But the melody that became the proper tune is the Hypo-ionian tune first offered by Walter in 1524. It is the one we offer in our edition, transposed to the lower fourth.

The original text, "*Es spricht der unweysen mund wol*," is given in WA 35, 441-443; the Walter melody is given in WA 35, 505. The translation, with minor revisions, is that by MacDonald, *Exotics*, pp. 64-66.

Cf. WA 35, 22.
Service Book and Hymnal of the Lutheran Church in America (1958), No. 259.
WA 35, 505.

"Although the Fools Say with Their Mouth"

WALTER 1524.

1. {Al - though the fools say with their mouth:
   {Their heart cares noth - ing for the truth,

"Great God, we mag - ni - fy him,"
In ac - tion they de - ny him. Their be-

ing is cor - rupt - ed quite; To God it is a

hor - rid sight; Not one of them works good - ness.

2 From heaven God downward cast his eye
Upon men's sons so many;
He set himself to look and spy
If he could find out any
Who all their understanding bent
To search his holy word, intent
To do his will in earnest.

3 Upon the right path there was none;
From it they all were straying;
Each followed fancies of his own,
Ill manners them betraying.
Not one there was who practiced good,
And yet they deemed in haughty mood
Their deeds must surely please him.

4 How long by lies will they be led,
Who vain attempts redouble,
And eat my people up as bread,
And live upon their trouble?
In God is not their confidence,
In need they ask not his defense,
They will themselves look after.

---

[1] Several hymnals have *e* in this place.
[2] Several hymnals have *c* in this place.

5 Therefore their heart is never still,
But always full of fearing.
Dwell with the good the Father will,
With them whose ears are hearing.
But ye despise the poor man's ways,
And scorn at everything he says
Concerning God his comfort.

6 Who will to Israel's scattered flock,
To Zion send salvation?
God will take pity on his folk,
And free his captive nation.
That will he do through Christ his Son;
And then is Jacob's weeping done,
And Israel filled with gladness.

"Would That the Lord Would Grant Us Grace"

[The 67th Psalm]

1523

Luther's *Order of Mass and Communion* had just been published in 1523, when his friend and co-worker Paul Speratus made a German translation of it.[1] This work appeared early in 1524. As a matter of fact, it must have left the press within the very first weeks of the year, for of the two copies which are still preserved one bears the handwritten inscription "January," and the other the date "*Anno* 1524, January 18." These inscriptions are significant for dating the hymn "Would That the Lord Would Grant Us Grace," for it was appended to Speratus' translation of *An Order of Mass and Communion*. Thus Luther wrote this paraphrase of Psalm 67 sometime during the latter part of 1523, probably at the same time he wrote his other Psalm paraphrases. Incidentally, this is the first missionary hymn of Protestantism.

The first publication of both text and music was on a broad sheet printed by Hans Knappe the Younger in Magdeburg in 1524. This print, too, is likely to have been published quite early in the year, for on May 6 of that year a man was arrested in Magdeburg for singing and selling the hymns "From Trouble Deep I Cry to Thee" and "Would That the Lord Would Grant Us Grace."[2] Another broadsheet (undated) was printed by Jobst Gutknecht, the publisher of the *Achtliederbuch*, in Nürnberg, which does not contain it. But it is found in the Erfurt enchiridia, Walter's Wittenberg hymnal, and in all subsequent collections.

Apparently, Luther thought of it as a "closing hymn." It is the only Psalm paraphrase that ends in an "Amen." It stands at the end of Speratus' translation, and it accords with Luther's suggestion in *An Order of Mass and Communion* that the service might close with either the Aaronic Benediction or Ps. 67:6-7.[3]

The proper melody for this hymn is the one first published on

---

[1] See p. 17.
[2] See p. 222.
[3] See p. 30.

232

Knappe's broadsheet. This Phrygian tune is an adaptation from an
older German hymn to the Virgin *"Maria du bist Gnaden voll."*[4]
It was soon accepted in all hymnals, and even in Wittenberg it replaced the Dorian tune originally used by Walter. The latter was
ultimately assigned to "To Jordan When Our Lord Had Gone" and
will be found with this baptismal hymn.[5]

The German text, *"ES wollt uns Gott genedig seyn,"* is given
in WA 35, 418-419. We offer the Phrygian tune in the version
of Knappe's broadsheet; for a slightly different rhythmical version, see WA 35, 491-492. The translation, with some revision, is
that by MacDonald, *Exotics,* pp. 77-78, with the exception of the
second half of the first stanza and the first half of the third stanza,
which were taken from Massie, *Martin Luther's Spiritual Songs,*
pp. 45-46.

Cf. Ameln, *"Es wolle Gott uns gnädig sein,"* *Jahrbuch für Liturgik und
Hymnologie,* III, 105-108 (including a facsimile of Knappe's broadsheet).
See p. 300.

"Would that the Lord Would Grant Us Grace"

MAGDEBURG 1524

1. Would that the Lord would grant us grace,
   And with clear shin-ing let his face
   With bless-ings rich pro-vide us,
   To life e-ter-nal light us; That we his
   gra-cious work may know, And what is his good pleas-ure,
   And al-so to the hea-then show Christ's rich-es
   with-out meas-ure And un-to God con-vert them.

2 Now let the heathen thank and praise
  The Lord with gladsome voices;
  Let all the world for joy upraise
  A song with mighty noises,
  Because thou art earth's judge, O Lord,
  And sin no more prevaileth;
  Thy word it is both bed and board,
  And for all folk availeth
  In the right path to keep them.

3 O let the people praise thy worth,
  In all good works increasing;
  The land shall plenteous fruit bring forth,
  Thy word is rich in blessing.
  May we be blest by Father, Son,
  Blest also by the Holy Ghost
  To whom by all be honor done,
  Whom all the world shall fear the most.
  Thus heartily say: Amen.

---

[1] Strassburg 1525 and later hymnals have half notes here and at all or more of the places marked with an asterisk.

234

"Come, the Heathen's Healing Light"

[*Veni Redemptor Gentium*]

1523

ince this Advent hymn appears in both the Erfurt enchiridia of 524 and Walter's hymnal of 1524, it may have been written for dvent, 1523. It is a quite literal translation of the *"Veni Re- emptor Gentium"* by Ambrose, except in the last stanza where uther substituted a doxology for the original words. There is also metrical change. Instead of the original Long Meter, Luther in- oduced a stanza of 7.7.7.7. He also made skilful changes in the elodic line. By ending the second verse on the mediant, he dded a cadence not found in the original hymn. He cleared way most of the ligatures and brought out the vigorous leap of fourth from *g* to *c*, making the first and last verses identical. hese changes, small though they may seem, change the character f the melody completely and make a Lutheran chorale of a me- ieval hymn.

This version is the one in the Erfurt enchiridia. The hymn as also included in Walter's Wittenberg hymnal of the same year, ut in a more melismatic form. We offer the melody as it ap- ears in the enchiridia. The German text, *"Nu kom der heyden Ieyland,"* is given in WA 35, 430-431; the melody is given in WA 5, 497. The translation of stanzas 3, 5, 6, and 7 is that by Mac-)onald, *Exotics*, pp. 39-40; the remaining stanzas were translated y the editor.

235

"Come, the Heathen's Healing Light"

ERFURT 1524

1. Come, the hea - then's heal - ing Light,

Hum - bly known a maid - en's child, Fill with won - der

all ·the earth God should grant it such a birth.

2 Not of flesh, nor of man's blood
Was incarned the Word of God.
By the Holy Ghost alone
Blossomed forth the virgin's womb.

3 Maiden she was found with child,
Chastity yet undefiled;
Many a virtue from her shone,
God was there as on his throne.

4 From the chamber of her womb,
From the royal hall he came.
Very man and God of grace
Forth he comes to run his race.

5 From the Father came his road,
And returns again to God;
Unto hell his road went down,
Up then to the Father's throne.

6 Equal with the Father, win
Vict'ry in the flesh o'er sin
Let the health which thou hast brought
In our mortal flesh be wrought.

7 Shine thy manger bright and clear,
Sets the night a new star there;
Darkness thence must keep away,
Faith dwells ever in the day.

8 Honor unto God be done;
Honor to his only Son;
Honor to the Holy Ghost,
Now, and ever, ending not.

"Jesus We Now Must Laud and Sing"

[A solis ortus cardine]

1523?

For Laudes on Christmas Day the *Antiphonale Romanum* prescribes the hymn *"A solis ortus cardine"* by the sixth-century bishop Coelius Sedulius. Several German translations of it had been made before Luther, the latest by Johannes Hutt, an Anabaptist of the group around Thomas Münzer. But Luther made no use of any of these. Indeed, he was the first translator to reverse the first and second halves of the first stanza so that the name of Jesus strikingly stands at the head of the whole hymn. Since this hymn first appeared in the Erfurt enchiridia of 1524 and in Walter's Wittenberg hymnal of 1524, it may have been written for Christmas, 1523.

Both sources retain the traditional plain-chant melody, but with a significant difference: while Walter and some of the later hymnals give the Gregorian melody unchanged with all its ligatures and curlicues, the enchiridia and the majority of later hymnals offer a radically simplified, syllabic version more suitable to congregational singing. Quite likely Luther took a hand in editing it according to his own concept of German plain song.[1] A later version of this simplified form came into general use with Klug's Wittenberg hymnal. For purposes of comparison, we offer all three forms of the melody in our edition (with the Walter melody transposed a fourth lower).

The German text, *"Christum wyr sollen loben schon,"* is given in *WA* 35, 431-433; all three forms of the melody are given in *WA* 35, 498-499. The translation is that by MacDonald, *Exotics,* pp. 42-43.

---

[1] See p. 55.

"Jesus We Now Must Laud and Sing"

WALTER 1524

ERFURT 1524

KLUG 1533

1. Je - sus we now must laud and sing, The

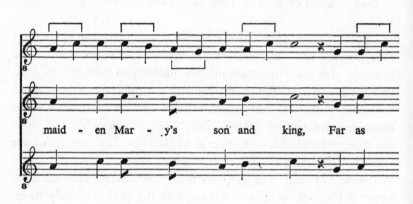

maid - en Mar - y's son and king, Far as

the bless - ed sun doth shine,

And reach-es to earth's ut - - most line.[1]

2 The blest Maker of all we view
  On a poor servant's body drew,
  The flesh to save at flesh's cost,
  Or else his creature would be lost.

3 From heaven high the godlike grace
  In the chaste mother found a place;
  A secret pledge a maiden bore—
  Which nature never knew before.

4 The tender heart, house modest, low,
  A temple of our God did grow;
  Whom not a man hath touched or known,
  By God's word she with child is grown.

5 The noble mother hath brought forth
  Whom Gabriel promised to the earth;
  Him John did greet in joyous way,
  While in his mother's womb he lay.

6 Right poorly lies in hay the boy;
  Th' hard manger caused him no annoy;
  A little milk made him content,
  Away who no bird hungry sent.

7 Therefore the heavenly choir is loud;
  The angels sing their praise to God,
  And tell poor men their flocks who keep
  He's come who makes and keeps the sheep.

8 Praise, honor, thanks, to thee be said,
  Christ Jesus, born of holy maid!
  With God, Father and Holy Ghost,
  Now and forever, ending not.

---

[1] Luther's construction.

"All Praise to Thee, O Jesus Christ"
1523?

The first stanza of this hymn was known long before the Reformation and was frequently sung on Christmas Day as the people's response to the sequence *"Grates nunc omnes."*[1] The earliest source for it is a Low-German manuscript from around 1370. The *Kyrioleis* marks it as a *Leise*, i.e., a vernacular hymn that developed from the acclamation *Kyrie eleison* and retained it at the end of every stanza. The complete text of this hymn originally appeared on a broadsheet printed in Augsburg, presumably by Melchior Ramminger. If this print—as is likely—appeared early in 1524, Luther may have written the hymn for Christmas, 1523.

The origin of the melody is uncertain. Lacking a pre-Reformation source for the music, we cannot tell whether it was traditional or Luther's own creation. But in keeping with his general practice, it would seem more likely that he retained the tune popularly associated with the words. Note the absence of an upbeat in the second line, which makes for an interesting alternation of iambic and trochaic rhythms.

We offer text and melody as they appeared in Walter's Wittenberg hymnal of 1524. The text, *"Gelobet seystu Jhesu Christ,"* is given in *WA* 35, 434-435; the music is given in *WA* 35, 499. The translation is that by MacDonald, *Exotics*, pp. 43-45.

"All Praise to Thee, O Jesus Christ"

WALTER 1524

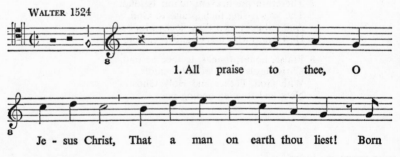

1. All praise to thee, O Je - sus Christ, That a man on earth thou liest! Born

---

[1] See p. 25, n. 31.

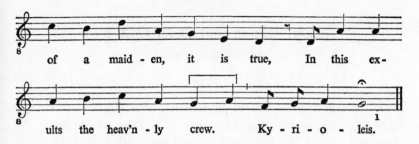

of a maid - en, it is true, In this ex-

ults the heav'n - ly crew. Ky - ri - o - leis.

2 The Father's only son begot
In the manger has his cot,
In our poor dying flesh and blood
Doth mask itself the endless good.
Kyrioleis.

3 Whom all the world could not enwrap,
Lieth he in Mary's lap;
A little child he now is grown,
Who everything upholds alone.
Kyrioleis.

4 In him the eternal light breaks through,
Gives the world a glory new;
A great light shines amid the night,
And makes us children of the light.
Kyrioleis.

5 The Father's Son, so God by name,
A guest in the world became,
And leads us from the vale of tears;
He in his palace makes us heirs.
Kyrioleis.

6 Poor to the earth he cometh thus,
Pity so to take on us,
And make us rich in heaven above,
And like the angels of his love.
Kyrioleis.

7 All this for us did Jesus do,
That his great love he might show.
Let Christendom rejoice therefore,
And give him thanks for evermore.
Kyrioleis.

---

[1] Kyrie eleison, a common contraction in medieval sacred folk song.

"Happy who in God's Fear Doth Stay"

[The 128th Psalm]

1524

In opposition to the medieval glorification of celibacy, Luther never tired of praising the married estate as a divine institution. No wonder he loved and frequently quoted the 128th Psalm! He made not only a German but also a Latin paraphrase of it.[1] The German hymn probably dates from the same period as the other early Psalm hymns. Possibly he was inspired to write it by a sermon on the wedding at Cana (John 2:1-11) which he preached on January 17, 1524.[2] It was assigned to the Epiphany season in Walter's and subsequent hymnals because of its reference to the Gospel for the Second Sunday after the Epiphany. The earliest sources for it are the Erfurt enchiridia and Walter 1524.

The hymnals of the sixteenth century offer four different melodies for this hymn. The enchiridia and related sources assign it the so-called "Tune of St. John Huss," i.e., the melody of "Jesus Christ, Our God and Savior."[3] The tune in Walter's Wittenberg hymnal of 1524 is a bright F major melody, but it is rhythmically rather intricate. Hymnals after Klug 1533 simplified the rhythm of this melody and altered the final cadence to end on the Tonic instead of the Dominant. A third melody found in editions of Walter's hymnal after 1537 failed to make its way in congregational use, and a fourth in the Dorian mode remained confined to the Strassburg hymnals.

In our edition we offer Walter's tune both in its original and in its simplified form, transposed to C major. The German text, *"Wol dem der ynn Gottes furcht steht,"* is given in WA 35, 437-438; all four melodies are given in WA 35, 501-502. The translation is that by MacDonald, *Exotics,* pp. 78-79.

---

[1] See WA 35, 603.
[2] See WA 15, 417-421.
[3] See p. 250.

"Happy who in God's Fear Doth Stay"

WALTER 1524

KLUG 1533

1. Hap - py who in God's fear doth stay,

And in it go - eth on his way;

Thine own hand shall thee find thy food,

So liv'st thou right, and all is good.

2 So shall thy wife be in thy house
Like vine with clusters plenteous,
Thy children sit thy table round
Like olive plants all fresh and sound.

3 See, such rich blessing hangs him on
Who in God's fear doth live a man;
From him the [old] curse away is worn,
With which the sons of men are born.

243

4 From Zion God will prosper thee;
Thou shalt behold continually
Jerusalem's now happy case,
To God so pleasing in her grace.

5 He will thy days make long for thee,
With goodness ever nigh thee be,
That thou with thy sons' sons may'st dwell.
And there be peace in Israel.

"Were God Not with Us at This Time"

[The 124th Psalm]

1524

When Luther, in his letter to Spalatin,[1] suggested several Psalms for versification, he did not mention the 124th. Perhaps he knew the paraphrase by his friend Justus Jonas, "*Wo Gott der Herr nicht bei uns hält,*"[2] or had even inspired it. This may have been the "poem of Justus Jonas, the provost" which Luther sent to Spalatin on January 14, 1524,[3] for in the same year it appeared in the Erfurt enchiridia. Nevertheless, Luther too wrote a hymn version of the same Psalm, "Were God Not with Us at This Time," which first appeared in Walter's Wittenberg hymnal of 1524. From then on, both hymns are found in all the basic collections. It is difficult to say why Luther duplicated the effort of his friend. To the modern ear Jonas' hymn sounds much smoother and more elegant. Luther's style appears rough-edged and craggy in comparison. However, Luther keeps closer to the Psalm and has three stanzas to Jonas' eight. Perhaps Luther found Jonas' hymn too long and wordy. From its place in the Walter collection and in later lists of *de tempore* hymns, Lucke conjectures that Luther's hymn was assigned to the Epiphany season.[4]

Three melodies have been associated with it. The first is the Dorian tune Walter offered in 1524, which passed into all the major hymnals as the proper tune for this hymn. A different melody in the Zwickau enchiridion of 1528 was not accepted elsewhere, and also the tune substituted in later editions of Walter (after 1537) could not compete with the original melody. We offer the original Dorian tune in our edition. The German text, "*Wer Gott nicht mit uns diese zeyt,*" is given in WA 35, 440-441; the three melodies are given in WA 35, 504-505. The translation is that by MacDonald, *Exotics*, p. 68.

---

[1] See p. 221.
[2] "If God Were Not upon Our Side." Cf. Julian, *Dictionary of Hymnology*, p. 605.
[3] WA, Br 3, No. 705, pp. 234-235.
[4] WA 35, 22.

"Were God Not with Us at This Time"

WALTER 1524

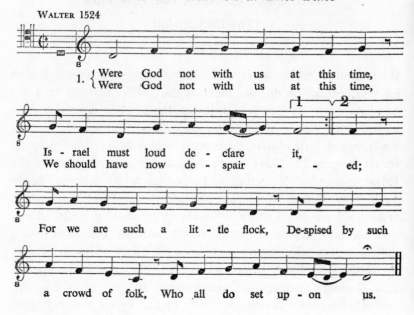

1. Were God not with us at this time,
Were God not with us at this time,
Is-rael must loud de-clare it,
We should have now de-spair - - ed;
For we are such a lit-tle flock, De-spised by such
a crowd of folk, Who all do set up-on us.

2 'Gainst us so angry is their mood,
If God had giv'n them tether,
Us they had swallowed where we stood,
Body and soul together.
We were like drowning men, like those
Above whose heads the waters close,
And sweep them down with fury.

3 Thank God! their throat he did not yet
Let swallow though it gaped;
As from a snare the bird doth flit,
So is our soul escaped.
The snare's in two, and we are through;
The name of God it standeth true,
The God of earth and heaven.

246

"In Peace and Joy I Now Depart"

[The Nunc Dimittis]

1524

This hymn was first published in Walter's Wittenberg hymnal of 1524. When it was written is uncertain, but perhaps it was for Candlemas (February 2) of the same year. At any rate, its place in Walter's collection, preceded and followed by Epiphany hymns, marks it as a hymn for the festival of the Presentation. Later it was also used as a funeral hymn and included in Klug's burial hymns of 1542.[1]

The only melody associated with it is a Dorian tune that appears in Walter's collection. It has the syncopations typical of sixteenth-century polyphonic *cantus firmi*, and with its bold broad steps, it may well be by Luther. We offer it in a form somewhat simplified from the way it appeared in Klug's hymnal of 1533 (and a fourth lower than in the original). The German text, *"Myt frid und freud ich far do hyn,"* is given in *WA* 35, 438-439; the melody in Walter's version is given in *WA* 35, 503-504. The translation is a revision of that by MacDonald, *Exotics*, pp. 109-110, with an assist in the third stanza from Catherine Winkworth's *Christian Singers of Germany* (Macmillan, 1869), p. 115.

---

[1] See pp. 325-331.

"In Peace and Joy I Now Depart"

KLUG 1533

1. In peace and joy . I now de - part, As God wants me. Con-tent and still is mind and heart, He doth save me. As my God hath prom-ised me, Death is be - come my slum - ber.

2 That is because Christ was God's Son,
  Our Savior true,
  Whom thou, O Lord, to me hast shown,
  And made me know
  As the life everlasting
  And health in pain and dying.

3 For thou in mercy unto all
  Hast set him forth.
  And to his kingdom thou dost call
  The whole wide earth
  Through thy precious wholesome word
  In ev'ry place resounding.

4 He is the health and happy light
  Of the heathen,
  To feed them and their eyes make bright
  Thee to see then.
  Of thy folk Israel he is
  The praise, joy, honor, pleasure.

248

"Jesus Christ, Our God and Savior"

1524

This hymn appeared first in the Wittenberg hymnal of 1524, in the Erfurt enchiridia, and on a broadsheet of the same year. In all these sources it bears the caption: "The hymn of St. John Huss, revised."[1] A Latin hymn of nine stanzas *"Jesus Christus nostra salus"* had been known since the fifteenth century and sometimes ascribed to John Huss (1366-1415), the Bohemian forerunner of the Reformation. Reminiscences of this hymn are found in the first, second, fourth, and sixth stanzas of Luther's chorale. But on the whole, the latter has little in common with its Latin counterpart. The word "revised" evidently refers to a complete theological revision. Where Huss speaks of the bread and food, Luther adds wine and drink. Where the Latin hymn is an encomium on the sacrament along the familiar lines of medieval mysticism, Luther presents the eucharist as the token of God's love and mercy, which requires no other preparation than faith and no other fruit than love. These are thoughts which in very similar words and phrases he had expressed in his sermons on Palm Sunday and Maundy Thursday in 1524.[2] It is not too farfetched to believe that the hymn was written about the same time. Note the unusual meter 8.8.7.8.

The strong Dorian melody also is of pre-Reformation origin, although assigned to a different text in the only medieval manuscript which preserves it. The numerous rhythmic and melodic variations in the early hymnals (see footnotes) seem to indicate that it was widely known in freely differing forms. The German text, *"Jhesus Christus unser Heyland,"* is given in WA 35, 435-437; the music is given in WA 35, 500-501. The translation is a revision of that by MacDonald, *Exotics,* pp. 103-105, with occasional appropriations from other sources. The translation of stanza 7 is by Massie, *Martin Luther's Spiritual Songs,* p. 76, and that of stanza 10 by Margaret Fuhlbohm, *Laudamus* (2nd ed.; Hannover: Schlüter, 1957), p. 35.

---

[1] *Verbessert.*
[2] *WA* 15, 481-509.

"Jesus Christ, Our God and Savior"

WALTER 1524

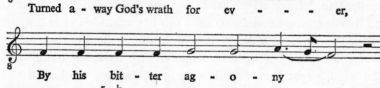

1. Je - sus   Christ,   our   God   and   Sav - ior,

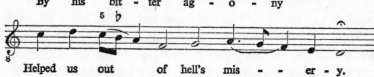

Turned a - way God's wrath   for   ev - - - er,

By   his   bit - ter   ag - o - ny

Helped us   out   of hell's mis - - er - y.

2 That we never should forget it
Gave he us his flesh to eat it,
Hidden in this bit of bread,
And to drink gave us his blood.

3 Whoso to this board repaireth,
Take good heed how he prepareth.
Who unworthy thither goes,
Thence death instead of life he knows.

---

[1] Other hymnals, such as Wittenberg 1524 and Klug 1533, have equal quarter notes, *a, g,* instead of the dotted rhythm.
[2] Klug 1533 and subsequent hymnals have two quarter notes, *f,* on "God and."
[3] Most other hymnals have two quarter notes, *f, e,* in this place.
[4] Later hymnals omit this rest and the two below.
[5] This slur appears in many different forms. For example, here are two variations:

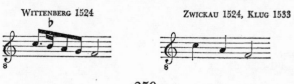

WITTENBERG 1524   ZWICKAU 1524, KLUG 1533

4 God the Father praise thou duly,
That he thee would feed so truly,
And for ill deeds by thee done
Up unto death has given his Son.

5 Have this faith, and do not waver,
'Tis food for every craver
Who, his heart with sin opprest,
Can no more for its anguish rest.

6 Such kindness and such grace to get,
Seeks a heart with agony great.
Is it well with thee? take care,
Lest at last thou shouldst evil fare.

7 Lo, he saith himself, "Ye weary
Come to me and I will cheer ye;
Needless were the doctor's skill
To the souls that be strong and well.

8 "Hadst thou any claim to proffer,
Why for thee then should I suffer?
This table is not for thee,
If thou wilt set thine own self free."

9 If such faith thy heart possesses,
And the same thy mouth confesses,
Fit guest then thou art indeed,
And this food thine own soul will feed.

10 Fruit of faith therein be showing
That thou art to others loving;
To thy neighbor thou wilt do
As God in love hath done to you.

"Let God Be Blest"

1524

In two of his writings Luther referred to a German hymn that enjoyed great popularity before the Reformation. In his *Von der Winckelmesse und Pfaffenweyhe* (*Of Secret Masses and Priestly Consecration*) of 1533,[1] he argued from the text of "Let God Be Blest" that communion under both forms had been known and accepted even before the Reformation. In *An Order of Mass and Communion*, 1523, he recommended the same hymn for use after communion, but suggested that the fifth and sixth lines (a prayer for the grace of receiving the sacrament from the hands of an ordained priest before death) were spurious and should be omitted.[2] He may well have been correct in this assumption, for melodically these two lines simply repeat a phrase that has been repeated before, and, of the two pre-Reformation sources, only one contains the verse in question. Luther adopted the medieval hymn minus this insertion and added two stanzas. Originally this had been a Corpus Christi *Leise* to be sung by the congregation between verses of the Latin sequence *"Lauda Sion Salvatorem"* ("Zion, Lift Thy Voice and Sing")[3] as the choir chanted it during the annual Corpus Christi procession. But in 1524 Luther discontinued the observance of Corpus Christi in Wittenberg, so it is not unlikely that he transformed the medieval Corpus Christi hymn into a Lutheran post-communion chorale to save a liturgical song that was popular with the people and that he himself treasured.

The chorale appeared in 1524 in Walter, and also in the Erfurt enchiridia, but without music. Possibly it was written the same year. The German text, *"Gott sey gelobet,"* is given in WA 35, 452-453; the melody is given in WA 35, 514-515. We offer the melody, which remained practically unchanged through all early Lutheran hymnals, in the version of Klug 1533. The translation, with some revisions, is that by MacDonald, *Exotics*, pp. 105-106.

---

[1] WA 38, 245-246.
[2] See pp. 36-37.
[3] Cf. Julian, *Dictionary of Hymnology*, pp. 662-664.

"Let God Be Blest"

KLUG 1533

1. {
Let God be blest, be prais - ed, and be
This his own flesh and blood to feed and

thank - ed, Who to us him - self hath grant - ed
save us. May we take well what he gave us.

Ky - ri - e - lei - - son. By thy ho - ly bod -

y with - out blame which from thine own moth - er

Mar - y came And by thy ho - ly blood Help us,

Lord, from all our need. Ky - ri - e - lei - son.

2 The holy body is for us laid lowly
Down in death, that we live holy;
No greater goodness he to us could render,
To make think of his love tender.
Kyrieleison.[2]

---

[1] Walter 1524 has here:

us him - self hath grant - ed.

[2] Another contraction for Kyrie eleison commonly used in medieval sacred folk song.

253

Lord, thy love so great hath in thee wrought
That thy blood to us hath marvels brought,
Of our debt paid the sum,
That God gracious is become.
   Kyrieleison.

3 God on us all his blessing free bestow now,
That in his ways we may go now!
Brotherly troth and fervent love ensuing,
Never so thy supper ruing.
   Kyrieleison.
Let thy Holy Ghost not forsake us,
Grant that of a sane mind he may make us,
That thy poor Christendom
Into peace and union come.
   Kyrieleison.

"Death Held Our Lord in Prison"

1524

Although this is an original hymn by Luther, its roots go deep into the Middle Ages. Around the year 1050, Vipo, court chaplain to Emperor Henry III, formed the mighty sequence "*Victimae Paschali laudes*,[1] which has become part of the Easter liturgy in the Roman rite. Its echo can be detected especially in the fourth stanza of Luther's chorale.

But long before Luther this same sequence had inspired a German folk song for Easter. The *Leise*, "*Christ ist erstanden*"[2] was widely known by the thirteenth century and retained its popularity until well into the eighteenth century.

The fact that Luther's chorale "Death Held Our Lord in Prison" appears in the earliest sources under the heading: "The Song of Praise '*Christ ist erstanden*' Amended," has puzzled many scholars, for it is known that Luther was extremely fond of "*Christ ist erstanden*," and his Easter chorale is in fact quite independent of the pre-Reformation folk song. Obviously this heading refers not to the text, but to the melody of Luther's hymn, which can be traced to that of the folk song.

The regular structure of this hymn should be noted. Of the seven stanzas, the first three and one-half rehearse the Easter message and the other three and one-half give the application. The meter consists of seven verses of seven syllables each and an eighth verse of eight syllables.

We offer the melody in two different versions. The first of these appears in the Erfurt enchiridia, in Walter's hymnal (first setting of the hymn), and in many later sources. The second forms the *cantus firmus* for the other two of Walter's three settings of this chorale and was preferred by later Wittenberg and Strassburg hymnals. The first tune provides for an Alleluia only in the first stanza. The German text, "*Christ lag ynn todes banden*," is given

---

[1] "Christians to the Paschal Victim." Cf. *The Hymnal of the Protestant Episcopal Church in the United States of America* (New York, 1940), No. 97.

[2] "Christ Is Arisen." Cf. *The Lutheran Hymnal* (St. Louis: Concordia, 1941), No. 187.

in *WA* 35, 443-445; the two versions of the melody are given in
WA 35, 506-507. No other tune was ever associated with this
hymn. The translation is a revision of that by MacDonald, *Exotics*,
pp. 52-54.

"Death Held Our Lord in Prison"

ERFURT 1524

WALTER
1524

1. Death held our Lord in pris - on,
   But he hath up a - ris - en,
For sin that did un - do us;
And brought our life back to us. There - fore we must
glad - some be, Ex - alt God, and thank - ful be,
And sing a - loud: Al - le - lu - ia!
Al - le - lu - ia! Al - le - lu - ia!

256

2 No man yet Death overcame—
All sons of men were helpless;
Sin for this was all to blame,
For no one yet was guiltless.
So Death came that early hour,
O'er us he took up his power,
And held us all in his kingdom. Alleluia!

3 Jesus Christ, God's only Son,
Into our place descending,
Away with [all] our sins hath done,
And therewith from Death rending
Right and might, made him a jape,
Left him nothing but Death's shape:
His ancient sting—he has lost it. Alleluia!

4 That was a right wondrous strife
When Death in Life's grip wallowed:
Off victorious came Life,
Death he has quite upswallowed.
The Scripture has published that—
How one Death the other ate.
Thus Death is become a laughter. Alleluia!

5 Here is the true Paschal Lamb
Which God himself attested.
That was on the tree of shame
In flaming passion roasted
His blood on our doorpost lies;
Faith holds that before Death's eyes;
The smiting angel can do nought. Alleluia!

6 So we keep high feast of grace,
Hearty the joy and glee is
That shines on us from his face:
The sun himself, ah! he is,
Who, by his brightness divine,
His light in our hearts makes shine:
The night of our sins is over. Alleluia!

7 We eat—and so we well fare—
Right Easter cakes sans leaven;
The old leaven shall not share
In the new word from heaven.
Christ himself will be the food,
Alone fill the soul with good:
Faith will live on nothing other. Alleluia!

"Jesus Christ, Our Savior True"

1524

Luther's second and shorter Easter hymn has no pre-Reformation pattern. He built it from themes frequently expounded in his Easter sermons. Only the form of it—a *Leise* ending in Kyrieleison—is typical of medieval German hymns. It appeared first in the Erfurt enchiridia and Walter's Wittenberg hymnal of 1524 and may have been written for Easter of the same year.

The original melody used in the enchiridia and (in a slightly differing version) by Walter is quite remarkable for its emphatic stress on important words and its vigorous leaps, irregular rhythm, and asymmetrical structure. Except for the numerous slurs, one might easily assume that it was composed by Luther. A second melody that Walter offers, he soon abandoned himself. Klug and later hymnals have a third melody, much simpler, but somewhat innocuous in comparison with the original. We offer the first and third melodies (the former in the version of the enchiridia and the latter a fifth lower). The text of the hymn appears in two versions. The earlier, represented by the enchiridia, has seven syllables in the first line; the latter, found in Walter and later hymnals, has eight. We follow the former and insert in the first line of the Klug melody a slur which is not in the original.

The German text, *"Jhesus Christus unser Heyland,"* is given in WA 35, 445; all three tunes are given in WA 35, 507-508. The translation is that by MacDonald, *Exotics,* pp. 54-55.

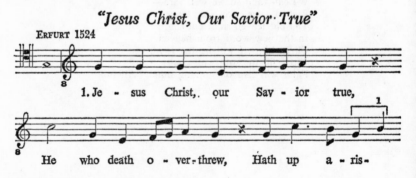

"Jesus Christ, Our Savior True"

ERFURT 1524

1. Je - sus Christ, our Sav - ior true,

He who death o - ver-threw, Hath up a - ris-

---

[1] Walter 1524 has a *b*-flat here.

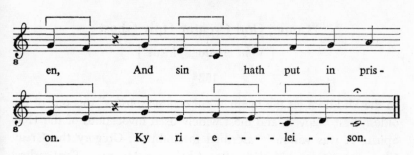

en,   And   sin   hath   put   in   pris-

on.   Ky - ri - e - - - - lei - - son.

KLUG 1533

1. Je - sus Christ, our Sav - - ior true,

He who death o - ver - threw, Hath up a - ris-

en,   And   sin   hath   put   in   pris-

on.   Ky - ri - e - lei - - - - son.

2 Born whom Mary sinless hath,
  Bore he for us God's wrath,
  Hath reconciled us—
  Favor God doth now yield us.
  Kyrieleison.

3 Death and sin, and life and grace,
  All in his hands he has.
  He can deliver
  All who seek the life-giver.
  Kyrieleison.

259

"Come, God Creator Holy Ghost"

["Veni creator spiritus"]

1524

In the Middle Ages the hymn "Veni creator spiritus" was one of the oldest, best beloved, and most widely used invocations of the Holy Spirit. It was variously ascribed to Ambrose, Gregory the Great, Charlemagne, or his chancellor Rhabanus Maurus. The earliest reference to it dates from the eleventh century. Its singing was marked with special dignity, the ringing of bells, the use of incense and the best vestments, etc. Its liturgical place was at Pentecost and at ordinations. Several German translations had been made before Luther wrote his, the last by Thomas Münzer.

But whereas Münzer had tried to smooth and fill in the brevity of the Latin text, Luther was intent on preserving the terse and compact style of the original. In fact, he tightened the logical sequence by exchanging the third and fourth stanzas and omitting the sixth. By this device he obtained three couplets of two stanzas each plus a doxology. The first two stanzas are a petition to the Holy Ghost to fill the hearts of the singers, the third and fourth ask for the gifts of the Spirit, especially for love, and the fifth and sixth seek preservation in the true faith. Again, the first two couplets are so organized that the first stanza always contains an invocation of the Holy Ghost and the second a description of his gifts.

This is the only one of Luther's three Pentecostal hymns which in Walter's hymnbook appeared in its proper place according to the church year. The other two are placed at the very beginning of the collection, an inconsistency which Lucke explains by suggesting that the major portion of Walter's book had been printed before the two hymns were finished.[1] In that case, this hymn would be the earliest of Luther's Pentecostal hymns.

Walter used the original, richly melismatic plain-chant melody for the German words, and in this the Strassburg hymnals followed him. But the Erfurt enchiridia had already offered a simplified syllabic version of the same melody for Luther's text. Later hym-

---

[1] WA 35, 23-24, 168-172.

nals brought this form into closer agreement with the original melodic line. Our edition offers both the earlier version from the Erfurt enchiridia and the later from Klug 1533.

The German text, "*Kom Gott schepfer heyliger geyst*," is given
in WA 35, 446-447; all three versions of the melody are given in
WA 35, 508-509. The translation is that by MacDonald, *Exotics*,
pp. 56-57.

"Come, God Creator Holy Ghost"

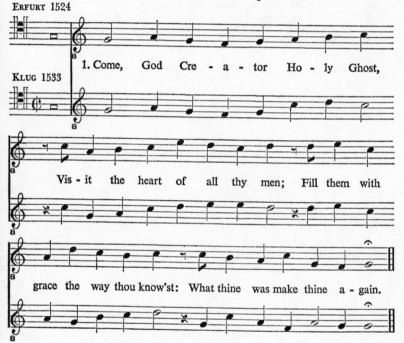

2 For thou art called the Comforter,
The blessed gift of God above,
A ghostly balm our quickener,
A living well, fire, and love.

3 O kindle in our minds a light;
Give in our hearts love's glowing gift;
Our weak flesh known to thee aright
With thy strength and grace uplift.

4 In giving gifts thou art sevenfold;
  The finger thou on God's right hand;
  His word by thee right soon is told,
  With clov'n tongues in every land.

5 Drive far the cunning of the foe;
  Thy grace bring peace and make us whole,
  That we glad after thee may go,
  And shun that which hurts the soul.

6 Teach us to know the Father right,
  And Jesus Christ, his Son, that so
  We may with faith be filled quite,
  Thee Spirit of both, to know.

7 Praise God the Father, and the Son,
  Who from the dead arose in power;
  Like praise to the Consoling One,
  Evermore and every hour.

"Now Let Us Pray to the Holy Ghost"

1524

The first stanza of this hymn is not by Luther. It is a German *Leise* (i.e., a sacred folk song in the vernacular, ending in Kyrie eleison) that was known since early in the Middle Ages. The famous thirteenth-century preacher, Berthold of Regensburg, commends it in one of his sermons and encourages the people to sing it. It became extremely popular and the people were permitted to intone it at Pentecost after the choir had sung the Latin sequence *"Veni sancte spiritus."* Luther regarded it highly. In *An Order of Mass and Communion* he named it as one of the few available hymns that could profitably be sung by the congregation.[1] Within a year after this reference he decided to add three stanzas to it and so converted the medieval *Leise* into a Lutheran chorale. In 1524 only Walter's collection contained this hymn, but soon it was accepted in every hymnal.

If—as has been suggested[2]—this hymn was not written until Walter's collection was printed and almost finished, it may be dated around Pentecost of the year 1524 (May 15), a time when Luther was greatly disturbed by the activities of Karlstadt, Münzer, and other enthusiasts and had ample reason to pray for preservation in the true faith.

The melody, too, is of pre-Reformation origin. Its strongly pentatonic character (it is built on the scale *d f g a c d*) suggests that it is a very old folk melody.

Our edition follows Ameln's facsimile edition of Klug's Wittenberg hymnal of 1533, fols. 14r-14v. The German text, *"Nu bitten wyr den heyligen geyst,"* is given in WA 35, 447-448; the melody in Walter's version is given in WA 35, 510. Differences between Walter and Klug are indicated in the footnotes. The translation is that by MacDonald, *Exotics*, p. 59, except for the second half of every stanza which had to be revised in the interest of singableness.

---

[1] See p. 25.
[2] See p. 260.

"Now Let Us Pray to the Holy Ghost"

Klug 1533

1. Now let us pray to the Ho - ly Ghost

For the true faith of all things the most, That in

our last mo - ments he may be - friend us And as home

we go, that he may tend us. Ky - ri - o - leis.

2 Thou noble light, shine as thou hast shone,
  Teach us to know Jesus Christ alone,
  Clinging to our Savior whose blood hath bought us
  Who to our true home hath again brought us.
  Kyrioleis.

3 Thou sweet Love, grant us favor, that so
  We feel within of thy love the glow,
  That we from our hearts may love true the others,
  And with peace and joy live as good brothers.
  Kyrioleis.

4 Thou comfort best in danger or blame,
  Help us to fear neither death nor shame,
  That we may not falter when all shall fail us
  And the foe with his taunts shall assail us.
  Kyrioleis.

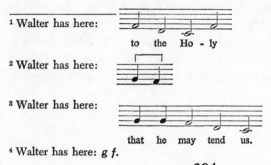

[1] Walter has here:

to the Ho - ly

[2] Walter has here:

[3] Walter has here:

that he may tend us.

[4] Walter has here: g f.

264

"Come, Holy Spirit Lord and God"

["Veni sancte spiritus"]

1524

In all of his hymns for Pentecost Luther made use of older materials. "Come, God Creator Holy Ghost" is the German version of a Latin hymn; "Now Let Us Pray to the Holy Ghost" is the extended form of a medieval German *Leise;* and "Come, Holy Spirit Lord and God" incorporates an older German antiphon. The first stanza was well known before the Reformation and has been preserved in several sources. Luther was extremely fond of it and remarked in his table talks, "The hymn 'Come, Holy Spirit Lord and God' was composed by the Holy Ghost himself, both words and music."[1] The German antiphon was based on a Latin antiphon *in vigilia pentacostes* "*Veni sancte spiritus, reple tuorum corda fidelium,*" which had been sung in Germany as early as the eleventh century and which was also prized by the Reformer.

For his own hymn he left the original medieval verse practically intact, but added two stanzas. If Lucke's assumptions are correct, the hymn was written about the same time as "Now Let Us Pray to the Holy Ghost," i.e., in May, 1524.[2] In that year the hymn appeared both in the Erfurt enchiridia and—as Number 2— in Walter's collection.

The melody offered in all the early sources is a simplified version of the rather melismatic plain-chant melody of the German sequence (the Latin antiphon has its own tune which was never used for the German versification). It almost has the form of a sequence; for since the melody of the first three lines is practically the same as the melody of the second three, each stanza becomes as it were a double versicle with appended Alleluia. In some of the later hymnals, such as Jobst Gutknecht's Nürnberg hymnal of 1531 and Klug 1533, the original, more melismatic form again

---

[1] *WA,* TR 4, 334, No. 4478.
[2] See p. 260. But Lucke's suggestion that the sixth line in the second stanza was prompted by the canonization of Bishop Benno of Meissen in June, 1524, seems quite farfetched.

made its appearance. But ultimately the version of 1524, which we present here in the form of the Erfurt enchiridia, was generally accepted as the proper tune for this chorale.

The text, *"Kom heyliger geyst herre Gott,"* is given in WA 35, 448-449; the melody is given in WA 35, 510-512. The translation is a revision of that by MacDonald, *Exotics*, pp. 57-58.

"Come, Holy Spirit Lord and God"

ERFURT 1524

8 1. Come, Ho - ly Spir - - it Lord and God,

8 Fill full with thine own gra - cious good The faith - ful ones'

8 heart, mind, de - sire; In them light of thy love the fire.

8 O Lord, through thy light's flash - es fast, In - to the

8 faith thou gath - ered hast The folk from ev - 'ry

land and tongue. This to thy praise, O our God,

be sung. Al - le - lu - ia, Al - le - lu - ia.

---

[1] After 1561 hymnals began to substitute *f d c* for *f e c* here and for "and tongue" below.
[2] The reading *a b a g* for the last Alleluia in most of the early sources is almost certainly a mistake.

2 Thou holy light, thou sure resort,
Let lighten us of life the Word,
Teach us to know our God aright
And call him Father with delight.
O Lord, protect us from strange lore,
That we may seek no masters more,
But Jesus with true faith solely,
And him with all our might trust wholly.
    Alleluia, Alleluia.

3 Thou holy fire, thou comfort sweet,
Now help us, glad with cheer complete,
That in thy service nought shake us,
From thee let trouble ne'er take us.
Lord, by thy power us prepare,
And make the weak flesh strong to bear,
That as good warriors we may force
Through life and death to thee our course.
    Alleluia, Alleluia.

"God the Father with Us Be"

1524

This hymn of invocation of the Holy Trinity seems to be patterned after medieval pilgrims' songs invoking the aid of the saints. Hymns that started, "St. Peter, with us be," "Dear St. Nicholas, with us be," or "St. Mary, with us be" were well known in the fifteenth century. Both words and music of such hymns to the saints are preserved in pre-Reformation sources, the words in a Crailshaim manuscript of 1480 and the melody in a tablature of 1524 by the Pforzheim organist Leonard Kleber. The melody was evidently well known, for the enchiridia of 1525 did not even bother to print the notes. A comparison of Kleber's tablature and Walter's version suggests that Luther adopted the melody without change. He retained the first five lines of the text with minor changes, replacing the appeal to the saints with an invocation of the three Persons of the Trinity, and he formed the concluding part differently, at least from those medieval versions that have been preserved.[1] Later Catholic hymnals, such as Vehe 1537 and Leisentrit 1567, combined the hymn with its medieval prototypes so as to include invocations both of the triune God and of the angels.

The structure of Luther's stanzas may be of interest. Marking the rimes of one stanza with letters, we arrive at the following scheme:

a b   a b

c d d d

c e e e

c f.

---

[1] Cf. the texts of the Crailshaim School Order, 1480, and of Luther (in Walter's hymnal of 1524):

Crailshaim 1480	Luther 1524
Virgin Mary with us be,	God the Father with us be,
Let us not fall to badness;	Let us not fall to badness;
Make us from all sinning free,	Make us from all sinning free,
And help us die in gladness.	And help us die in gladness.
'Gainst the devil well us ware,	'Gainst the devil well us ware,
Mary Virgin undefiled.	[8 more lines]
Help us with the angels' guild	
So shall we sing: Alleluia.	Let us then sing: Alleluia.

If we compare the music we notice that the "c" verses, ending in the same rime, are also melodically identical. In passing it may also be noted that the first two lines of the music contain the germ of the well-known chorale tune *"Jesus, meine Zuversicht (Ratisbon)."*

Luther's chorale made its first appearance in Walter's hymnal of 1524, ostensibly as a hymn for Trinity and/or the Trinity season. Later it was also appointed for weddings.

The melody, practically the same in all early Lutheran hymnals, is offered as given in Schumann 1539, but transposed down a fourth. The German text, *"Gott der vater won uns bey,"* is given in *WA* 35, 450; the melody is given in *WA* 35, 512. The translation is that by MacDonald, *Exotics*, pp. 60-61.

"God the Father with Us Be"

SCHUMANN 1539

God the Fa - ther with us be,·
Make us from all sin - ning free,

Let us not fall to bad - ness;
And help us die in glad - ness.

'Gainst the dev -
Let us whol -

il well us ware, And keep our faith from fail -
ly trust thy care, With all good Chris - tians shar -

ing, Our hope in thee from quail - ing. Our hearts
ing, Es - cape the dev - il's snar - ing, Him with

up - on thee stay - ing.
God's weap - ons dar - ing.

A - men, now! so

may we fare! Let us then sing: Al - le - lu - ia!

2 Jesus Savior with us be,
Let us not fall to badness;
Etc.

3 Holy Spirit with us be,
Let us not fall to badness;
Etc.

---

[1] Walter 1524 and other early hymnals have *g* instead of *a* in this place. But *a* seems to be the better and more original reading, for it is also found in Kleber's notation of the pre-Reformation hymn.

"In One True God We All Believe"
1524

Luther's hymn on the Creed is based on an earlier medieval verse, preserved with notes and with Latin and German words in a Breslau manuscript of 1417. He used the first two lines of the original German text and, with a few significant changes, also the medieval melody. But as a paraphrase of the three articles of the Creed this hymn is really his own.

The medieval hymn summarized the Creed in a single stanza. Luther sets forth the work of creation and preservation, redemption, and sanctification in three stanzas devoted to the three Persons of the Trinity. Some of the basic emphases found later in his catechisms are found here already. At the same time he strengthened the metrical structure of the hymn. For the irregular lines of the medieval hymn he substituted eight-syllable verses throughout, but avoided any suggestion of monotony by starting his verses alternately with an upbeat and downbeat and ending them with masculine and feminine rimes in turn. Every stanza consists of four and four and two verses, each part forming a logical unit. Walter's Wittenberg hymnal of 1524 is the earliest source for this chorale. Here it appears with "God the Father with Us Be," apparently as a proper hymn for Trinity. But in the following year the Erfurt enchiridion put it under the heading "The *Patrem* or the Creed."[1] Both in the Strassburg *Kirchenamt* of 1524/25 and in Luther's *German Mass* of 1526 it was used as a substitute for the Latin Credo of the mass, a function which soon was universally accepted in the Lutheran liturgy.[2]

---

[1] *Patrem* is the first word of the Nicene Creed in the mass as the choir responds to the intonation by the priest *"Credo in unum Deum."*

[2] Lucke, following Friedrich Spitta (*Monatsschrift für Gottesdienst und Kirchliche Kunst.*, XI, 220), seeks to prove in WA 35, 174-175, that the liturgical use of the chorale was not Luther's original intention and only the example of the Strassburg liturgy and other hymnals prompted him to use it in lieu of the Creed. But this argument is very strained. In keeping with his policy of substituting German chorales for Latin chants, Luther could hardly help thinking of this hymn as a paraphrase of the Creed in the mass.

We offer the melody in the version of Klug 1533 because it seems more felicitous than Walter's and was accepted in most subsequent hymnals. A simplified form without the melisma at the beginning and end appeared in the Zwickau hymnal of 1525[3] and a few others, but failed to gain universal acceptance. The German text, *"Wyr gleuben all an eynen Gott,"* is given in *WA* 35, 451-452; the melody is given in *WA* 35, 513. The translation of the first stanza is that by MacDonald, *Exotics*, p. 89; the other stanzas are translated by the editor, with an assist from an unknown translator in *Laudamus*, pp. 30-31, for the second stanza and from MacDonald, *op. cit.*, p. 90, for the third stanza.

"In One True God We All Believe"

KLUG 1533

1. In one true God we all be-lieve,
Mak-er of the earth and heav-en; Who, us as
chil-dren to re-ceive, Hath him-self as Fa-ther
giv-en. Now and hence-forth he will feed us, Soul
and bod-y will sur-round us, 'Gainst mis-chanc-es

---

[3] See *WA* 35, 514.
[4] Walter 1524 has here *g a* instead of *e f*.

he will heed us, Nought shall meet us that shall wound us. He watch - es o'er us, cares, de - fends; And ev - 'ry - thing is in his hands.

2 And we believe in Jesus Christ,
His own Son, our Lord and Master
Who beside the Father highest
Reigns in equal might and glory.
Born of Mary, virgin mother
By the Spirit's operation
He was made our elder brother
That the lost might find salvation;
Slain on the cross by wicked men
And raised by God to life again.

3 We all confess the Holy Ghost
With the Father and the Savior
Who the fearful comforts most
And the meek doth crown with favor.
All of Christendom he even
In one heart and spirit keepeth.
Here all sins shall be forgiven;
Wake too shall the flesh that sleepeth.
After these suff'rings there shall be
Life for us eternally.

---

[5] Walter 1524 has here *d* instead of *e*.

273

"In the Midst of Life We Are"

["Media vita"]

1524

An oft-repeated story tells of a monk from the convent of St. Gall in Switzerland who watched workmen build a bridge across a yawning gorge in the Alps and felt inspired to write the hymn "Media vita in morte sumus" ("In the Midst of Life We Are in Death"). The monk is supposed to have been Notker Balbulus, the Stammerer (d. 910), the writer of many famous sequences and the first medieval composer about whom we know more than generalities. Unfortunately, the same sources that prove his authorship for many sequences make no mention of the "Media vita" and give no support to the attractive story which only came to light seven hundred years after Notker's death. In fact, it is not too likely that the "Media vita" hails from St. Gall, for it is found in English manuscripts of the eleventh century, two hundred years before it makes its appearance in codices of St. Gall. Furthermore, the Trisagion, which forms the second part of the hymn, has ancient Greek beginnings, and its melody is not unrelated to the music of the same words in the Improperia for Good Friday.

But no matter who the author was, the "Media vita" enjoyed enormous popularity during the Middle Ages. It was used not only in memory of the departed, but also as a prayer hymn, a battle song, and even as a charm. Several German versions were current before the Reformation. Luther may have known one of these; the text and music of his hymn echo some of their phrases. Nevertheless, he decisively altered the character of the hymn as a whole. While the pre-Reformation hymn was an almost frantic cry for help in mortal danger, Luther, by putting the fifth line in the indicative, made the hymn not only a petition for help, but an assurance of grace and a confession of God's goodness. And by adding a second and third stanza he deepened (on the basis of I Cor. 15:56) the prayer for help in death to a petition for forgiveness of sins. The melody, too, with its ascent to d in the second, fourth, and last lines sounds bolder and more confident than in its medieval form. Here as elsewhere, Luther altered the music in the direction of the folk song. At least the first two lines are reminiscent of the folk ballad of *Tannhäuser*.[1]

We do not know if certain events in Luther's own life inspired the writing of this hymn. Lucke surmises that the tragic death by drowning of Melanchthon's friend Wilhelm Nesen on July 5, 1524, which deeply affected Luther, led to his version of "*Media vita*."[2] But Luther—as indeed his whole age—was always so aware of the brevity and transience of human life that he hardly needed a shock such as this to turn his thoughts to death.

The enchiridia offer this hymn without a tune. We give the Phrygian tune which remained the only melody for this hymn, as it appears in Walter's Wittenberg hymnal of 1524. The German text, "*Mitten wyr im leben sind*," is given in WA 35, 453-454; the melody is given in WA 35, 515-516. The translation is a revision of that by MacDonald, *Exotics*, pp. 107-108.

"In the Midst of Life We Are"

WALTER 1524

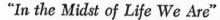

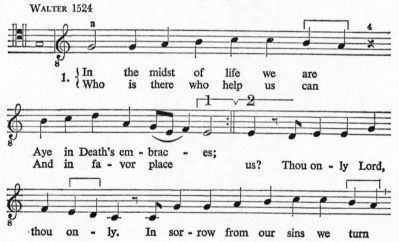

---

[1] See F. M. Böhme, *Altdeutsches Liederbuch* (Leipzig, 1925), No. 21, p. 82.
[2] WA 35, 130-132.
[3] Here the later hymnals (Klug 1533, etc.) have a quarter note.
[4] Here the later hymnals omit the rest.

That have made thy an-ger burn. Ho - .ly and right-eous God,

Ho - ly and might - y God, Ho - ly and lov - ing gra - cious

Sav - ior, Ev - er - last - ing God, Let us not be drown-

ed In the pains of bit - ter death. Ky - ri - e - lei - son.

2 In the midst of death behold
Hell's jaws gaping at us!
Who will from such dire distress
Free and scathless set us?
That dost thou, Lord, thou only.
It fills thy tender heart with woe
We should sin and suffer so.
Holy and righteous God,
Holy and mighty God,
Holy and loving gracious Savior,
Everlasting God,
Let us not be daunted
By hell's hollows all aglow.
Kyrieleison.

3 In the midst of pains of hell,
Us our sins are baiting;
Whither shall we flee away
Where a rest is waiting?
To thee, Lord Christ, thee only.
Outpoured is thy precious blood,
For our sins sufficing good.
Holy and righteous God
Holy and mighty God,
Holy and loving gracious Savior,
Everlasting God,
Let from thee us fall not
From the comfort of thy faith.
Kyrieleison.

---

5 Here and at the following six similar places (quarter note, rest) the later
hymnals have a half note and no rest.

"These Are the Holy Ten Commands"
1524

Several hymns on the Ten Commandments had been written before the Reformation. Whether or not Luther knew them is a moot question. If he did, he did not use them, but created two versions of his own. Apparently he considered it very important for the church to have hymns on the Ten Commandments. This attitude requires a word of explanation, for to the modern mind the whole idea of writing a hymn on the Ten Commandments seems preposterous. We have become so accustomed to think of poetry as an expression of the personal feelings and emotions of the writer that we cannot conceive of a merely "utilitarian" use of poetry. Hymnody in our own age has been defined as "lyrical religion." We find it difficult to think of a merely didactic hymn without sentimental overtones.

But Luther proceeded from different premises. Very soberly he thought of the hymn as a means of instilling the Word of God in the people. While some of his hymns were born out of his most personal experience and reflected the struggles and victories of his own faith, others were mere versifications of the Catechism. And it is hardly surprising that the demands of the law in the Ten Commandments did not inspire him to such lofty joy as the message of the gospel and justification by faith. Nevertheless, he wanted both law and gospel to be expressed in verse to instruct the common people and firmly ground them in the whole plan of salvation. As early as 1525 these hymns were sung in the weekday services during Lent when the sermons were on the Catechism.[1] According to the Wittenberg church order of 1533, the choir boys were supposed to sing this hymn before catechism sermons and the other hymn on the Ten Commandments[2] afterward. Incidentally, the Genevan psalter and the early English psalters also contained hymns on the Ten Commandments.[3]

---

[1] See pp. 68-69.
[2] "Man, Wouldst Thou Live All Blissfully," in this volume, pp. 280-281.
[3] Cf. Julian, *Dictionary of Hymnology*, p. 932; Douglas, *Church Music in History and Practice*, p. 220.

Luther assured its immediate reception by assigning to it the melody of the pre-Reformation pilgrims' hymn *"In Gottes Namen fahren wir"*[4] ("We Journey in the Name of God"), sung since the thirteenth century. We offer the melody as it appears in the Erfurt enchiridia and later Wittenberg hymnals. The rhythmical deviations of Walter's version noted in the music are a telling example of the habit of sixteenth-century composers to introduce rhythmical complications in an otherwise simple *cantus firmus*. The Strassburg hymnals offer two other melodies, neither of which succeeded in replacing the pilgrims' *leise*.

The German text, *"Dis sind die heylgen zehn gebott,"* is given in *WA* 35, 426-428; all three melodies are given in *WA* 35, 495-497. The translation is a revision of that by MacDonald, *Exotics*, pp. 84-87.

"These Are the Holy Ten Commands"

ERFURT 1524 [5]

1. These are the ho - ly Ten Com-mands Which came to us from God's own hands By Mo - ses who o - beyed his will On top of Si - nai's high hill. Ky - rio - leis.

2 I am the Lord thy God alone;
Of gods besides thou shalt have none;
Thou shalt thyself trust all to me,
And love me right heartily.
Kyrioleis.

---

[4] Cf. Böhme, *Altdeutsches Liederbuch*, No. 568, p. 677.
[5] The notes marked by an asterisk are doubled in value by Walter 1524.

3 Thou shalt not speak like idle word
   The name of God who is thy Lord;
   As right or good thou shalt not praise
   Except what God does and says.
   Kyrioleis.

4 Thou shalt keep holy the seventh day,
   That rest thou and thy household may;
   From thine own work thou must be free,
   That God his work have in thee.
   Kyrioleis.

5 Honor thou shalt and shalt obey
   Thy father and [thy] mother alway;
   To serve them ready be thy hand,
   That thou live long in the land.
   Kyrioleis.

6 In wrathfulness thou shalt not kill,
   Nor hate, nor take revenge for ill,
   But patience keep and gentle mood,
   And e'en to thy foe do good.
   Kyrioleis.

7 Thy marriage bond thou shalt keep clean,
   That even thy heart no other mean;
   Thy life thou must keep pure and free,
   Temperate, with fine chastity.
   Kyrioleis.

8 Steal not thy neighbor's goods or gold,
   Nor profit by his sweat or blood.
   Open thou wide thy kindly hand
   To the poor man in thy land.
   Kyrioleis.

9 Thou shalt not lying stories bear,
   Nor 'gainst thy neighbor falsely swear;
   His innocence thou shalt rescue,
   And hide his shame from man's view.
   Kyrioleis.

10 Thy neighbor's wife or house to win
   Thou shalt not seek, nor aught within;
   But wish that his such good may be
   As thine own heart wish for thee.
   Kyrioleis.

11 To us come these commands, that so
   Thou, son of man, thy sins mayst know,
   And make thee also well perceive
   How before God man should live.
   Kyrioleis.

12 May Christ our Lord help us in this,
   For he our mediator is;
   Our own work is a hopeless thing,
   'Tis wrath alone it can bring.
   Kyrioleis.

279

"Man, Wouldst Thou Live All Blissfully"

1524

This is the shorter of Luther's two hymns on the Ten Commandments. It has five stanzas. While the other hymn allowed one stanza for each commandment, plus one opening and two closing stanzas, this hymn has a peculiar staggered arrangement: After the introductory first stanza, the second stanza deals with the First Commandment, the third with the Second and Third, the fourth with the Fourth, Fifth, and Sixth, and the fifth with the Seventh to Tenth. Thus every stanza has one commandment more than the one before.

The earliest source for this hymn is Walter's Wittenberg hymnal of 1524, and the Phrygian tune used there remained the only one associated with it. It shows remarkable similarities to some of Luther's other tunes. The second line recalls the second line of "Vom Himmel Hoch,"[1] and the third and fourth lines are an inverted reflection of the first and second lines of "Aus tiefer Not."[2] Perhaps it too was framed by the Reformer.

The German text, "Mensch wiltu leben seliglich," is given in WA 35, 428-429; the melody is given in WA 35, 497. The translation, with minor revisions, is that by MacDonald, Exotics, pp. 87-88.

---

[1] The tune for "From Heaven on High I Come to You"; see p. 290.
[2] The Phrygian tune for "From Trouble Deep I Cry to Thee"; see p. 223.

"Man, Wouldst Thou Live All Blissfully"

WALTER 1524

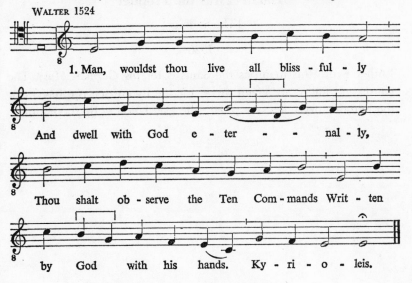

1. Man, wouldst thou live all bliss - ful - ly

And dwell with God e - ter - - nal - ly,

Thou shalt ob - serve the Ten Com - mands Writ - ten

by God with his hands. Ky - ri - o - leis.

2 Thy God and Lord I am alway;
No other god shall make thee stray;
Thy heart must ever trust in me;
Mine own kingdom shalt thou be.
    Kyrioleis.

3 My name to honor thou shalt heed
And call on me in time of need.
Thou shalt hallow the sabbath day
So in thee I work alway.
    Kyrioleis.

4 Father and mother thou shalt hold
In honor next to me, thy Lord.
None kill nor yield to anger wild,
And keep thy wedlock undefiled.
    Kyrioleis.

5 From any one to steal beware;
'Gainst none thou shalt false witness bear;
Thy neighbor's wife thou shall not eye—
Let his be his willingly.
    Kyrioleis.

281

"Isaiah 'Twas the Prophet"

[The Sanctus]

1526

Luther wrote this hymn as the Sanctus for his *German Mass*. The words and music are given there; for the hymn, see pp. 82-83; for the introductory notes, see p. 60. The translation is by the editor.

"Our God He Is a Castle Strong"

[The 46th Psalm]

1527/28?

Interminable controversies have been fought over the date of the writing of "Our God He Is a Castle Strong." The earliest extant hymnal that has it is Andrew Rauscher's Erfurt hymnal of 1531. But it is supposed to have been in Joseph Klug's Wittenberg hymnal of 1529, of which no copy exists, and before that in the Hans Weiss Wittenberg hymnal of 1528, also lost. Beyond these dates we have only conjecture. Scholars have combed the writings of Luther and his friends for phrases and expressions reminiscent of "Our God He Is a Castle Strong." They have examined Luther's personal life and the religious and political events in the critical years between 1521 and 1530. A good case can be made for almost any year in this period, and we have to be content with the knowledge that this hymn more than any other epitomizes Luther's thought and personal experience. He did not write it to express his own feelings, but to interpret and apply the 46th Psalm to the church of his own time and its struggles. That it should have lain on Luther's desk for a number of years before it was published is hardly in keeping with his general practice. He wrote hymns not as a means of self-expression, but to serve his fellow-believers. We can therefore assume that it was written sometime during the years 1527 or 1528, not long before it was published.

While no one questions the bold originality of thought and expression in the text, Luther has sometimes been accused of plagiarism in regard to the melody. Scholars have tried to detect in it snatches of pre-Reformation plain chant and folk song. It would be foolish to dispute certain reminiscences of the music with which Luther had grown up. No creative genius lives in a vacuum; he cannot avoid using all sorts of ready-made idioms for his building blocks. The value of the melody for "Our God He Is a Castle Strong" consists not in its absolute originality—it reminds one most strongly of Luther's earlier martyrs' hymn[1]—but in its basic in-

---

[1] "A New Song Here Shall Be Begun," in this volume, pp. 211-216.

283

tegrity and strength. This is no patchwork of bits and pieces taken from here and there, but a masterpiece of musical expression. The melody reflects not only the general mood of the text, but gives strong rhythmical emphasis to the important words.

Our transcription of the melody follows Klug's Wittenberg hymnal of 1533, transposed a fourth lower. The German text, '*EIn feste burg ist unser Gott*," is given in *WA* 35, 455-457; the music is given in *WA* 35, 518. The translation, with minor revisions, is that by MacDonald, *Exotics*, pp. 66-67.

"Our God He Is a Castle Strong"

Klug 1533

[1] Since Seth Calvisius, *Harmonia Cantionum Ecclesiasticarum* (Leipzig, 1597), a *b* has been used here instead of an *a*.

[2] In the first edition of Walter's hymnal that contains "Our God He Is a Castle Strong," the edition of 1544, Walter changed this figure.

[3] Since Georg Rhau, *Neue Deutsche Gstl. Gesänge* (Wittenberg, 1544), an *f*-sharp has been used here instead of an *f*.

[4] Since the 1561 hymnal of the Bohemian Brethren, an *f* has been used here instead of a *g*.

2 'Tis all in vain, do what we can,
Our strength is soon dejected.
But He fights for us, the right man,
By God himself elected.
Ask'st thou who is this?
Jesus Christ it is,
Lord of Hosts alone,
And God but him is none,
So he must win the battle.

3 And did the world with devils swarm,
All gaping to devour us,
We fear not the smallest harm,
Success is yet before us.
This world's prince accurst,
Let him rage his worst,
No hurt brings about;
His doom it is gone out,
One word can overturn him.

4 The word they shall allow to stand,
Nor any thanks have for it; [1]
He is with us, at our right hand,
With the gifts of his spirit.
If they take our life,
Wealth, name, child and wife—
Let everything go:
They have no profit so;
The kingdom ours remaineth.

---

[1] *Or:* Nor any choice have in it.

"Grant Peace in Mercy, Lord, We Pray"

[Da pacem Domine]

1528/29?

The Latin antiphon *"Da pacem Domine in diebus nostris"* ("Give Peace, Lord, in Our Time") is recorded as early as the tenth century. Luther's translation appears in Rauscher's hymnal of 1531 and was most likely also included in the lost Klug hymnal of 1529. In 1528 the Turks were pressing against the bastions of the West, and Luther called on young and old to overcome the enemy by the fervency of their prayer. It was evidently for this purpose that he furnished a chorale-like version of the traditional antiphon. Perhaps he also arranged the melody. Only the first line bears a faint similarity to the traditional plain chant; the rest is more strongly reminiscent of the melody to "Lord, Keep Us Steadfast in Thy Word"[1] and the Ambrosian hymn "Come, the Heathen's Healing Light,"[2] on which the former is based. This hymn was often appended to "Lord, Keep Us Steadfast in Thy Word" and sung after the sermon.

Our transcription of the music follows Klug's Wittenberg hymnal of 1533. The German text, *"Verley uns frieden gnediglich,"* is given in WA 35, 458; the melody is given in WA 35, 521. The translation is by the editor.

---

[1] See pp. 304-305.
[2] See pp. 235-236.

"Grant Peace in Mercy, Lord, We Pray"

KLUG 1533

Grant peace in mer - cy, Lord, we pray,

Peace in our time, O send us! For there is

none on earth but thee, None oth - er to de -

fend us. On - ly thou, Lord, canst fight for us.

---

[1] Schumann 1539 and other later hymnals give an *f* instead of *g*.

[2] Here and at the asterisks Klug 1543 and his later hymnals and Johann Spangenberg, *Cantiones Ecclesiasticae* (Magdeburg, 1545), give a quarter note instead of a half note.

[3] Gutknecht, *Kirchengesänge* (Nürnberg, 1531), Klug 1543 and his later editions, and Spangenberg 1545 give *f e* instead of *f*.

[4] In Spangenberg 1545 and other later hymnals this line is as follows:

None oth - er to de - fend us.

[5] In Gutknecht 1531 and other later hymnals this line is as follows:

On - ly thou, Lord, canst fight for us.

287

"Lord God, Thy Praise We Sing"

1531

This is Luther's translation of the *Te Deum*. It is included with Luther's liturgical chants; see pp. 171-175.

"From Heaven on High I Come to You"

1534/35

While Luther's earlier Christmas hymns had been translations from the Latin, this one is entirely his own. When he wrote it in 1534 or 1535 his children were just old enough to sing it. Indeed, some scholars maintain that the hymn is a miniature Christmas pageant for the family, with the angel singing stanzas 1-5, individual children stanzas 7-14, and stanzas 6 and 15 sung by the whole group. Be that as it may, in this hymn Luther certainly followed his own axiom: "If we wish to train children, we must become children with them."[1] No other hymn of his is as simple and intimate in content and as folk-like in structure. The first stanza is actually patterned after a pre-Reformation secular folk song, a singing game popular with the young people in Luther's time, that began with the lines:

> Good news from far abroad I bring,
> Glad tidings for you all I sing.
> I bring so much you'd like to know
> Much more than I shall tell you though.[2]

After this verse the singer would propose a riddle to one of the girls, and unless she could solve it, she had to give him her wreath.

Originally Luther used the lilting melody of this folk song for his Christmas carol. It is found in the earliest extant source, the Klug hymnal of 1535, and many subsequent hymnals. But with the increasing popularity of "From Heaven on High I Come to You," he must have felt that the hymn deserved its own melody. The new music first appeared in the Schumann hymnal of 1539 and ultimately became the proper tune. Quite likely Luther wrote it himself, for it has the same beginning and the same strong emphasis on the upper tonic that are found in his melodies for "A

---

[1] See p. 67.
[2] Böhme, *Altdeutsches Liederbuch*, No. 271, p. 350.

New Song Here Shall Be Begun"[3] and "Our God He Is a Castle Strong."[4]

The earlier folk-song melody was ultimately assigned to "From Heaven the Angel Troop Came Near," where it will be found in our edition.[5] A third tune by Johann Walter[6] failed to make its way.

We present the hymn with its second tune, i.e., Luther's own melody. The text, *"Vom himel hoch da kom ich her,"* is given in *WA* 35, 459; the melody is given in *WA* 35, 524. The translation is that by MacDonald, *Exotics*, pp. 45-48.

"From Heaven on High I Come to You"

SCHUMANN 1539

1. From heaven on high I come to you. I bring a sto-ry good and new; Of good-ly news so much I bring; Of it I must both speak and sing.

2 To you a child is come this morn,
A child of holy maiden born,
A little babe so sweet and mild—
Your joy and bliss shall be that child.

3 It is the Lord Christ, our own God.
He will ease you of all your load;
He will himself your Savior be,
And from all sinning set you free.

---

[3] See pp. 211-216.
[4] See pp. 283-285.
[5] See p. 307.
[6] *WA* 35, 525; Zahn, *Die Melodien der deutschen evangelischen Kirchenlieder,* I (1889), No. 345.

4 He brings you all the news so glad
Which God the Father ready had—
That you shall in his heavenly house
Live now and evermore with us.

5 Take heed then to the token sure,
The crib, the swaddling clothes so poor;
The infant you shall find laid there,
Who all the world doth hold and bear.

6 Hence let us all be gladsome then,
And with the shepherd folk go in
To see what God to us hath given,
With his dear honored Son from heaven.

7 Take note, my heart; see there! look low:
What lies then in the manger so?
Whose is the lovely little child?
It is the darling Jesus-child.

8 Welcome thou art, thou noble guest,
With sinners who dost lie and rest,
And com'st into my misery!
How thankful I must ever be!

9 Ah Lord! the maker of us all!
How hast thou grown so poor and small,
That there thou liest on withered grass,
The supper of the ox and ass?

10 Were the world wider many fold,
And decked with gems and cloth of gold,
'Twere far too mean and narrow all,
To make for thee a cradle small.

11 The silk and velvet that are thine,
Are rough hay, linen not too fine,
Yet, as they were thy kingdom great,
Thou liest in them in royal state.

12 And this hath therefore pleased thee
That thou this truth mightst make me see—
How all earth's power, show, good, combined,
Helps none, nor comforts thy meek mind.

13 Dear little Jesus! in my shed,
Make thee a soft, white little bed,
And rest thee in my heart's low shrine,
That so my heart be always thine.

14 And so I ever gladsome be,
Ready to dance and sing to thee
The lullaby thou lovest best,
With heart exulting in its guest.

15 Glory to God in highest heaven,
Who his own Son to us hath given!
For this the angel troop sings in
Such a new year with gladsome din.

291

"To Me She's Dear, the Worthy Maid"

1535/45

At first acquaintance this hymn appears to be an oddity. The first stanza sounds like a secular love song. The meter of twelve lines—some long, some very short—is complex, and the melody is quite intricate due to an abundance of syncopations, flourishes, and time changes. Quite clearly, this is not a typical "chorale," and one is not surprised to find that it disappeared from common use more quickly than any other hymn Luther wrote. Nevertheless, it has a legitimate place in a complete edition of Luther's hymns, and its unusual form is really conditioned by its content.

Early sixteenth-century people were deeply moved by eschatological portents, hopes, and fears. Luther himself expected the imminent end of the world and saw in the religious struggles of his day the apocalyptic contest between Christ and the Antichrist. These sentiments received additional impetus from the turbulent events of 1534. In that year some Jews expected the coming of their messiah. One "David Moses" appeared as such and was heralded by his apostle Solomon Malchu. In the same year the reign of the Anabaptists in Münster reached its height. Luther could not remain unmoved by these events. He turned to the Apocalypse and found there the church depicted by the figure of the woman who though persecuted by the devil still is protected by God. Since our hymn (without a tune) first appeared in Joseph Klug's Wittenberg hymnal of 1535, Luther may have composed it in 1534 as a hymn of comfort to the church under the cross. And since here as elsewhere he preserved the imagery of Scripture and addressed the church as the "elect lady," it can hardly be termed surprising that he employed that poetico-musical form which in his time was used to "praise one's lady," namely, the *Hofweise*.[1] Hence the intricate structure of both text and melody. As in "From Heaven on High I Come to You"[2] he had paraphrased a singing game popular among the young people of his day, so in "To Me She's Dear, the Worthy Maid" he utilized

---

[1] See pp. 196-197.
[2] See pp. 289-291.

the style of sixteenth-century love lyrics. Whether or not he used either the words or melody of an actual secular song can no longer be determined. Some of the phrases, both verbal and musical, can be traced to other folk songs or *Hofweisen*. But barring further discoveries, we will have to credit Luther with the words and with the melody which followed ten years later in Babst 1545.

The German text, *"Sie ist mir lieb die werde magd,"* is given in *WA* 35, 462-463; the original melody is given in *WA* 35, 525. The translation, with minor revisions, including an assist in the second stanza from Massie, *Martin Luther's Spiritual Songs,* is that by MacDonald, *Exotics,* pp. 70-71.

"To Me She's Dear, the Worthy Maid"

BABST 1545

1. To me she's dear, the wor - - thy maid,
   Praise, hon - or, vir-tue of her are said;

And I can-not for - get her;
Then all I love her bet - - - - - - - ter.

I seek her good, And if I should Right e - vil fare,

I do not care, She'll make up for it to

me, With love and truth that will not tire, Which she will

ev - er show me; And do all my de-sire.

2 She wears of purest gold a crown
  Twelve stars their rays are twining;
  Her raiment, glorious as the sun,
  And bright from far is shining.
      Her feet the moon
      Are set upon.
      She is the bride
      With the Lord to bide.
  Sore travail is upon her;
  She bringeth forth a noble Son
  Whom all the world must honor,
  Their king, the only one.

3 That makes the dragon rage and roar,
  He will the child upswallow;
  His raging comes to nothing more;
  No jot of gain will follow.
      The infant high
      Up to the sky
      Away is heft,
      And he is left
  On earth, all mad with murder.
  The mother now alone is she,
  But God will watchful guard her,
  And the right Father be.

"All Glory, Laud, and Praise Be Given"

1537

This is Luther's version of the Gloria in Excelsis. It is included
with Luther's liturgical chants; see pp. 184-188.

"Our Father in the Heaven who Art"

1539

The writing of this hymn may have been prompted by Luther's desire to furnish a hymn for every part of the catechism. Many other people had tried to versify the Lord's Prayer in the Middle Ages and the sixteenth century. But Luther's version is outstanding, for every stanza begins with an almost literal rendering of the Lord's Prayer phrase by phrase, followed by the catechetical interpretation of its meaning in the remaining lines. The hymn seems to have been first published in 1539 on a broadsheet now lost. In the same year it appeared in Valentin Schumann's Leipzig hymnal, not however with Luther's other hymns, but in a later section of the book. Perhaps it did not come to the publisher's attention until the book was partially set or even printed.

This is one of two hymns for which an original draft in Luther's hand is known.[1] It shows not only earlier and inferior versions of some of the verses with Luther's own corrections, but also the tune he had originally sketched out for it. This melody bears some of the characteristic marks of Luther's own melodies. The start on the upper tonic recalls "A New Song Here Shall Be Begun,"[2] "Our God He Is a Castle Strong,"[3] and "From Heaven on High I Come to You";[4] the third, fourth, and last lines echo phrases from "Isaiah 'Twas the Prophet."[5] Nevertheless, he was evidently not content with this melody. Schumann 1539 and all later hymnals[6] offer a more subdued and devotional tune that can be traced to the melody of Michael Weisse's hymn on the Lord's Prayer *"Begehren wir mit Innigkeit"* in the 1531 hymnal of the Bohemian Brethren. Whether Luther was responsible for the adaptation of

---

[1] For a facsimile, see Moser, *Die Melodien der Lutherlieder,* facing p. 81.
[2] See pp. 211-216.
[3] See pp. 283-285.
[4] See pp. 289-291.
[5] See pp. 82-83.
[6] Two other melodies given by Georg Rhau, *Neue geistliche Gesänge* (Wittenberg, 1544), failed to find acceptance elsewhere. They can be found in Zahn, *Die Melodien der deutschen evangelischen Kirchenlieder,* II, Nos. 2563-2564.

this melody to his Lord's Prayer is hard to say. It is not as bold and vigorous as some of the tunes that can with greater likelihood be ascribed to him. At any rate, he must have preferred the mood of the melody ultimately chosen, even though its progression does not reflect the emphasis of the text as closely as his earlier sketch.[7] We offer both melodies.

The German text, *"Vater unser im Himelreich,"* is given in *WA* 35, 463-467; both melodies are given in *WA* 35, 527. The translation, with minor revisions, is that by MacDonald, *Exotics,* pp. 91-93.

"Our Father in the Heaven who Art"

SCHUMANN 1539

1. Our Fa - ther in the heaven who art,

Who tell - est all of us, in heart Broth - ers to be, and

on thee call, And wilt have prayer from us all, Grant that

the mouth not on - ly pray, From deep - est heart, O help its way.

---

[7] Cf. Markus Jenny, *"Die beiden Weisen zu Luthers Vaterunser-Lied,"* Ameln et al. (eds.), *Jahrbuch für Liturgik und Hymnologie,* VI, 115-118.

LUTHER MS.

1. Our Fa - ther in the heaven who art,

Who tell - est all of us, in heart Broth - ers to be, and

on thee call, And wilt have prayer from us all, Grant that

[sic]

the mouth not on - ly pray, From deep - est heart, O help its way.

2 Hallowed be thy name, O Lord;
   Amongst us pure, O keep thy word,
   That we too may live holily,
   And keep in thy name worthily.
   Defend us, Lord, from lying lore;
   Thy poor misguided folk restore.

3 Thy kingdom come now here below,
   And after, up there, evermo'.
   The Holy Ghost his temple hold
   In us with graces manifold.
   The devil's wrath and greatness strong,
   Crush, that he do thy church no wrong.

4 Thy will be done the same, Lord God,
   On earth as in thy high abode;
   In pain give patience for relief,
   Obedience in love and grief;
   All flesh and blood keep off and check
   That 'gainst thy will makes a stiff neck.

5 Give us this day our daily bread,
   And all that doth the body stead;
   From strife and war, Lord, keep us free,
   From sickness and from scarcity;
   That we in happy peace may rest,
   By care and greed all undistrest.

6 Forgive, Lord, all our trespasses,
   That they no more may us distress,
   As of our debtors we will let
   Pass all the trespasses and debt.
   To serve make us all ready be
   In honest love and unity.

297

7 Into temptation lead us not.
E'en though the foe makes battle hot
Upon the right and the left hand,
Help us with vigor to withstand,
Firm in the faith, armed 'gainst a host
Through comfort of the Holy Ghost.

8 From all that's evil free thy sons—
The time, the days are wicked ones.
Deliver us from endless death;
Comfort us in our latest breath;
Grant us also a blessed end,
Our spirit take into thy hand.

9 Amen! that is, let this come true!
Strengthen our faith ever anew,
That we may never be in doubt
Of that we here have prayed about.
In thy name, trusting in thy word,
We blithely say Amen, O Lord.

"To Jordan When Our Lord Had Gone"

1541

With the publication in 1539 of his hymn on the Lord's Prayer, Luther had furnished a hymn for every part of the Catechism except baptism. He filled this gap in 1541. Actually, the earliest hymnals in existence which contain this chorale are Klug's Wittenberg hymnal of 1543, Johann Walter's Magdeburg hymnal of the same year, and Rödinger's Magdeburg hymnal, published not before 1542. It also appears in an appendix to Schumann's Leipzig hymnal of 1543. But a Low-German Lübeck hymnal of 1556, now lost, contained this hymn with the date 1541—evidently copied from an earlier broadsheet.[1] We are therefore safe in assuming that it was written in or before 1541.

All the hymnals assign to it the Dorian melody which Walter in 1524 had offered for "Would That the Lord Would Grant Us Grace."[2] This Dorian tune, with its vigorous fourth in the first, third, fifth, and sixth lines, is strongly reminiscent of "Dear Christians, Let Us Now Rejoice"[3] and may well be an original Luther melody. We offer it following Walter 1524, but transposed a fourth lower. The German text, "*Christ unser HErr zum Jordan kam*," is given in *WA* 35, 468-470; the melody is given in *WA* 35, 490-491. The translation, with minor revisions,[4] is that by MacDonald, *Exotics*, pp. 98-100.

---

[1] *WA* 35, 281.
[2] See p. 234.
[3] See p. 219.
[4] The first half of the second stanza and the second half of the sixth stanza are from Massie, *Martin Luther's Spiritual Songs*, pp. 69-71.

"To Jordan When Our Lord Had Gone"

WALTER 1524

1. To Jordan when our Lord had gone,
He took his baptism of Saint John,

His Father's pleasure willing,
His work and task fulfilling; There-in he

would appoint a bath To wash us from defile-

ment, And also drown that cruel death In his blood

of atonement; A new life he would give us.

2 So hear ye all and well receive
What God does call baptism
And what a Christian should believe
To shun error and schism.
Water indeed, not water mere
In it can do his pleasure,
His holy Word is also there
With Spirit rich, unmeasured;
He is the one baptizing.

3 This clearly he to us by word
Hath shown, nor less by vision;
The Father's voice men plainly heard,
At Jordan tell his mission.
He said, This is my own dear Son,
In whom I'm well contented;
To you I send him, every one—
That you may hear, I've sent him,
And follow what he teaches.

4 Also God's Son himself here stands
  In all his manhood tender;
  The Holy Ghost on him descends,
  In dove's appearance hidden,
  That not a doubt should ever rise
  That, when we are baptized,
  All the three persons do baptize;
  And so, here recognized,
  Will make their dwelling with us.

5 Christ to his followers says: Go forth,
  Give to all men acquaintance
  That lost in sin lies the whole earth,
  And must turn to repentance.
  Who trusts and is baptized, each one
  Is thereby blest for ever;
  Is from that hour a new-born man,
  And thenceforth dying never,
  The kingdom shall inherit.

6 But in this grace who puts no faith,
  Abides in his trespasses
  And is condemned to endless death
  Deep down in hell's abysses.
  His holiness avails him not
  Nor aught which he is doing;
  His in-born sin brings all to nought,
  And maketh sure his ruin;
  Himself he cannot succor.

7 The eye but water doth behold,
  As from man's hand it floweth;
  But inward faith the power untold
  Of Jesus Christ's blood knoweth.
  Faith sees therein a red flood roll,
  With Christ's blood dyed and blended,
  Which hurts of all kinds maketh whole,
  From Adam here descended,
  And by ourselves brought on us.

301

"Herod, Why Dreadest Thou a Foe"

[*Hostis Herodes impie*]

1541

This is a German translation of the Latin hymn "*Hostis Herodes impie*" by Coelius Sedulius (d. *ca.* 540). Like "*A solis ortus cardine*," which inspired Luther's "Jesus We Now Must Laud and Sing,"[1] "*Hostis Herodes*" was extracted from a much longer acrostic hymn on the whole life of Christ. It dealt with the traditional themes of the Epiphany: the Magi, the baptism of Jesus, and the wedding feast at Cana.

While a German version by Thomas Münzer had appeared as early as 1524, Luther's hymn was not published until 1543, when it was incorporated in Klug's Wittenberg hymnal. The date of writing, however, seems to be two years earlier. A New Testament in the Jena library contains a handwritten copy of it by Luther's friend and amanuensis Georg Rörer with the significant remark: "The blessed Luther finished this hymn, as the added note shows, on December 12, 1541."[2] Apparently Rörer had taken a copy from Luther's original draft (incidentally, without the fifth stanza). The "added note" would then appear to be the date the poet wrote under his lines.

Neither Klug 1543 nor Babst 1545 offer any music for this hymn. Both of them refer instead to the melody for "Jesus We Now Must Laud and Sing."[3] But Wolff Köpfl's Strassburg hymnal of 1545 and Johann Spangenberg's *Cantiones Ecclesiasticae* of the same year offer the proper plain-chant melody for "*Hostis Herodes impie*,"[4] which we offer in the Köpfl 1545 version. The German text, "*Was furchstu, Feind Herodes, seer*," is given in WA 35, 470-471; the melody is given in Zahn, *Die Melodien der deutschen evangelischen Kirchenlieder*, I, No. 361. The translation is that by MacDonald, *Exotics*, pp. 50-51.

---

[1] See pp. 237-239.
[2] See WA 35, 268.
[3] See pp. 238-239.
[4] Not a more melismatic version of "*A solis ortus*" as Moser erroneously asserts in WA 35, 528; cf. also Zahn, *Die Melodien der deutschen evangelischen Kirchenlieder*, I (1889), No. 361.

"Herod, Why Dreadest Thou a Foe"

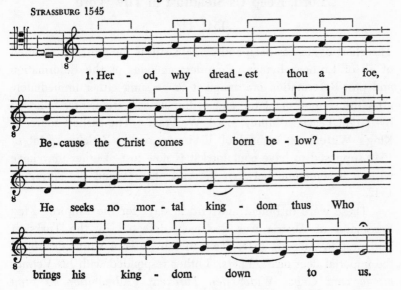

STRASSBURG 1545

1. Her - od, why dread - est thou a foe,
Be - cause the Christ comes born be - low?
He seeks no mor - tal king - dom thus Who
brings his king - dom down to us.

2 After the star the Wise Men go,
That light the true light them did show;
They signify with presents three,
This child God, Man, and King to be.

3 In Jordan baptism he did take,
This Lamb of God, for our poor sake;
Thus he who never did a sin,
Hath washed us clean both out and in.

4 A miracle straightway befell:
Six pots of stone they saw, who tell,
Of water full, which changed its sort,
And turned to red wine at his word.

5 Praise, honor, thanks to thee be said,
Jesus, born of the holy maid;
With Father and with Holy Ghost,
Now, and henceforward, ending not.

303

"Lord, Keep Us Steadfast in Thy Word"

1541/42?

This short hymn has been and perhaps still is the most widely used of all of Luther's hymns. Countless agendas of the Reformation and post-Reformation era assign it to be sung either immediately after the sermon or at the end of the service, frequently followed by "Grant Peace in Mercy, Lord, We Pray."[1] The earliest source is Klug's Wittenberg hymnal of 1543. An earlier Zwickau print of 1542 supposed to have contained it is now lost. Luther may have written it sometime between the end of 1541 and the spring of 1542.

These were turbulent and critical days for the Empire. King Ferdinand of Austria was decisively defeated by the Turks at Budapest in August, 1541. Two months later a storm destroyed the imperial fleet near Algiers. Luther responded with his *Vermanunge zum Gebet Wider den Türcken*[2] (*Admonition to Pray Against the Turk*). The Elector requested pastors to offer special prayers for divine help and protection. Our hymn may have been written with this in mind, for Luther repeatedly stressed the children's prayers as the best defense against the Turks.

But many people took bitter offense at the juxtaposition of "Turk" and "papist" in the second line of the first stanza. In predominantly Catholic principalities the hymn was forbidden, and after the interim of 1548, even Lutherans attempted to revise this line. Under the influence of pietism it was commonly changed to a petition for protection from the enemies of the Word, and today the original version has almost completely disappeared from use. But it must be remembered that at the time of writing not only the Turks but also many of the European princes loyal to Rome were ready to liquidate Lutheranism by force. Francis I of France, e.g., who posed as a defender of the church, made common cause with the Sultan against the Empire. These were the conditions that inspired Luther's prayer for protection against both pope and Turk.

---

[1] See pp. 286-287.
[2] WA 51, 585-625.

The melody bears the marks of Luther's own hand. Clearly it is patterned after Ambrose's *"Veni Redemptor Gentium."*[3] But the bold steps of the chorale are excellently suited to the mood of the words and make it truly congregational.

We offer text and melody after the oldest source, Klug's Wittenberg hymnal of 1543. Valentin Babst's Leipzig hymnal of 1545 and many later sources double the value of the notes marked by an asterisk and insert a quarter rest at the place indicated by a plus sign. The German text, *"ERhalt uns HErr bey deinem Wort,"* is given in *WA* 35, 467-468; the music is given in *WA* 35, 528. The translation, with minor revisions, is that by MacDonald, *Exotics,* p. 69.

"Lord, Keep Us Steadfast in Thy Word"

KLUG 1543

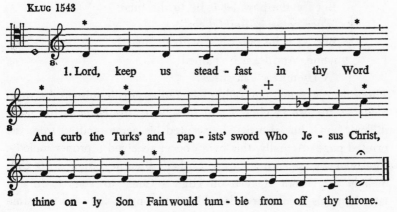

1. Lord, keep us stead - fast in thy Word
And curb the Turks' and pap - ists' sword Who Je - sus Christ,
thine on - ly Son Fain would tum - ble from off thy throne.

2 Proof of thy might, Lord Christ, afford,
For thou of all the lords art Lord;
Thine own poor Christendom defend,
That it may praise thee without end.

3 God Holy Ghost, who comfort art,
Give to thy folk on earth one heart;
Stand by us breathing our last breath,
Lead us to life straight out of death.

---

[3] *The Service Book and Hymnal of the Lutheran Church in America* (1958), No. 155, notes that Luther's tune is based on the Latin hymn tune *Jesu, dulcedo cordium,* but the earliest source for the latter is the *Antiphoner,* published in Poitiers in 1746. Cf. Maurice Frost, *Historical Companion to Hymns Ancient and Modern* (London: Wm. Clowes, 1962), p. 345.

"From Heaven the Angel Troop Came Near"
1543

This is Luther's last Christmas hymn. It appeared in the 1543 edition of Klug's hymnal. Students of Luther's hymns have noted its sterner tone as compared with his earlier Christmas hymns. The last three verses breathe an air of defiance similar to "Our God He Is a Castle Strong" and "Lord, Keep Us Steadfast in Thy Word."

It is also one of two hymns that are known in Luther's own writing.[1] Particularly revealing is the following postscript which Luther added to the hymn:

Either to the tune: *"A solis ortus"*[2] ⎫
Or: *"Vom Himmel Hoch"*[3] ⎬ in church ⎭
But for the boys let it be to the tune:
"Puer natus in Bethlehem."[4]
But let it be published without my
name. And let it be named:
"A Hymn for Christmas."

These words show not only that Luther distinguished between melodies for use in church and in school (the latter is the more difficult one), but also that he wanted his name omitted from the printed page. Actually, this hymn never received a proper melody. The hymnals appearing during Luther's lifetime assigned his own melody for "From Heaven on High I Come to You" to it.[5] In later hymnals it inherited the older folk-song melody for the same hymn. This is the tune we offer, following Klug's hymnal of 1535. The German text, *"Vom Himel kam der Engel schar,"* is given in WA 35, 471-472; the melody is given in WA 35, 524. The translation, with slight revisions, is that by MacDonald, *Exotics,* pp. 48-49.

---

[1] For a facsimile of the manuscript, see WA 35, 636-637. The manuscript of the other hymn "Our Father in the Heaven who Art" is preserved only in a facsimile in C. V. Winterfeld, *Dr. Martin Luthers deutsche geistliche Lieder* (Leipzig, 1840), Appendix.
[2] See pp. 238-239.
[3] See p. 290.
[4] "A Child Is Born in Bethlehem." See Zahn, *Die Melodien der deutschen evangelischen Kirchenlieder,* I, No. 192a.
[5] See p. 290.

"From Heaven the Angel Troop Came Near"

Klug 1535

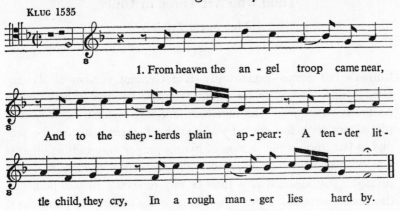

1. From heaven the an - gel troop came near,

And to the shep - herds plain ap - pear: A ten - der lit -

tle child, they cry, In a rough man - ger lies hard by.

2 In Bethlehem, David's town of old,
As Prophet Micah has foretold;
'Tis the Lord Jesus Christ, I wis,
Who of you all the Savior is.

3 And ye may well break out in mirth,
That God is one with you henceforth;
For he is born your flesh and blood—
Your brother is the eternal Good.

4 What can death do to you, or sin?
The true God is to you come in.
Let hell and Satan raging go—
The Son of God's your comrade now.

5 He will nor can from you go hence;
Set you in him your confidence.
Let many battle on you make,
Defy them—he cannot forsake.

6 At last you must approval win,
For you are now of God's own kin,
For this thank God, ever and aye,
Content and patient all the day. Amen

"Thou who Art Three in Unity"

[*O lux beata Trinitas*]

1543

Luther's last hymn—significantly—is a German version of the ancient Vesper hymn "*O lux beata Trinitas*," commonly ascribed to Ambrose (340-397). The fact that in Klug's hymnal of 1543 it is placed not with the other hymns of the Reformer but as the second-to-last item in the section of hymns proper may indicate that it was written while the book was already in the process of being printed. The absence of a tune or any reference to one points in the same direction. Later hymnals give the traditional plain-chant tune, one version of which appears in Babst's Leipzig hymnal of 1545 and the other in Köpfl's Strassburg hymnal of the same year. We offer both versions. The German text, "*Der du bist drey in einigkeit*," is given in WA 35, 473; the melodies are given in WA 35, 529. The translation is that by MacDonald, *Exotics*, p. 61.

"Thou who Art Three in Unity"

BABST 1545

STRASSBURG 1545

1. { Thou who art three in u - ni - ty,
{ A true God from e - ter - ni - ty,

The sun with day with - draws his shine,

Light - en us with thy light di - vine.

2 At morn we praise thee with the day,
At evening also to thee pray;
Our poor song glorifieth thee
Now, ever, and eternally.

3 To God the Father praise be poured;
To God the Son, the only Lord;
To the consoling Holy Ghost;
Now and forever, ending not. Amen[1]

---

[1]The hymnals offer no music for the "Amen." Presumably it was sung on the closing note of the hymn.

PREFACES TO HYMNALS AND
OTHER MUSICAL COLLECTIONS

INTRODUCTION

Several of the hymnals and other musical collections which appeared in Wittenberg and other nearby cities during Luther's lifetime contained prefaces written by the Reformer. Publishers were eager to carry Luther's recommendation. In an era before the advent of the copyright when piracy was common among printers and when the Lutheran hymns were reprinted everywhere—often in badly garbled versions[1]—Luther's preface could be taken to indicate that a given hymnal had been approved by him, if not edited under his supervision. For a list of hymnals prepared under Luther's supervision, see pp. 191-194.

Luther gladly used this opportunity to express his views on music and its place in the church. These brief prefaces contain a whole philosophy of music and afford an insight into his concept of art and culture and their relation to the gospel.

---

[1] See pp. 317-318; 333-334.

Preface to the Wittenberg Hymnal

1524

Translated by Paul Zeller Strodach
Revised by Ulrich S. Leupold

Luther took personal interest in the publication of his hymns. While countless copies of them were printed without his knowledge or authorization, some of the best hymnals of the period appeared in Wittenberg and were compiled under his personal supervision.

The first of these is the *Spiritual Hymn Booklet* of 1524, often called the *Walter Choir Book*. Of all the hymnals published in 1524, this is the most ambitious and comprehensive, and the only one that follows the church year. It contains thirty-seven chorales in polyphonic settings by Johann Walter, Luther's trusted musical adviser. All but five of these hymns are German, and twenty-four of them are by Luther. This earliest hymnal prepared under Luther's auspices offers his hymns in highly artistic musical settings for the choir. As church choirs were composed primarily of boys and older students at school, these settings were supposed to implant the gospel through music in the hearts and minds of the young.

Luther wrote this preface for the Wittenberg hymnal of 1524 to indicate his personal interest in the work and its purpose. From there it passed into many later hymnals. The German text, *Vorrhede Martini Luther,* is given in WA 35, 474-475; the following translation is a revision of P. Z. Strodach's translation in *PE* 6, 283-284.

Preface by Martin Luther

That it is good and God pleasing to sing hymns is, I think, known to every Christian; for everyone is aware not only of the example of the prophets and kings in the Old Testament who praised God

315

with song and sound, with poetry and psaltery, but also of the common and ancient custom of the Christian church to sing Psalms. St. Paul himself instituted this in I Corinthians 14 [:15] and exhorted the Colossians [3:16] to sing spiritual songs and Psalms heartily unto the Lord so that God's Word and Christian teaching might be instilled and implanted in many ways.

Therefore I, too, in order to make a start and to give an incentive to those who can do better, have with the help of others compiled several hymns, so that the holy gospel which now by the grace of God has risen anew may be noised and spread abroad.

Like Moses in his song [Exod. 15:2], we may now boast that Christ is our praise and song and say with St. Paul, I Corinthians 2 [:2], that we should know nothing to sing or say, save Jesus Christ our Savior.

And these songs were arranged in four parts[1] to give the young—who should at any rate be trained in music and other fine arts—something to wean them away from love ballads and carnal songs and to teach them something of value in their place, thus combining the good with the pleasing, as is proper for youth. Nor am I of the opinion that the gospel should destroy and blight all the arts, as some of the pseudo-religious[2] claim. But I would like to see all the arts, especially music, used in the service of Him who gave and made them. I therefore pray that every pious Christian would be pleased with this [the use of music in the service of the gospel] and lend his help if God has given him like or greater gifts. As it is, the world is too lax and indifferent about teaching and training the young for us to abet this trend. God grant us his grace. Amen.

---

[1] Actually most of the arrangements are for five parts.
[2] Or super-religious, a reference to the enthusiasts who condemned and, when possible, destroyed sacred art of any kind.

316

Preface to the Weiss Hymnal

1528

Translated by Paul Zeller Strodach
Revised by Ulrich S. Leupold

The enormous popular response to the hymns of Luther and his friends resulted in countless reprints of his hymns and hymnals; almost a hundred Lutheran hymnals were published in Luther's lifetime. Without copyright laws, Luther's hymns were fair prey for every printer who wanted to cash in on the tremendous demand for them. Some of these reprints were done with care, but others, prepared in great haste to scoop the market, circulated the Wittenberg hymns in badly corrupted versions.[1]

Luther dealt with this situation in his *New Preface by Martin Luther*. The earliest extant source for this preface is the hymnal published by Andrew Rauscher of Erfurt in 1531. But Rauscher's hymnal is a reprint of Joseph Klug's Wittenberg hymnal of 1529, which is lost. Lucke[2] has made a good case for the assumption that Klug in turn borrowed it from Hans Weiss's Wittenberg hymnal of 1528. The German text, *Ein newe Vorrede Marti. Luth.*, is given in *WA* 35, 475-476; the following translation is a revision of P. Z. Strodach's translation in *PE* 6, 285-286.

A New Preface
by Martin Luther

Now there are some who have given a good account of themselves and augmented the hymns so that they by far surpass me and are my masters indeed. But others have added little of worth. And since I realize that there is going to be no end to this haphazard and arbitrary revision which goes on from day to day, and that

---

[1] Cf. the verse on the title page of Klug 1543 and Babst 1545, in this volume, p. 332.
[2] *WA* 35, 50.

even our first hymns are more and more mutilated with each reprinting, I fear that this booklet will ultimately fare no better than good books everywhere, namely, to be corrupted and adulterated by blunderheads until the good in it will be lost and only the bad remain. Similarly, we see in St. Luke 1 [:1-4] that in the beginning everyone wanted to write a gospel, until the true gospel was all but lost among so many gospels. The same thing happened to the books of SS. Jerome, Augustine, and many others. In a word, there must be mouse dirt with the pepper.[1]

In order to prevent this as far as possible, I have reviewed this booklet again and printed the hymns of our group separately with the names of the authors, something that I had heretofore avoided for fear of vainglory, but that I am now forced to do, lest worthless hymns by others be sold under our name. I have placed other hymns which we think are good and the most useful in the second section.

I beg and admonish all who love the pure Word no more to "improve" or enlarge our booklet without our knowledge. But if it should be "improved" without our knowledge, let it be known that such is not the booklet published by us in Wittenberg. After all, everyone can compile his own booklet of hymns and leave ours intact, as we beg, desire, and herewith declare to be our wish. For we would like to safeguard the value of our own currency, not begrudging anyone else the privilege of coining a better one for themselves, in order that God's name alone be praised and not ours. Amen.

---

[1] A common proverb; cf. WA 51, No. 371.

A Preface for All Good Hymnals
1538

Translated by Paul Nettl
Revised by Ulrich S. Leupold

Johann Walter (1496-1570), Luther's musical friend and adviser, was, like most musicians of his time, not only a composer but also a poet. He contributed a number of hymns to the early Lutheran hymnals. In 1538 he published a rimed encomium of music, *Lob und Preis der löblichen Kunst Musica*[1] (*Glory and Praise of the Laudable Art of Music*), a didactic poem of 335 verses in which he developed a whole theology of music along the lines of Luther's scattered remarks on music. The Reformer provided the rimed introduction, entitled *A Preface for All Good Hymnals*.

Artists of the sixteenth century liked to personify the arts, sciences, virtues, etc. It was a common device of painters, sculptors, and poets to represent music as a lady. Luther followed this trend when he put his preface on the lips of "Dame Music" and had her extol her own gifts.

Actually, *A Preface for All Good Hymnals* was not printed in any hymnal in Luther's lifetime, except in Joseph Klug's hymnal of 1543, where it was appended at the end. The German text, *Vorrhede auff alle gute Gesangbücher*, is given in WA 35, 483-484. The translation, with minor revisions, is that by Paul Nettl, *Luther and Music*, pp. 65-66.

A Preface for All Good Hymnals

Dame Music [speaks:]

Of all the joys upon this earth
None has for men a greater worth
Than what I give with my ringing
And with voices sweetly singing.
There cannot be an evil mood
Where there are singing fellows good,

---

[1] Published in Wittenberg: Georg Rhau, 1538.

There is no envy, hate, nor ire,
Gone are through me all sorrows dire;
Greed, care, and lonely heaviness
No more do they the heart oppress.
Each man can in his mirth be free
Since such a joy no sin can be.
But God in me more pleasure finds
Than in all joys of earthly minds.
Through my bright power the devil shirks
His sinful, murderous, evil works.
Of this King David's deeds do tell
Who pacified King Saul so well
By sweetly playing on the lyre
And thus escaped his murderous ire.[1]
For truth divine and God's own rede
The heart of humble faith shall lead;
Such did Elisha once propound
When harping he the Spirit found.[2]
The best time of the year is mine[3]
When all the birds are singing fine.
Heaven and earth their voices fill
With right good song and tuneful trill.
And, queen of all, the nightingale
Men's hearts will merrily regale
With music so charmingly gay;
For which be thanks to her for aye.
But thanks be first to God, our Lord,
Who created her by his Word
To be his own beloved songstress
And of *musica* a mistress.
For our dear Lord she sings her song
In praise of him the whole day long;
To him I give my melody
And thanks in all eternity.

---

[1] Cf. I Sam. 16:23.   [2] Cf. II Kings 3:15.
[3] It is not quite clear whether the original reads *"mein"* or *"Maien,"* i.e.,
"mine" or "May." The thought in either case is that spring with the music
of the birds is more than others the season of music.

320

Preface to Georg Rhau's
Symphoniae iucundae

1538

Translated by Ulrich S. Leupold

In its infancy Lutheran church music was fortunate to have a publisher as forward looking, imaginative, and energetic as the Wittenberg printer Georg Rhau (1488-1548). A musician and composer, he was an early predecessor of J. S. Bach at St. Thomas in Leipzig and had contributed a mass for twelve voices for the opening of the disputation between Luther and Eck in 1519.[1] At this time or soon after he became an adherent of Luther. He moved to Wittenberg in 1523 and opened a printing firm that produced volume after volume of liturgical music for the Lutheran church service. Between 1538 and 1545 he published twelve carefully-edited collections in which he offered a complete repertory of masses, vespers, antiphons, responsories, and hymns, in both Latin and German and by the best composers of his day. The initial two volumes of this ambitious series were the *Symphoniae iucundae* (*Delightful Symphonies*)[2] and the *Selectae Harmoniae quatuor vocum de passione Domini (Selected Harmonies of the Passion of Our Lord for Four Voices)*. The first one contained fifty-two motets for the Sundays of the church year, the second motets and other choral works for Lent. The prefaces for these two collections were written by Luther and Melanchthon respectively. The following translation of Luther's *Preface to Georg Rhau's Symphoniae iucundae* is based on the Latin text, *Martinus Luther Musicae Studiosis*, given in *WA* 50, 368-374.

Martin Luther to the Devotees of Music

Greetings in Christ! I would certainly like to praise music with all my heart as the excellent gift of God which it is and to commend it to everyone. But I am so overwhelmed by the diversity

---

[1] Cf. *LW* 31, 309-325.
[2] The word "symphony" had none of its present meaning. It signified any piece of music for several parts, whether instrumental, vocal, or both.

and magnitude of its virtue and benefits that I can find neither beginning nor end or method for my discourse. As much as I want to commend it, my praise is bound to be wanting and inadequate. For who can comprehend it all? And even if you wanted to encompass all of it, you would appear to have grasped nothing at all. First then, looking at music itself, you will find that from the beginning of the world it has been instilled and implanted in all creatures, individually and collectively. For nothing is without sound or harmony.[1] Even the air, which of itself is invisible and imperceptible to all our senses, and which, since it lacks both voice and speech, is the least musical of all things, becomes sonorous, audible, and comprehensible when it is set in motion. Wondrous mysteries are here suggested by the Spirit, but this is not the place to dwell on them.[2] Music is still more wonderful in living things, especially birds, so that David, the most musical of all the kings and minstrel of God, in deepest wonder and spiritual exultation praised the astounding art and ease of the song of birds when he said in Psalm 104 [:12], "By them the birds of the heaven have their habitation; they sing among the branches."

And yet, compared to the human voice, all this hardly deserves the name of music, so abundant and incomprehensible is here the munificence and wisdom of our most gracious Creator. Philosophers have labored to explain the marvelous instrument of the human voice: how can the air projected by a light movement of the tongue and an even lighter movement of the throat produce such an infinite variety and articulation of the voice and of words? And how can the voice, at the direction of the will, sound forth so powerfully and vehemently that it cannot only be heard by everyone over a wide area, but also be understood? Philosophers for all their labor cannot find the explanation; and baffled they end in perplexity; for none of them has yet been able to define or demonstrate the original components of the human voice, its sibilation and (as it were) its alphabet, e.g., in the case of laughter—to say nothing of weeping. They marvel, but they do not understand. But such speculations on the infinite wisdom of God, shown in this

---

[1] Literally, "sounding number."
[2] Luther probably thought of the influence of the Holy Spirit on the spirit of man.

single part of his creation, we shall leave to better men with more time on their hands. We have hardly touched on them.

Here it must suffice to discuss the benefit[3] of this great art.[4] But even that transcends the greatest eloquence of the most eloquent, because of the infinite variety of its forms and benefits. We can mention only one point (which experience confirms), namely, that next to the Word of God, music deserves the highest praise. She is a mistress and governess of those human emotions[5]—to pass over the animals—which as masters govern men or more often overwhelm them. No greater commendation than this can be found— at least not by us. For whether you wish to comfort the sad, to terrify the happy, to encourage the despairing, to humble the proud, to calm the passionate, or to appease those full of hate— and who could number all these masters of the human heart, namely, the emotions, inclinations, and affections that impel men to evil or good?—what more effective means than music could you find? The Holy Ghost himself honors her as an instrument for his proper work when in his Holy Scriptures he asserts that through her his gifts were instilled in the prophets, namely, the inclination to all virtues, as can be seen in Elisha [II Kings 3:15]. On the other hand, she serves to cast out Satan, the instigator of all sins, as is shown in Saul, the king of Israel [I Sam. 16:23].

Thus it was not without reason that the fathers and prophets wanted nothing else to be associated as closely with the Word of God as music. Therefore, we have so many hymns and Psalms where message and music[6] join to move the listener's soul, while in other living beings[7] and [sounding] bodies[8] music remains a language without words.[9] After all, the gift of language combined with the gift of song was only given to man to let him know that he should praise God with both word and music, namely, by proclaiming [the Word of God] through music[10] and by providing

---

[3] *Usus.*
[4] Literally, "thing."
[5] *Affectuum.*
[6] *Sermo et vox.*
[7] Luther thinks, e.g., of birds.
[8] I.e., for example, instrumental music.
[9] *Sine sermone gesticulatur.*
[10] *Sonora praedicatione.*

sweet melodies with words. For even a comparison between different men will show how rich and manifold our glorious Creator proves himself in distributing the gifts of music, how much men differ from each other in voice and manner of speaking so that one amazingly excels the other. No two men can be found with exactly the same voice and manner of speaking, although they often seem to imitate each other, the one as it were being the ape of the other.

But when [musical] learning is added to all this and artistic music which corrects, develops, and refines the natural music, then at last it is possible to taste with wonder (yet not to comprehend) God's absolute and perfect wisdom in his wondrous work of music. Here it is most remarkable that one single voice continues to sing the tenor,[11] while at the same time many other voices play around it, exulting and adorning it in exuberant strains and, as it were, leading it forth in a divine roundelay, so that those who are the least bit moved know nothing more amazing in this world. But any who remain unaffected are unmusical indeed and deserve to hear a certain filth poet[12] or the music of the pigs.

But the subject is much too great for me briefly to describe all its benefits. And you, my young friend, let this noble, wholesome, and cheerful creation of God be commended to you. By it you may escape shameful desires and bad company. At the same time you may by this creation accustom yourself to recognize and praise the Creator. Take special care to shun perverted minds who prostitute this lovely gift of nature and of art with their erotic rantings; and be quite assured that none but the devil goads them on to defy their very nature which would and should praise God its Maker with this gift, so that these bastards purloin the gift of God and use it to worship the foe of God, the enemy of nature and of this lovely art. Farewell in the Lord.

---

[11] Luther refers to the polyphonic style of his time which gave the melody to the tenor in long notes while the other voices provided a tracery of counterpoints in livelier rhythms.
[12] Luther uses the strong term *merdipoeta* to refer to Simon Lemnius, a humanist and poet who in the same year had drawn the ire of Luther with a collection of poems slandering prominent persons in Wittenberg and eulogizing the cultured, but profligate Archbishop Albrecht of Mainz; cf. WA 50, 350-351.

Preface to the Burial Hymns

1542

Translated by Paul Zeller Strodach
Revised by Ulrich S. Leupold

Several hymnals published in Wittenberg during Luther's lifetime were devoted exclusively to burial hymns. The first of these, published by Joseph Klug in Wittenberg in 1542, contained eight Latin chants and six German chorales. Luther supplied the preface, in which he outlined the guiding principles for the reform of the burial service. Here as elsewhere he did not condemn pomp and ceremony as such. He was able to interpret proper decorum at a burial as an expression of Christian hope. But he failed to detect this hope in the requiem masses of the Roman church with its morbid preoccupation with the fate of the departed and its frantic intercession for them. Luther deplored the doleful character of traditional funerals and wanted the whole funeral rite to be an expression of confident trust.

The German text, *Dem Christlichen Leser, D. Mart. Luther*, is given in *WA* 35, 478-483; the following translation is a revision of P. Z. Strodach's translation in *PE* 6, 287-292. The editor translated the rimed biblical verses.

Preface to the Burial Hymns
To the Christian Reader

Dr. Martin Luther

St. Paul exhorts the Thessalonians [I Thess. 4:13-18] not to sorrow over the dead as others who have no hope, but to comfort each other with God's Word as having a certain hope of life and of the resurrection of the dead.

It is little wonder if those are sad who have no hope. Nor can they be blamed for it. Since they are beyond the pale of faith in Christ, they must either cherish this temporal life as the only thing worthwhile and hate to lose it, or they must expect that

325

after this life they will receive eternal death and the wrath of God in hell and must fear to go there.

But we Christians, who have been redeemed from all this by the dear blood of the Son of God, should by faith train and accustom ourselves to despise death and to regard it as a deep, strong, and sweet sleep, to regard the coffin as nothing but paradise and the bosom of our Lord Christ, and the grave as nothing but a soft couch or sofa, which it really is in the sight of God; for he says, John 11 [:11], "Our friend Lazarus has fallen asleep," and Matthew 9 [:24], "The girl is not dead but sleeping."

Thus, too, St. Paul in I Corinthians 15 [:42-44] bans from his sight every ugly aspect of death in our mortal body and brings to the fore a wholly delightful and joyous picture of life when he says: "What is sown is perishable, what is raised is imperishable. ... It is sown in weakness, it is raised in power. It is sown a natural body, it is raised a spiritual body."

Accordingly, we have removed from our churches and completely abolished the popish abominations, such as vigils, masses for the dead, processions, purgatory, and all other hocus-pocus on behalf of the dead. And we do not want our churches to be houses of wailing and places of mourning any longer, but *Koemeteria*[1] as the old fathers were wont to call them, i.e., dormitories and resting places.

Nor do we sing any dirges or doleful songs over our dead and at the grave, but comforting hymns of the forgiveness of sins, of rest, sleep, life, and of the resurrection of departed Christians so that our faith may be strengthened and the people be moved to true devotion.

For it is meet and right that we should conduct these funerals with proper decorum in order to honor and praise that joyous article of our faith, namely, the resurrection of the dead, and in order to defy Death, that terrible foe who so shamefully and in so many horrible ways goes on to devour us.

Thus the holy patriarchs, Abraham, Isaac, Jacob, Joseph, and others, conducted their burials with much splendor and left explicit directions concerning them. Later the kings of Judah made

---

[1] Hence the English word "cemetery."

a great show and pomp over the dead with costly incense and all sorts of rare and precious spices, all of which was done to spite the stinking and shameful Death and to praise and confess the resurrection of the dead and thus to comfort the sad and the weak in faith.

Here also belong the traditional Christian burial rites, such as that the bodies are carried in state, beautifully decked, and sung over, and that tombstones adorn their graves. All this is done so that the article of the resurrection may be firmly implanted in us. For it is our lasting, blessed, and eternal comfort and joy against death, hell, devil, and every woe.

This is also why we have collected the fine music and songs which under the papacy were used at vigils, masses for the dead, and burials. Some fine examples of these we have printed in this booklet and we, or whoever is more gifted than we, will select more of them in the future. But we have adapted other texts to the music so that it may adorn our article of the resurrection, instead of purgatory with its torment and satisfaction which lets their dead neither sleep nor rest. The melodies and notes are precious. It would be a pity to let them perish. But the texts and words are non-Christian and absurd. They deserve to perish.

It is the same in other matters where they outdo us by far. They have the most beautiful services, gorgeous cathedrals, and splendid cloisters. But the preaching and teaching that goes on inside is a blasphemy and for the most part serves not God but the devil. For he is the prince and god of this world and must therefore have of everything the most elegant, precious, and beautiful.

They also possess superb gold and silver monstrances and pictures, adorned with precious stones and jewels. But inside are dead bones, as likely as not from the flaying ground. Likewise they own exquisite vestments, chasubles, palliums, copes, caps, and mitres. But who is under these or clothed in them? Lazy bellies, evil wolves, and godless swine who persecute and profane the Word of God.

And indeed, they also possess a lot of splendid, beautiful songs and music, especially in the cathedral and parish churches. But these are used to adorn all sorts of impure and idolatrous texts.

327

Therefore, we have unclothed these idolatrous, lifeless, and foolish texts, and divested them of their beautiful music. We have put this music on the living and holy Word of God in order to sing, praise, and honor it. We want the beautiful art of music to be properly used to serve her dear Creator and his Christians. He is thereby praised and honored and we are made better and stronger in faith when his holy Word is impressed on our hearts by sweet music. God the Father with Son and Holy Spirit grant us this. Amen.

But we do not hold that the notes need to be sung the same in all the churches. Let every church follow the music according to their own book and custom. For I myself do not like to hear the notes in a responsory or other song changed from what I was accustomed to in my youth. We are concerned with changing the text, not the music.

If the graves should be honored in other ways, it would be fine to paint or write good epitaphs or verses from Scripture on the walls above (where there are such) so that they may be seen by those who go to a funeral or to the cemetery, namely, these or the like:

He has fallen asleep with his fathers and has been gathered to his people [Gen. 25:8].

I know that my Redeemer lives, and that he will awaken me out of the earth: And I shall be clothed with my skin, and in my flesh I shall see God. Job 19 [:25-26].

I lie me down and sleep; I wake again, for the Lord sustains me. Psalm 3 [:5].

I lie down and sleep in complete peace. Psalm 4 [:8].

I shall behold thy face in righteousness: I shall be satisfied, when I awake, with thy likeness. Psalm 17 [:15].

God will redeem my soul from the power of Sheol, for he has accepted me. Psalm 49 [:15].

Precious in the sight of the Lord is the death of his saints. Psalm 116 [:15].

On this mountain the Lord will remove the covering that covers all peoples, and the veil that is spread over all nations. He will swallow up death forever. Isaiah 25 [:7-8].

Thy dead shall live and arise in the body. Awake and sing, you who lie under the earth, for thy dew is as the dew of a green field. Isaiah 26 [:19].

Go, my people, into a chamber, and shut the door behind you. Hide yourself for a little while until the wrath is past. Isaiah 26 [:20].

The righteous is taken away from the evil. And those who have walked uprightly enter into peace and rest in their chambers. Isaiah 57 [:1-2].

Thus says the Lord; Behold, I will open your graves, O my people, and cause you to come up out of them. Ezekiel 37 [:12].

Many that lie sleeping under earth will awake, some to everlasting life, and some to shame and contempt. Daniel 12 [:2].

I will redeem them from hell and rescue them from death. O death, I will be poison to you. O hell, I will be a plague to you. Hosea 13 [:14].

I am the God of Abraham, and the God of Isaac, and the God of Jacob. God is not the God of the dead, but of the living. Exodus 3 [:6] and Matthew 22 [:32].

This is the will of the Father who sent me, that I should lose nothing of all that he has given me, but raise it up at the last day. John 6 [:39].

No one lives to himself, and no one dies to himself. If we live, we live to the Lord, and if we die, we die to the Lord. Whether we live therefore, or die, we are the Lord's. For to this end Christ died, and rose, and became alive again, that he might be Lord both of the dead and living [Rom. 14:7-9].

If in this life only we have hope in Christ, we are of all men most miserable. I Corinthians 15 [:19].

For as in Adam all die, so also in Christ shall all be made alive. I Corinthians 15 [:22].

Death is swallowed up in victory. O death, where is thy sting? O hell, where is thy victory? The sting of death is sin, and the power of sin is the law. But thanks to God, who has given us the victory through our Lord Jesus Christ. I Corinthians 15 [:54-57].

Christ is my life and dying my gain. Philippians 1 [:21].

329

Just as we believe that Jesus died and rose again, even so will God bring those who sleep in Jesus with him. I Thessalonians 4 [:14].

Such verses and inscriptions would more fittingly adorn a cemetery than other secular emblems, such as shields and helmets.

But if anyone should have the gift and desire to put these verses into good rimes, that would help to have them read more gladly and remembered more easily. For rime and verse make good sayings and proverbs which serve better than ordinary prose.[2]

Luke 2 [:29-32]

In peace departed I this world;
For mine own eyes have seen the Lord
Thy Savior, God, who was to come
A light for all of Christendom.
While I in this my tomb remain,
Until my Lord returns again.

Luke 2 [:29-32]

With peace and joy in sweet repose,
Gladly will I mine eyelids close
And go to sleep the grave within.
For mine eyes have the Savior seen,
Whom thou for all of us hast given
To open us the gate of heaven,
That he should be the light divine
Which shall upon the gentiles shine,
And unto Israel to raise
Glory and everlasting praise.

John 11 [:25-26]

Christ is the truth, he is the life,
And resurrection he will give.
Who trust in him will life obtain,

---

[2] The translator offers no apology for the following rimes. They are as irregular as Luther's own. See pp. 197-201.

Though he may in the grave have lain.
Who lives and trusts, will never die,
But praise him in eternity.

Job 19 [:25-26]
This was my comfort while I lived
I said: he lives who has me saved.
He whom I trusted in my pain,
Will cover me again with skin
So that I from the grave shall rise
And live with him in paradise.
In my flesh shall I see the Lord.
This is confirmed by his own word.

The German hymns, "In Peace and Joy I Now Depart,"[3] "In One True God We All Believe,"[4] "Now Let Us Pray to the Holy Ghost,"[5] and "We Lay this Body in the Grave,"[6] may be sung alternately on returning home from the interment. In the same way one may use the Latin songs, *"Iam moesta quiesce,"*[7] *"Si enim credimus,"*[8] *"Corpora Sanctorum,"*[9] *"In pace sumus,"*[10] etc.

---

[3] See pp. 247-248.
[4] See pp. 271-273.
[5] See pp. 263-264.
[6] *"Nun lasst uns den Leib begraben,"* a burial hymn by Michael Weisse. Cf. Julian, *Dictionary of Hymnology*, p. 822.
[7] "Despair Not, O Heart, in Thy Sorrow," a hymn by Aurelius Prudentius (348-413). See the *Service Book and Hymnal of the Lutheran Church in America* (1958), No. 297.
[8] "If We Believe that Jesus Died and Rose Again," a responsory on I Thess. 4:14. This chant is contained in Klug's burial hymns.
[9] "The Bodies of the Saints Are Buried in Peace," an antiphon for Laudes for feasts of martyrs. This chant is in the *Antiphonale Romanum*.
[10] "We Are at Peace." The editor was unable to identify this chant.

331

Preface to the Babst Hymnal

1545

Translated by Paul Zeller Strodach
Revised by Ulrich S. Leupold

The most complete and most carefully edited hymnal to appear in Luther's lifetime was published by Valentin Babst in Leipzig in 1545, the year before Luther died. The preface he wrote for it was his last contribution to hymnody. However, he does not seem to have been actively involved in editing this hymnal, for the two mistakes he points out in the preface appear uncorrected in the hymnal.

The German text, *Vorrhede D. Mart. Luth.*, is given in WA 35, 476-477. The following translation is a revision of P. Z. Strodach's translation in *PE* 6, 293-295. The verse preceding the preface first appeared on the title page of the Klug hymnal of 1543 and was then reprinted on the title page of the Babst hymnal of 1545. The text is given in the bibliographical notes to these hymnals in *WA* 35, 331-333.

A Warning by D. Martin Luther

Many false masters now hymns indite
Be on your guard and judge them aright.
Where God is building his church and word,
There comes the devil with lie and sword.

A New Preface by D. Martin Luther

The 96th Psalm [:1] says, "Sing to the Lord a new song. Sing to the Lord all the earth." For in the Old Covenant under the law of Moses, divine service was tedious and tiresome as the people had to offer so many and varied sacrifices of all they possessed, both in house and field. And since they were restive and selfish, they performed this service unwillingly or only for the sake of temporal gain. As the prophet Malachi asks in the first chapter [:10], "Who is there even among you that would shut the doors for nought or kindle a light on my altar for nothing?" Now with a heart as lazy and unwilling as this, nothing or nothing good can be sung. Heart and mind must be cheerful and willing if one is to sing. Therefore, God abrogated the service that was rendered so indolently and reluctantly, as he in the same place continues: "I have no pleasure in you, says the Lord of hosts, and I will not accept an offering from your hand. For from the rising of the sun to its setting my name is great among the nations, and in every place incense is offered to my name, and a pure offering: for my name is great among the nations, says the Lord of hosts" [Mal. 1:10-11].

Thus there is now in the New Testament a better service of God, of which the Psalm [96:1] here says: "Sing to the Lord a new song. Sing to the Lord all the earth." For God has cheered our hearts and minds through his dear Son, whom he gave for us to redeem us from sin, death, and the devil. He who believes this earnestly cannot be quiet about it. But he must gladly and willingly sing and speak about it so that others also may come and hear it. And whoever does not want to sing and speak of it shows that he does not believe and that he does not belong under the new and joyful testament, but under the old, lazy, and tedious testament.

Therefore, the printers do well if they publish a lot of good hymns and make them attractive to the people with all sorts of ornamentations,[1] so that they may move them to joy in faith and to gladly sing. In such pleasing fashion the book by Val[en]tin Babst has been prepared. God grant that it may cause great loss and harm to the Roman pope,[2] who through his damned, intolerable, and abominable laws has caused nothing but howling, mourning, and grief in all the world. Amen.

But I must also give this warning: the burial hymn "We Lay this Body in the Grave"[3] bears my name; but it is not mine, and

---

[1] Babst's hymnal was lavishly fitted with numerous illustrations and decorative designs on every page. It is the finest piece of printing of all the early Lutheran hymnals.
[2] The name of the printer Babst rimes with the German word for pope: *Pabst.*
[3] *"Nun lasst uns den Leib begraben."* See p. 331, n. 6.

hereafter it should not be credited to me. Not that I condemn it; for it pleases me very much, and a good poet wrote it, one named Johannes Weiss[4] (only that on the sacrament he has come close to the enthusiasts). But I will not palm off anyone's work as my own.

And in "From Trouble Deep I Cry to Thee"[5] the reading should be: "Everyone must fear thee."[6] Whether by mistake or deliberately, in most books this is made to read "everyone must be afraid."[7] For the expression "that thou mayest be feared" [Ps. 130:4] is a Hebrew idiom. Compare Matthew 15 [:9], "In vain they fear[8] me with the commandment of men," and Psalm 14 [:4-5] and Psalm 53 [:4-5], "They have not called upon God. They fear where there is nothing to fear," i.e., they show great humility, and bow and scrape in their worship, which worship I do not want. So also here the meaning is this: Since forgiveness of sins cannot be found except with thee, they must cease from all their idolatry and willingly bow and bend before thee, humble themselves, hold thee alone in honor, take their refuge in thee, and serve thee as those who live by thy grace and not by their own righteousness, etc.

---

[4] Luther means Michael Weisse (ca. 1480-1534), the great hymn writer and hymnbook editor of the Bohemian Brethren.
[5] Luther refers to the sixth line of the second stanza. See p. 224.
[6] *Des muss dich fürchten jedermann.*
[7] *Des muss sich fürchten jedermann.*
[8] The Masoretic text and the Vulgate version both have "fear" in the Isaiah text (Isa. 29:13) quoted here by Jesus.

A MOTET
"I SHALL NOT DIE, BUT LIVE"

1545

Translated by Ulrich S. Leupold

INTRODUCTION

One of Luther's musician friends was Ludwig Senfl (*ca.* 1492- *ca.* 1555), the ablest German composer of his time. Luther may have met him in Innsbruck in 1510, when Luther was on his way to Rome, or in Augsburg in the year 1518. At any rate, he sent Senfl a very cordial letter in 1530, while he was following the negotiations in Augsburg from the Coburg fortress with mounting impatience and anger. In his melancholy mood he requested the famous composer to arrange for him the antiphon *"In pace in id ipsum"*[1] for many voices.

Luther wrote to Senfl: "This melody has comforted me from boyhood, and even more now that I understand the words. . . . I hope that the end of my life is at hand. The world hates and scorns me and I in turn am disgusted with the world and despise it. May the Good Shepherd take my soul. That is why I am beginning to sing this song more frequently; but I would like to hear it in parts. If you do not have or should not know the melody, I shall send you the music, and you may set it after my death if you so desire."[2]

Senfl, however, complied with Luther's request in a very thoughtful manner; for instead of the requested *"In pace,"* he chose another of Luther's favorite verses, "I shall not die, but live, and declare the works of the Lord."[3] This was the verse Luther had written with its plain-chant notes on the wall of his study on the Coburg.[4]

---

[1] Ps. 4:8, "I will both lay me down and sleep: for thou, Lord, only makest me dwell in safety."

[2] *WA*, Br 5, No. 1727, p. 639.

[3] Ps. 118:17. In Latin this verse begins *Non moriar, sed vivam.* Senfl's motet, which is more elaborate than Luther's and is for five voices instead of four, was found by Theodore Kroyer in a manuscript of the Zwickau Rathsbibliothek, but with one part, the *Altus,* missing (cf. *Vierteljahrsschrift für Musikwissenschaft,* VI, 122 f.). This missing part was recovered by Müller-Blattau in the library of the University of Königsberg (cf. *Zeitschrift für Musikwissenschaft,* VI, 235 f.).

[4] As late as 1550 this inscription was seen by Matthaeus Ratzeberger; cf. An-

Apparently, Luther was so fond of this verse that he tried his hand at a polyphonic arrangement of the same *cantus firmus*.[5] A motet on this *cantus firmus* was published under Luther's name in the drama *Lazarus* by Joachim Greff (Wittenberg, 1545). While it must be admitted that many things which Luther did not write were credited to him in his lifetime, it seems more than coincidental that the only motet for which he is named as the composer utilizes an antiphon that we know to have been especially dear to him. And the general calibre of his musicianship[6] makes the assignment logical and likely.

Our edition follows R. von Liliencron's edition in *WA* 35, 537, except that the music has been transposed one tone higher than the original. The original title is *Non moriar sed vivam D. Martin Lutheri IIII vocum aus seinem schönen Confitemini*.

---

drew Poach, *Christlicher Abschied aus diesem sterblichen Leben des lieben theuren Mannes Matthaei Ratzebergers*, 1559.
[5] This *cantus firmus*, as the tenor part shows, is really the eighth psalm tone in the florid canticle version.
[6] See pp. 202-203.

"I Shall Not Die, But Live"

INDEXES

INDEX OF NAMES AND SUBJECTS

INDEX TO SCRIPTURE PASSAGES

2:14 –21
2:29-30 – 132
2:29-32 – 247, 330
7:50 – 121
8:48 – 121
10:42 – 14
14:7-10 – 47
22:20 – 30, 81
24:50-51 – 30

John
1:14 – 131
1:19-28 – 76-78
1:29 – 67
2:1-11 – 242
3:16-18 – 66
6:39 – 329
11:11 – 326
11:25-26 – 330
16:24 – 139
19:34 – 27
20:17 – 135

Acts
20:28-31 – 125

Romans
4:25 – 67
5:12 – 66
5:15-21 – 66
6:9 – 134
13 – 66
14:5 – 31
14:7 – 38
14:7-9 – 329
14:17 – 31
14:26-27 – 38
15:2 – 48
15:5-6 – 61

I Corinthians
1:10 – 61
2:2 – 316
4:1-5 – 73
4:1-8 – 84-86
6:12 – 47
8:1 – 47
8:8 – 31
11:19 – 45, 49
11:25 – 30, 81
11:25-26 – 34
11:26 – 137
11:29 – 105
14:15 – 316
14:26-31 – 11
14:27 – 12
14:38 – 34
14:40 – 47
15:19 – 329
15:22 – 329
15:42-44 – 326
15:54-57 – 329
15:56 – 274

II Corinthians
1:24 – 48
9 – 64
10:8 – 48
13:10 – 39

Galatians
4:31 – 31
5:13 – 67
6:2 – 33
6:7 – 105

Ephesians
4:8 – 135
5:22-24 – 114

5:25-29 – 114
5:32 – 115

Philippians
1:21 – 329
2:1-4 – 46
2:2 – 61

Colossians
3:16 – 36, 316

I Thessalonians
4:13-18 – 325
4:14 – 330, 331
5:21 – 22

II Thessalonians
2:3-4 – 19, 35

I Timothy
3:1-7 – 124
4:4-5 – 31, 124

II Timothy
2:20 – 49
2:21 – 50

Hebrews
12:6 – 67

James
3:2 – 33

I Peter
5:2-4 – 126
5:8 – 45

Revelation
12 – 292

Body, 10 on 13 Caledonia
Display, Bulmer and Caledonia
Paper, Standard White Antique 'RRR'